Praise for *Bryson City Tales*

With homespun warmth, my friend Dr. Walt Larimore tells stories that integrate the science and art of medicine. Walt is a brilliant lifelong learner who is patient-centered. *Bryson City Tales* portrays medical practice as something deeply personal, relational, and spiritual.

Randy Alcorn, author of *Deadline* and *The Treasure Principle*

What a delightful work! *Bryson City Tales* brims with the charm, color, and character of the North Carolina mountains and its unique folk. Dr. Larimore's gifted storytelling makes us wince, gasp, laugh, and cry with these charming people and their "fresh out of training" doctor. A television script writer could only hope to do as well as this over-the-shoulder peek at real-life medical drama in a small town.

Richard A. Swenson, M.D., physician, futurist, researcher, and best-selling author of *Margin*

Walt Larimore has the gift. His fine book brings before the reader a vivid world inhabited by colorful people. We see the tragedy and triumph of their lives, and like a master, Doc Larimore employs the old show-business adage, "Make 'em laugh—make 'em cry!" If you are seeking a book that delights and informs, you need look no further than *Bryson City Tales.*

Gilbert Morris, best-selling author of the House of Winslow series, the Appomattox series, and *The Edge of Honor*

The title *Bryson City Tales* is a modest cover for a lot of personal true stories that illustrate some highly profound principles. How does a young doctor manage to integrate his background of high academic medical training and simple Christian faith into the hurly-burly of established human relationships in a mountain community? This sounds like heavy stuff, but it turns out to be light—almost hilarious—reading.

Paul Brand, M.D., coauthor of *Fearfully and Wonderfully Made* and *The Gift of Pain*

I became an M.D. because doctors were my heroes growing up, and many of them still are—including Walt Larimore, M.D., the author of *Bryson City Tales. Bryson City Tales* shows the character, motives, surprises (awakenings), and disappointments of a first-year small-town family doctor. I loved it. I laughed. I cried. And, most important, my faith has been reinforced that there still are loving and caring docs out there.

Paul Meier, M.D., cofounder of the Meier New-Life Clinics and author of fifty-two books

Books by Dr. Walt Larimore

10 Essentials of Highly Healthy People

Alternative Medicine (coauthored with Dónal O'Mathúna)

Bryson City Tales

Bryson City Seasons

Going Public with Your Faith: Becoming a Spiritual Influence at Work (coauthored with William Carr Peel)

The Highly Healthy Child

Lintball Leo's Not-So-Stupid Questions About Your Body

Why A.D.H.D. Doesn't Mean Disaster (coauthored with Dennis Swanberg and Diane Passno)

S R'S FIRST

N

les

W M.D.

ZONDERVAN™
GRAND RAPIDS, MICHIGAN 49530 USA

We want to hear from you. Please send your comments about this book to us in care of zreview@zondervan.com. Thank you.

ZONDERVAN™

Bryson City Tales

Requests for information should be addressed to:

Zondervan, *Grand Rapids, Michigan 49530*

Library of Congress Cataloging-in-Publication Data

Larimore, Walter L.

Bryson City tales : stories of a doctor's first year of practice in the Smoky Mountains / Walt Larimore.

p. cm.

ISBN 0-310-24100-6 (hardcover)

1. Walter L. Larimore. 2. Physicians—North Carolina—Bryson City—Biography. 3. Medicine, Rural—North Carolina—Bryson City. I. Title.

R154. L267 A3

610'.92—dc21

2001008039

Softcover ISBN 0-310-25670-4.

Illustration by William Rozek
Interior design by Todd Sprague

Printed in the United States of America

05 06 07 08 09 10 /❖ DC/ 10 9 8 7 6 5 4 3

To Barb,
the love of my life

and to Bryson City and her people. These selected stories represent only a small portion of all that could be told. These people, our "southern highlanders," represent—at least once you come to know them—a warm and gentle people. They slowly took me in. They slowly welcomed me. They always taught me. This volume is, in a way, my thanks to them—for who they are and for what they meant to me and my family.

A Word from the Author

Some of the characters revealed herein are real—they still reside in Bryson City—and Barb and I have had the pleasure of visiting with many of them over the last year. The vast majority, but not all, are still friends and still friendly. Others have moved to other towns, to other places. Some keep in touch with me from time to time.

Other characters described in this tome are composites of real people and bear names that are purely fictional—primarily to protect the identities of those who formed the origin of the story itself. In many cases the name, gender, and age of patients have been changed to protect the confidentiality and privacy of my many patients who never planned or wanted to have their stories appear in the public square. Therefore, those readers who think they recognize a friend or acquaintance in these pages should consider it a most unlikely coincidence.

Many of the most influential characters mentioned in this book have passed on and will have no opportunity to tell their side of the same story. Some, I suspect, would be pleased with what has been recorded about their impact on my life. Others, I'm sure, would protest—perhaps vociferously.

Indeed, most (but not all) of the stories actually happened—although not all occurred exactly as they are written. Some artistic license was employed in the timing of certain events.

Looking back over the decades at the events occurring at the dawn of my medical career, I suspect that similar accounts could have been recorded by countless other family physicians in rural America with, of course, some personal variations. This writing is intended to be more a record of this type of practice and the personal and professional growth it produces in almost any young physician than the full autobiography of a single one.

Contents

Acknowledgments

As I write these acknowledgments, the Swain County Maroon Devils have just won the 2001 North Carolina state football championship. I wish I had been there with them. I am so appreciative of the Swain County High School athletic department, coaches, and fans. Being allowed to serve as their team physician was one of the highest honors of my professional career. A special thank-you is due from me to Coach Boyce Dietz.

The idea for this book started with an informal lunch at Zondervan in Grand Rapids, Michigan. Scott Bolinder, executive vice president and publisher; Lyn Cryderman, vice president and associate publisher; Cindy Hays Lambert, senior acquisitions editor; and several staff members were meeting with Barb and me to discuss a series of books on medical topics. During lunch, Lyn said, "Walt, tell us about your first year in practice." I began to relate some of these stories. We laughed and our eyes got misty, and with some stories we were deeply moved. At the conclusion of our lunch, Scott, Lyn, and Cindy had decided to publish the "Tales." Therefore, I must first and foremost acknowledge that the birth of *Bryson City Tales* is due to Scott's, Lyn's, and Cindy's encouragement and affirmation.

A special thank-you is owed Cindy Hays Lambert, who tirelessly worked with me during the development of this book. Cindy's care, her coaching and direction, and her friendship and handholding during every phase of the growth of this "baby" were instrumental in the process of coming to a final manuscript. She single-handedly took the raw stories of a writing neophyte and assisted him in shaping the final work. Cindy, I appreciate what you have done—but most of all I appreciate who you are.

The editors who labored over the final manuscript, Traci Mullins and Dirk Buursma, are owed my eternal gratitude for their loving care and molding of the *Tales*. My administrative assistant, Donna Lewis, unselfishly assisted in manuscript review and in many, many research arrangements. Thanks, Donna.

Most of the places mentioned in *Bryson City Tales* can still be visited. I'm forever grateful for the lovely evenings, meals, and repose that Barb and I had (and that can still be had) at the Hemlock Inn, the Fryemont Inn, and the Frye-Randolph House (now called the Randolph House).

I'm in debt to the trustees, administration, and staff of Swain County Hospital—which is still there (although the birthing suites and operating rooms are gone—the former shut down when Dr. Pyeritz and I left town, and the latter closed when Dr. Mitchell was buried). These men and women will always command my respect and thanks.

Barb and I are so appreciative of the provision of our home in Bryson City. The house still stands—although I have no idea what happened to our bench. Last time we checked, it was no longer there. Dr. Pyeritz's and my medical office still stands—as do at least two of the Christmas trees we planted there. The practice football field, the county football stadium, the Bryson City cemetery, the Road to Nowhere, the courthouse, Clampitt's Hardware Store, and WBHN are all still there. Super Swain Drugs, Hardee's, Dr. Bacon's orchard, and Swain Surgical Associates are no longer there—but Na-Ber's Drive-In is!

Louise Thomas was still at the hospital—at least the last time I visited. To this very day, I appreciate her smile, laughs, and hugs—which are more precious now than ever. I pray that she and "Dr. Pat," her lifetime love, will both see this work in print. I expect her to fuss at me over some of the stories I've told about her.

I so appreciate Mr. Earl Douthit. He is now retired and still lives in Bryson City—in the same home described in the *Tales*. I acknowledge the expertise of Fred Moody—who still practices there. I want to acknowledge Bill and Ruth Adams—who can still be found tending their inn. Dr. Nordling has retired, and Dr. Sale left medicine to become a pastor in Bryson City.

During 2001, Barb and I returned to Bryson City twice to do research for the *Tales*. Returning sixteen years after leaving was a bit anxiety provoking. How would we be received? Would we be remembered? Ever gracious, the men and women whom we had come to admire and love so much warmly welcomed us back.

We owe the proprietors of the Hemlock Inn an immense debt of thanks. To John Shell, Mort White, and Lainey White, as well as to their staff at the inn, an immense thank-you for your assistance with our research and for providing your ever-gracious and warm hospitality and your prayers. Lainey is John and Ella Jo's daughter. Ella Jo has passed away. I so wish I could have seen her face as she read these *Tales*. I can hear her laughter even now.

Katherine has sold the Fryemont Inn and moved away. Nevertheless, we enjoyed visiting the inn. The meals there are as delicious as we remember.

Others who unselfishly assisted with my research include Dean and Preston Tuttle; Diana Owle; Elizabeth Ellison; Dr. Paul Sale; R.P. and Sally Jenkins; Troy, Tammy, and Trey Burns; Debbie Wilson; the wonderful kids at The Gathering; Monty and Dianna Clampitt; Dr. David and Beth Zimmerman; Reva Blanton; John and Rita Mattox; Jon and Virginia Molinato; Margaret Iorio; Dr. Mike and Kim Hamrick. I appreciate their assistance. Last but not least, I appreciate the research assistance of the Swain County Chamber of Commerce.

Rick Pyeritz, M.D., and Ray Cunningham, M.D., have also moved from Bryson City—but they still practice medicine. Ray and Nancy Cunningham are precious friends. Surviving my first year of practice would have been unbearable without their support and love. Rick Pyeritz was my partner, colleague, teacher, and confidant for seven years. He was our family physician. His love and care for the Larimores is forever appreciated and will never be forgotten. Rick remains one of my dearest friends.

Drs. Bacon, Mitchell, and Mathieson, as well as Marcellus Buchanan, have all passed away. I wish I could thank them today for all they contributed. I also appreciate the contribution of "Walter"—who is still living near Bryson City on an undisclosed farm in a hidden hollow but is still as beautiful as the first day I saw her, although getting up in years.

Last but not least, I love and appreciate Kate and Scott. Their original contribution to *Bryson City Tales* cannot be understated. Their permission to allow their dad to share their stories with you is recognized and deeply appreciated. I love them so very much. Of all the roles that the Lord has allowed me on this earth, other than being their mother's best friend and husband, none is more precious to me than the role of being their daddy.

Walter L. Larimore, M.D.
Colorado Springs, Colorado

Foreword

by Gilbert Morris

For most men the most dreaded words in the language are, "Did you take the trash out?" or "We have to talk!" For a novelist, however, the most dreaded words are, "Would you please read my manuscript and tell me what you think?"

I get numerous requests of this nature, and being the good fellow that I am, I usually agree. One dear lady's work was very bad, and I tried gently to put her off. She kept badgering me to read more of her work, and finally after driving me nearly crazy, she asked, "Do you think there's enough *fire* in my work?" I heard myself saying, "Lady—there's not enough of your work in the fire!" This was unkind, and I had to do penance by reading the awful stuff and being extra nice to her.

Walt Larimore's work does *not* belong in the fire! It belongs in the library of every person who has had, is having, or will ever have medical problems (which means all of us!)

I freely admit I have had problems with doctors. Others may tell lawyer jokes, but *I* tell doctor jokes. I have a mental file of horror stories about physicians who have failed me, and since I have a memory like a zebra, I never forget! When I sat down to read Walt Larimore's manuscript, even before I read the first page I was preparing the speech I'd be forced to give to Walt. "Walt, stick to doctoring people, and let *real* writers handle the books."

Two aspects of *Bryson City Tales* gave me great pleasure: First, it gave me new insight into how doctors are made, and second, I simply *enjoyed* the fine writing.

Like most people, I am somewhat frightened of doctors. They ask me to trust them, to put my life in their hands. They are powerful people, and as someone has once said, "Power corrupts, and absolute power corrupts absolutely." But in this book we see the human side of one man who is humbled by his own limitations. The curtain is drawn back, and we see behind the scenes of the drama. As Walt Larimore is thrust into the cosmos of a small southern town, he makes mistakes, he rushes in where angels fear to tread, he makes enemies. Living through the very human problems of a young physician trying to make it, just like the rest of us ordinary mortals, gave me fresh insight into the world of medicine.

Bryson City Tales also pleased me because it is so readable. After having taught creative writing for twenty-five years and written quite a few novels, I have one criterion that I apply to writing: Is this book fun to read? I found out years ago that teachers, preachers, and writers had better do whatever they have to in order to entertain those who sit under them! And Walt Larimore has the gift. As a novelist, I harbor a hope that he never turns his hand to writing novels, for he has the talent for it—and I don't need the competition! His fine book brings before the reader a vivid world inhabited by colorful people. We see the tragedy and the triumph of their lives, and like a master, Doc Larimore employs the old show-business adage, "Make 'em laugh—make 'em cry!"

We cry when a young woman loses her baby, but we laugh at the man of ninety-eight years who's about to be married to a young woman and comes to Larimore for a premarital exam. When the good doctor (worried about the old man's health) warns him tactfully that sex can be dangerous under certain conditions, the old man stares at him and says, "Well, Doc, if she dies, she dies."

If you are seeking a book that delights and informs, you need look no further than *Bryson City Tales!*

Gilbert Morris
December 20, 2001

BRYSON CITY *Tales*

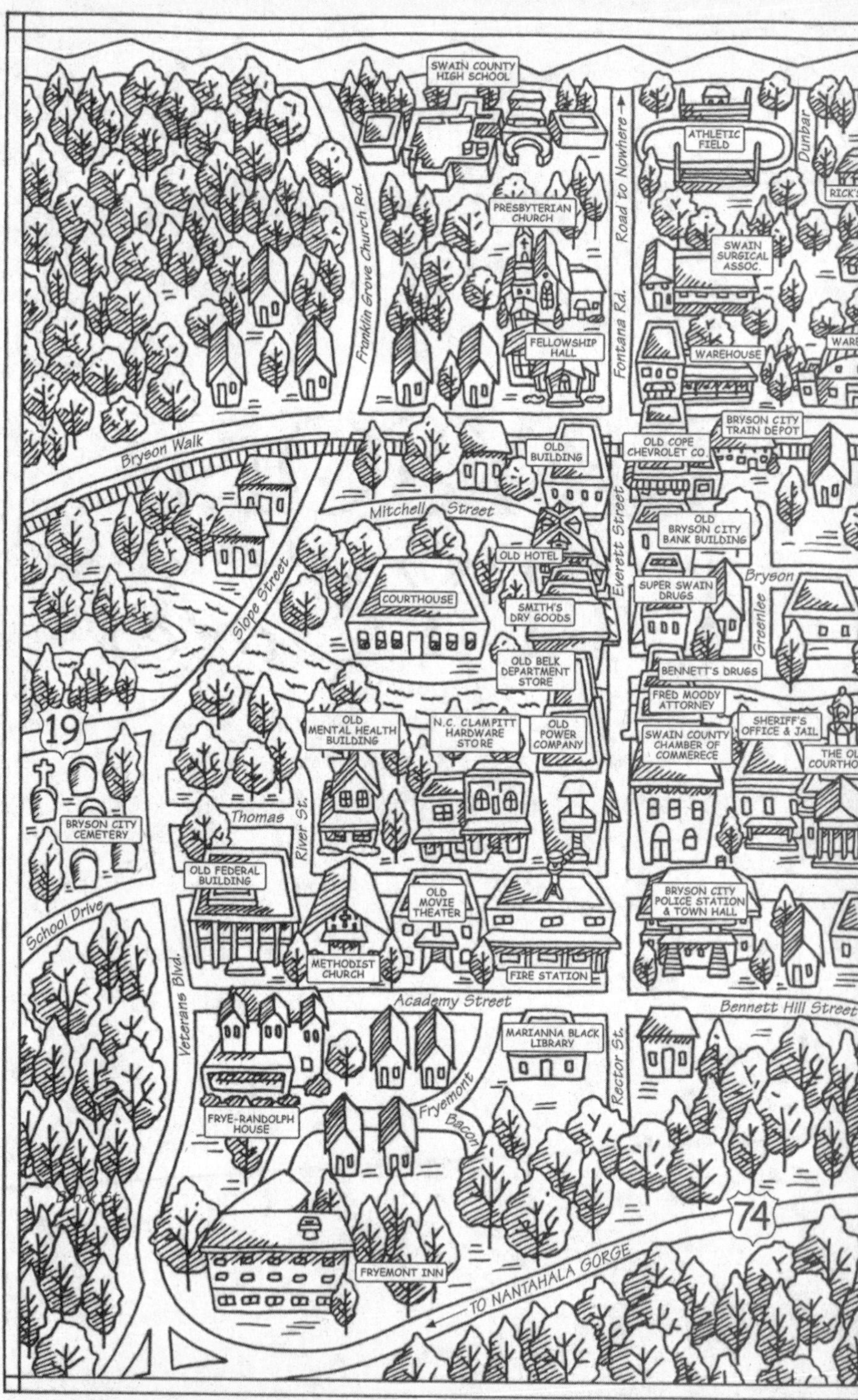

SWAIN COUNTY HIGH SCHOOL
ATHLETIC FIELD
Dunbar
RICK'S
PRESBYTERIAN CHURCH
Franklin Grove Church Rd.
Road to Nowhere
SWAIN SURGICAL ASSOC.
FELLOWSHIP HALL
Fontana Rd.
WAREHOUSE
BRYSON CITY TRAIN DEPOT
Bryson Walk
OLD BUILDING
OLD COPE CHEVROLET CO.
Mitchell Street
Everett Street
OLD BRYSON CITY BANK BUILDING
OLD HOTEL
Bryson
Slope Street
COURTHOUSE
SMITH'S DRY GOODS
SUPER SWAIN DRUGS
Greenlee
OLD BELK DEPARTMENT STORE
BENNETT'S DRUGS
FRED MOODY ATTORNEY
19
OLD MENTAL HEALTH BUILDING
N.C. CLAMPITT HARDWARE STORE
OLD POWER COMPANY
SHERIFF'S OFFICE & JAIL
SWAIN COUNTY CHAMBER OF COMMERECE
Thomas
River St.
BRYSON CITY CEMETERY
OLD FEDERAL BUILDING
OLD MOVIE THEATER
BRYSON CITY POLICE STATION & TOWN HALL
School Drive
Veterans Blvd.
METHODIST CHURCH
FIRE STATION
Academy Street
Bennett Hill Street
MARIANNA BLACK LIBRARY
Rector St.
Fryemont
Bacon
FRYE-RANDOLPH HOUSE
74
FRYEMONT INN
TO NANTAHALA GORGE

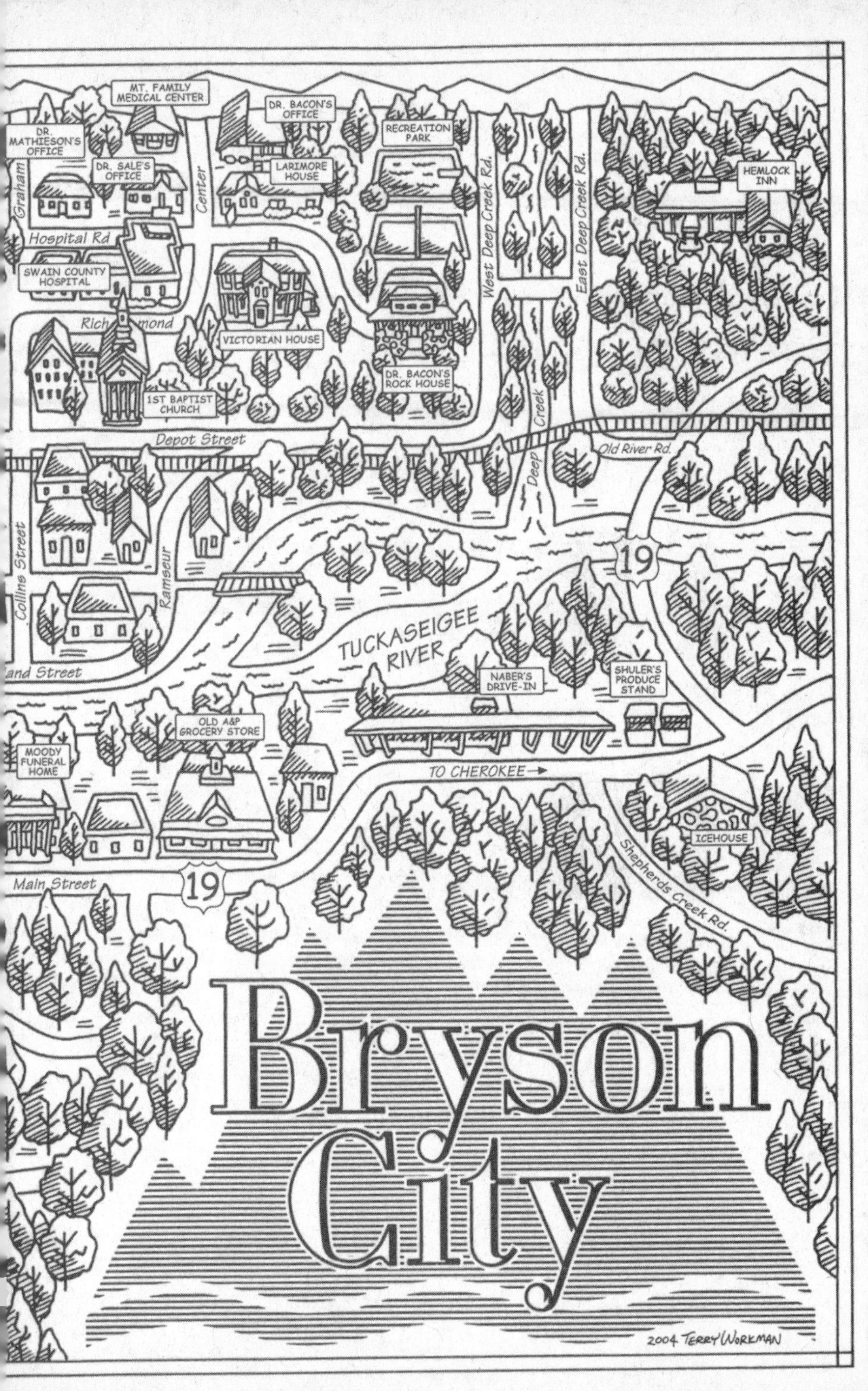
MT. FAMILY MEDICAL CENTER
DR. BACON'S OFFICE
DR. MATHIESON'S OFFICE
RECREATION PARK
DR. SALE'S OFFICE
LARIMORE HOUSE
HEMLOCK INN
Graham
Center
West Deep Creek Rd.
East Deep Creek Rd.
Hospital Rd
SWAIN COUNTY HOSPITAL
Richmond
VICTORIAN HOUSE
DR. BACON'S ROCK HOUSE
1ST BAPTIST CHURCH
Depot Street
Creek
Deep
Old River Rd.
Collins Street
Ramseur
19
TUCKASEIGEE RIVER
and Street
NABER'S DRIVE-IN
SHULER'S PRODUCE STAND
OLD A&P GROCERY STORE
MOODY FUNERAL HOME
TO CHEROKEE
ICEHOUSE
Shepherds Creek Rd.
Main Street
19
Bryson City
2004 TERRY WORKMAN

chapter one

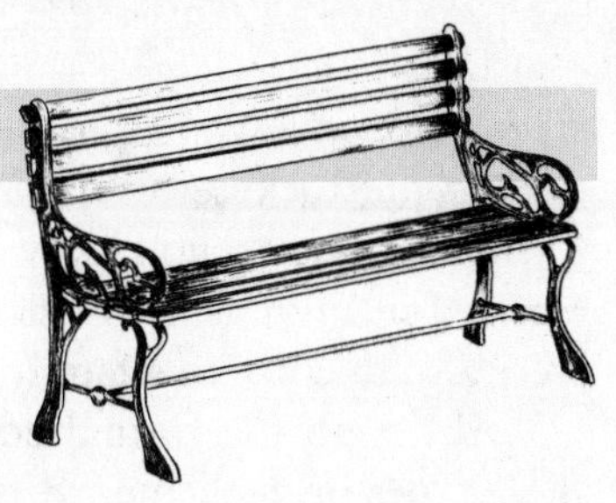

THE MURDER

They didn't tell me about this in medical school. And they sure didn't prepare me for this in my family medicine residency. Of course, like all well-trained family physicians, I knew how to provide for the majority of the medical needs of my patients in hospitals and nursing homes. Naturally I had been taught the basics of how to practice medicine in the office setting. But I was quickly discovering that physicians who headed into the rural counties of the Smoky Mountains in the third quarter of the twentieth century needed to know much more than these basics.

I don't remember any school or residency lessons on the peculiar calls I would receive from national park rangers telling of a medical emergency in the Great Smoky Mountains National Park. "Wilderness medicine," at least when I first started practice, was not in my black bag.

I don't remember any preparation for the unique medical emergencies faced by the Swain County Rescue Squad. Search-and-rescue medicine wasn't in my repertoire either, nor were the river rescues I would be involved with on the county's four rivers—the Tuckaseigee, the Nantahala, the Oconaluftee, and the Little Tennessee. And I know for certain that I had no training in caring for animals or livestock—but, sure enough, those calls were also to come to a family physician in the Smoky Mountains.

Although my formal education had not prepared me for these types of medicine, when the need arose to learn and practice them, I felt up to the challenge. Although I was often perplexed by some of the unique aspects of practicing medicine in a rural—and, I first thought, somewhat backward—community, I didn't find the demands particularly distressing. My first murder case, however, was a different story.

I had just moved a month before, with my wife, Barb, and our nearly-three-year-old daughter, Kate, from my residency in family medicine at the Duke University Medical Center in Durham, North Carolina, to Swain County, in the heart of the Great Smoky Mountains. The county had only 8,000 residents, but occupied over 550 square miles. However, the federal government owned 86 percent of the land—and much of it was wilderness. Over 40 percent of the Great Smoky Mountains National Park is contained within the borders of Swain County, which is also home to the eastern band of the Cherokee Indians, to one of the more southern sections of the Appalachian Trail, and to the beginning of the Blue Ridge Parkway.

The doctors in the county seat—the small town of Bryson City, North Carolina—rotated the on-call assignment. When we were on call, we were responsible for a twenty-four-hour period of time, from 7:00 A.M. to 7:00 A.M. We were on call for all of the patients in Swain County General Hospital's forty beds, the Mountain View Manor Nursing Home, the Bryson City and Swain County jails, and the hospital emergency room. We also provided surgical backup for the physicians in nearby Robbinsville, which had no hospital, and for the physicians at the Cherokee Indian Hospital, located about ten miles away in Cherokee, which had a hospital but no surgeons. While on call, we were also required to serve as the county coroner.

Since pathology-trained coroners lived only in the larger towns, the nonpathologist physicians in the rural villages often became certified as coroners. We were not expected to do autopsies—only pathologists were trained to perform these—but we were expected to provide all of the nonautopsy responsibilities required of a medical examiner.

Having obtained my training and certification as a coroner while still in my family medicine residency, I knew the basics of determining the time and cause of death, gathering medical evidence, and filling out the copious triplicate forms from the state. Not sure that I was adequately prepared, but proud to be the holder of a fancy state-provided certificate of competence anyway, I thought I was ready to begin practice in Bryson City—ready to join my colleagues as an inexperienced family physician as well as a neophyte medical examiner. It was not long after our arrival that I was required to put my new forensic skills to work.

I had finished a fairly busy evening in the emergency room—my first night on call in my first week of private practice in this tiny Smoky Mountain town—and, after seeing what I thought would be the evening's last patient, I crossed the street to our home, hoping for a quiet night and some much-needed sleep. Sometime between sleep and sunrise, the shrill ring of the phone snatched me from my slumber.

"Dr. Larimore," barked an official voice. "This is Deputy Rogers of the Swain County Sheriff's Department. We're at the site of an apparent homicide and need the coroner up here. I've been notified that you are the coroner on call. Is that correct, sir?"

"Ten-four," I replied, in my most official coroner-type voice.

"Then, sir, we need you up at the Watkins place. Stat, sir."

"Ten-four." Boy, did I ever feel official and important as I placed the phone in its cradle.

I rolled over to inform Barb of the advent of my first coroner's case. She didn't even wake up. Nevertheless, I sat upright on the edge of the bed, beginning to feel the adrenaline rush of my first big professional adventure, when I suddenly moaned to myself and fell back into the bed. *Where in the world is the Watkins place?* I thought to myself. I hadn't a clue. But I knew who would—Millie the dispatcher.

I hadn't yet met Millie face-to-face, but already I felt I knew her after only a short time in town. Every doctor knew Millie, and she knew everything about every doctor—where they would be and what they would be doing at almost any time of any day. Equally important to me was that Millie knew where everyone's "place" was.

So I phoned dispatch. She answered quickly and barked, almost with a snarl, "Swain County Dispatch. What you want?"

"Millie, this is Dr. Larimore."

There was a long pause, then a condescending, "Yes, I know."

I'd heard the older doctors refer to Millie's "always courteous" and "helpful" demeanor. *What was up with the dispatcher tonight?* I wondered.

"Millie, where is the Watkins place?"

A big sigh was followed by a clipped statement of the obvious: "Son, it's the scene of a crime tonight."

Now I was feeling myself getting a bit impatient. "Right ... Millie, I need to get up there."

There was another long pause, then another condescending, "Yes, I know."

I was quiet for a moment, then, almost pleading—in fact, begging—I said, "Millie, I need to know how to *get* there!"

Millie sighed again and—almost reluctantly, it seemed—gave me directions to the Watkins place.

A fifteen-minute drive from our home—smack-dab on the top of Hospital Hill—down winding mountain roads brought the on-call coroner to the scene of the crime. It wasn't hard to find, with police and sheriff cars—their red lights blazing in the cool mountain air—gathered around a small frame house, bathing it in the whitewash of headlights. The border of the lawn—a small picket fence—was already surrounded with yellow crime-scene tape.

I parked outside the ring of official vehicles and quickly walked up to the house. It looked so small, so innocent, and so all-American. Deputy Rogers met me at the tape to lift it up and issue a warning: "Doc, it's pretty gruesome in there."

Obviously, I thought, *you don't understand that I am a trained professional.* As would soon become painfully clear, I didn't have a clue what I was about to walk into.

The sheriff met me at the door and shook my hand. This was our first meeting. A tall, bulky man, he looked more like an NFL linebacker than my preconceived idea of a small-county sheriff.

"Pleased to meet you, son. This your first case?"

"Yes, sir. It sure is."

He motioned to the yard, and we walked out several feet to speak in confidence. He reached into his shirt pocket to pull out a pack of cigarettes. Partially shaking out a couple, he offered me one.

"No thanks, Sheriff."

He put one to his lips, lit it, and took a long drag.

"Son, it isn't pretty in there. There was a woman and her daughter a visitin' the man who owns the home. I'm not sure why. They was in the bedroom sittin' on the bed. Apparently there was another man that come up to visit. He wasn't expected or welcome. Apparently the entire crew had been drinkin' a bit."

I was to come to learn that "drinkin' a bit" meant they were soused.

He went on. "Anyways, an argument commenced and apparently the fella that lived here grabbed a loaded shotgun out of his closet. The two fellas began to tussle a bit. The gun went off. So did the head of one of the fellas."

He paused for a moment, for effect and for another long drag. For the first time he looked at me, eyeball-to-eyeball.

"Son, all I need you to certify is that this fella is dead and the cause of death. Then we'll ship the body over to the morgue in Sylva. The pathologist will do the autopsy tomorrow."

"No problem, Sheriff."

He crushed out the half-smoked cigarette and then turned to return to the house. I followed.

We entered a living room that couldn't have been more than ten by fourteen feet. There was barely room for a small TV, a small sofa and chair, and a small table. To the left, a doorway led to a small kitchen. To the right was a doorway to a small bedroom—maybe eight by ten feet in size. Most of the space was occupied by a twin bed. Just to the side of the bed was a body. The boot-clad feet were lying together, the toes pointing up. The blue jeans and the plaid shirt looked quietly peaceful. However, there was nothing above the shirt. In fact, the shirt *ended at the wall*—almost as though the head were stuck in a hole in the wall.

The wall. It was then that I noticed that the walls were an unusual color and texture. The nausea and near-wretch overwhelmed me as the shock of what I was seeing registered in my mind. Plastered on the walls and the ceiling and the bed and the floor were thousands of globs of brain and skull and scalp and hair. Only a small section of the bed was clean.

The sheriff, as though reading my thoughts, commented, "The girls were sittin' on the bed. They was covered with brains and blood when we got here. The clean spot on the bed was where they was sittin'. One of my lady detectives has taken them over to the safe house in Sylva. They'll be seein' the victim's advocate right away."

A combination of shakes, cold sweats, and the sure feeling of an approaching faint now replaced the rush of nausea. I backed out of the bedroom and sat on the sofa in the living room.

The sheriff followed me into the living room. "Don't feel bad, son," he said, trying to comfort me. "I felt the same way the first time I seen a murder like this."

"Oh, I feel just fine," I moaned. "I'm just sitting here to reconstruct the events of the crime." The sheriff was experienced and kind enough to allow my delusion to remain intact. He patted me on the back as he turned to walk out of the house. "Deputy Rogers is here to help you with anything you need," he said.

After a few minutes the nausea and weakness passed. "Deputy, let's go to work."

Alongside the investigating detective I supervised the examination of the room, the collection of evidence, and the police photographer. We then moved the body away from the wall. It was still warm and soft—no evidence of stiffness, no coldness. This killing was fresh.

The neck seemed normal but was only connected to a small piece of the back and base of the skull. The inside of the skull—what little was left—was strangely beautiful, glistening white, still moist and warm. There was nothing left of the head. The shock and nausea had receded, and now my training and limited experience took over as I, almost mechanically, finished the evidence collection.

As soon as I had all the information I needed, I jumped into my car and headed away from the scene. I fought to focus my mind on the medical data and to shut out my emotional reactions to the horror. So often in residency we had to stuff our emotions deep into our subconscious—there to lie hidden, not talked about, not explored, not released.

I thought, *This isn't the medical center—this is a little town—now my home. These folks—the victim and the survivors—I don't know them, but in a sense they are my new neighbors.* I thought of the woman and her daughter. *Who are they? Will they be OK? Will they—can they—ever recover from witnessing such a horrible tragedy? Will* I *ever recover?*

My mind was a swirling cacophony of emotions. Suddenly I felt a strange sensation on my cheeks—my own tears. I pulled off the road, turned off the engine, and lay my forehead on the steering wheel. Three years of residency—of learning to be a doctor—with all of its anxiety and failure and repressed emotion erupted out of its repose like the deep waters of a dam that had just burst. I sobbed and sobbed. After a bit, I collected myself and blew my nose. I found myself wondering, *Who am I crying for? Myself, or for this senseless tragedy? Maybe both,* I thought.

I heard a noise and turned to see the hearse, followed by Deputy Rogers in his squad car, drive by me and down the hill—probably heading toward Moody Funeral Home. After the cars drove by, my eyes were drawn to what appeared to be, in the half-moon's light, a football field—and beyond it, a cemetery. *What an unusual combination,* I thought. In a sense, one represented my past. Then I felt goose bumps on my arms as I realized that the other represented my future. I was between the two. *What would be said,* I wondered, *when life ended for me? What would my tombstone say?*

I had no idea what my future in this small town might hold. I again bowed my head onto the steering wheel. *Father in heaven,* I prayed silently, haltingly, and confusedly. I continued, *Thank you for the skills and training you have given me. Guide my use of them, and grant me your wisdom. I don't want my life to end like this man's did tonight. I want my life to mean something. I ask you to use me. I ask for your peace.*

I felt suddenly refreshed—strangely peaceful. I smiled at the cemetery. *Not just yet*, I said silently to the rolling knoll of tombstones. *Not just yet!*

I started the car and headed back toward Hospital Hill. When I arrived at the house, I walked around back and sat down on the wrought-iron bench just outside our back door. The view was stunning—looking up the Deep Creek Valley and into the Great Smoky Mountains National Park. I filled my lungs with the crisp fall mountain air.

I thought about my decision to move to the Smoky Mountains to practice medicine. *What were you thinking when you accepted a position in this little town? Was it these mountains?* The second thoughts and self-doubt that plague every young physician flooded my mind. *Am I just a do-gooder? Am I trying to be some sort of Brother Teresa? Was I wrong to bring my pregnant wife and young child to these rural mountains? Some of the local doctors don't really want me here anyway. Should I just leave? Have I made the worst mistake of my life?*

There were no answers that night. But as I sat there looking out over the mountains—which had been viewed by several generations of Smoky Mountain physicians before me—a fragile sense of peace came over me. *No*, I thought. *This is where I'm supposed to be. At least for now.*

The wind was picking up, and I began to feel chilled. I got up off the bench to go inside. I scrubbed my hands and face and then crawled into bed. As I wrapped my trembling arms around my sleeping wife, Barb didn't stir. After four years of medical school and three years of residency, she was used to me leaving at night, sometimes several times a night, to respond to emergencies at the hospital. She slept well that night. I did not.

Here I was in a warm and safe home, with a precious daughter and incredible wife. I was in an amazing profession in a stunningly beautiful location. But the self-doubts had come crawling into the house with me. *Was this all a mistake?* I thought again. *One big mistake?*

part one

REWIND: FIRST STOP IN BRYSON CITY

chapter two

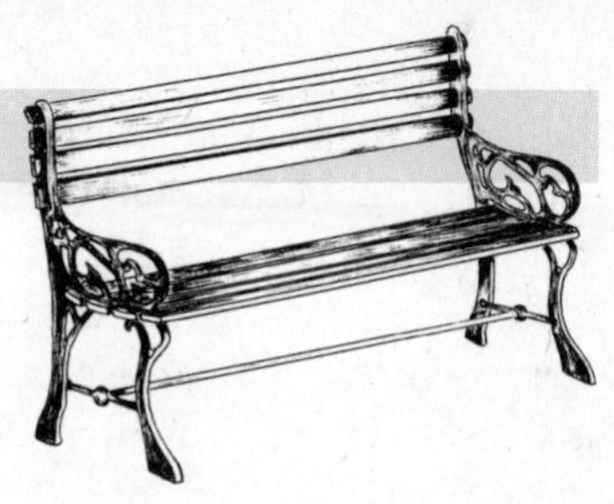

The Arrival

It was October, nearly one year before the murder. I was in the last year of my residency training at Duke University. During my residency, Barb and I had fallen in love with North Carolina and her people. I would finish my training the next summer, and I needed to find a place to ply my trade. We were also looking for a place to raise our family—a special place where we might even spend the rest of our lives.

During residency, we would use our vacation time and the rare long weekend to look around the state for places in which to both live and practice. First, we looked at the Outer Banks and along the beaches of the southeastern part of the state. None of these sites really clicked with us. Then we looked at small towns in the midlands. But after one trip to the Smoky Mountains, we knew that was where our hearts were calling us.

And then, there we were, driving toward the heart of the Smokies for my interview with the board at Swain County Hospital. Barb and I had spent hours and hours reviewing information from each potential practice site—information sent by the local hospital or the town's Chamber of Commerce. The packets would often include appeals from local political officials that extolled the benefits of their locale and why a physician could experience permanent bliss only by choosing to practice in their town or area. Conspicuously absent was any explanation as to why, if their town was so perfect, they were not already overrun with doctors.

Quite frankly, our motive for agreeing to an interview in Bryson City was because we had friends who had camped and hiked there and who had lauded its natural beauty and its relative isolation. So we wanted to see the area, but we were pretty sure we would ultimately end up in one of the many other towns whose public-relation materials were so much more attractive. One by one, however, the towns had been checked off our list. Now only Bryson City remained. Would this town open her arms to us? And if so, would we feel called to accept her embrace?

As we drove along, I glanced over at my wife of nearly seven years. Barb, my best friend, reclined in the passenger seat, fast asleep on a fluffy pillow. The so-called air-conditioning of our aging Toyota Corolla was laboring to keep the car cool and gently blowing Barb's blond bangs off her forehead. I smiled. I felt fortunate to be married to such a remarkable woman. We had known each other since we were five years old, growing up in Baton Rouge, Louisiana. Voted by her high school class as the most likely to succeed, Barb had earned her bachelor of science degree in English education at Louisiana State University, where she had been both the sweetheart of my fraternity—and of me. We were married during our last year of college, and then Barb had been a teacher in New Orleans, Louisiana, and in Durham, North Carolina—first putting me through medical school and then through family medicine residency. At LSU, she had been awarded a Ph.T. degree—Putting Hubby Through!

Our first child had been born during my internship. I was on an emergency-room rotation—forty hours on and eight hours off, followed by forty more on and eight more off. Barb's water broke five weeks before Katherine Lee was due, and our premature daughter was born on the night before Halloween during one of my eight-hours-off periods. Although I had been a physician for less than a year, in medical school I had delivered several hundred babies in the charity hospital system in Louisiana. I had taken care of many more in the nursery. I had seen babies of all sizes, shapes, colors, and looks. And, speaking quite objectively, I had never seen a more beautiful baby than Kate!

But when Kate was about four months old, Barb became very concerned that our daughter wasn't progressing normally. Our family doctor tried to reassure us, but over the next two months Barb became more and more concerned. Finally we were referred to an elderly, but gentle and wise, pediatric neurologist. After his exam of Kate, he told us that he too was concerned. It was the first assurance Barb had received that her maternal instincts were accurate. The neurologist then ordered a special brain X ray called a CT scan.

I vividly remember when Dr. Renuart broke the terrible news. "Barb and Walt, Kate has cerebral palsy."

He let the words sink in and then continued. "Two-thirds to three-quarters of her brain has died and has dissolved away. This must have happened at some time during the pregnancy, and I suspect we'll never know what caused it. Maybe it was a knot in the umbilical cord; maybe it was just a kink. But somehow her brain lost oxygen and nutrients and died. On the right side, she has no brain at all—just water. On the other side, she has about one-half of the normal brain mass."

We were in shock. He continued. "Barb and Walt, Kate will grow physically. She'll probably grow to a normal adult size. She'll be bigger, but she'll never be better. She'll probably never walk, she'll never talk, she'll never think abstractly. You'll just have to take her home and love her the way she is."

He was quiet. The waiting room was quiet. It was as though the sun had set permanently and the lights had gone out. The room seemed colder, the world crueler.

Our marriage suffered. We suffered. I now understand why over 70 percent of couples with a child who has a disability end up divorced. But with the help of several terrific neighbors and a caring faith community and church, Barb and I got through our first two difficult years with Kate. Our marriage became stronger as Kate became stronger. In her development she was already defying the experts' prognoses. And right now she was snoozing contentedly in her car seat in the back of the yellow Toyota.

When we crossed the Swain County line, a remarkable transformation took place in the geography. The mountains seemed to be higher—and they seemed greener and lusher. There seemed to be more open space and less clutter and development. I breathed in deeply as I took in the vistas looking north, into the Great Smoky Mountains National Park, mountain ridge after mountain ridge as far as the eye could see.

I left the four-lane highway at the Hyatt Creek/Ela exit and found myself on a small two-lane country road that followed a wide, slow-moving river. Suddenly the air cooled and Barb stirred. "Are we there, honey?" she asked through a yawn and a prolonged stretch.

"I think this is it."

She returned her seat to its full, upright, and locked position and started to look around.

"It's beautiful, Walt," she whispered.

We were both awestruck at the scenery. It may have been the first moment we knew that this is where we might be for a while. Barb pulled out the directions to the inn where we were to spend the night. It was a Sunday afternoon, and our interview at the hospital was scheduled for the next morning.

Winding up the side of the Tuckaseigee River valley, we drove slowly to admire the fall wildflowers adorning the sides of the road. The leaves were beginning to turn a hundred shades of yellow and orange and red. We came upon a quaint house with a beautiful flower-and-vegetable garden to the side. A small sign by the driveway announced *The Douthits*. I hit the brakes, coming to a sudden stop.

"What is it, honey?" asked my startled wife.

"The Douthits. Isn't that the name of the administrator of the Swain County Hospital?"

"I think so. Why?"

"Do you think this might be their house? Shouldn't we stop in and say hi?"

"Might not hurt."

I put the car in reverse and pulled into the driveway. I went to the door while Barb gently aroused Kate from her slumber. The small ranch-style house was well kept. The yard was nicely manicured with a variety of fruit trees. The garden at the side of the house was a profusion of color—with flowers and vegetables. Someone in this home both loved the land and knew how to tend it.

After knocking a time or two, I could see what appeared to be the woman of the house approaching the front door. There was a small window in the door through which she peered at me, obviously not recognizing me. However, instead of opening the door, she began to walk away. I was perplexed.

Then I heard her call out, "Judy, one of your little friends is here to see you."

I felt the color rising in my cheeks. Through medical school and residency, professors and teachers always accused me of looking too young to be a doctor. This was almost always the first comment of any new patient I saw—a source of considerable irritation for me. I wanted to look older, more distinguished. But my youthful appearance wouldn't cooperate with my ambition.

Soon a striking young woman, who appeared to be in her late teens or early twenties, bounded to the door. Clearly she was gleeful about whomever she thought might be at the door. Without looking through the window, she flung the door open. She was in full smile, her shoulder-length dark hair glistening in the sunlight as she playfully tossed it back. Then her eyes met mine and took on the look of confusion. She quickly realized that I was not the eagerly anticipated visitor and that she, in fact, had no idea who I was. The smile melted into a frown, and she slammed the door shut.

I thought, *This is awfully strange behavior!* As she disappeared down the hall, she called out, "Dad, I don't have a clue who that is at the door." All was quiet for a moment or two. I didn't know whether to knock again or to leave. As I was pondering the options, a man rounded the corner and headed toward the door. Like his wife, he gazed through the window at me and, like her, looked equally perplexed. At least he opened the door.

He was a handsome middle-aged man, executive appearing in looks but dressed in casual slacks and a crisp short-sleeved Oxford shirt. "How may I help you, young man?" he inquired. By now, Barb was walking toward the door, with Kate in her arms. He glanced at her, and then his countenance softened and he began to smile. Before I could answer, he asked, "Are you Dr. Larimore?"

I was relieved to see that we had very likely chosen the right home. "I am! I am indeed." Barb was now at my side. "This is Barb and our daughter, Kate."

"Come in. Please come in."

As we entered, he called out, "Margie, it's the Larimores!"

He showed us into a small but comfortable living room with a picture window revealing a spectacular view of the Alarka Mountains, which lay south of town. There wasn't a building or structure in sight. I was mesmerized by the striking panorama.

"Please. Please make yourselves comfortable," Mr. Douthit said. "I knew you were coming in tonight. The Shells are expecting you at the inn."

As we took a seat on a plush couch, a friendly and pleasant-looking woman appeared from the kitchen carrying a tray of iced tea and drinking glasses.

"Dr. and Mrs. Larimore," our host said, "this is my wife, Margie."

As she placed the tray on the coffee table, her smile was radiant, and we could see where Judy's smile had come from. "It is so good to meet you," she declared as she shook our hands. "Please make yourself at home. I've brought some sweet tea, and I'll bring some cookies in a moment." She glanced over at Kate, resting in Barb's arms. "And who is this?" inquired Mrs. Douthit.

"This is Kate," Barb answered. "She's almost two years old."

"Earl and I can't *wait* to be grandparents, but I'm afraid that's a few years away. James and Judy are both in college and haven't found their spouses just yet." Margie's friendly chatter put us at ease, and we leaned back in the couch and began to enjoy an unhurried visit with the Douthits.

Earl had been the administrator of the hospital since its inception, he told us. It was chartered as a not-for-profit community hospital in 1948 with one idea in mind: offering top-quality medical care to the people of Swain County and the surrounding areas from conception until death. Swain County Hospital opened its doors two years later, in 1950, with twenty beds, and had expanded several times to its current capacity of forty beds. Earl smiled as he related the rather difficult childhood the hospital had endured. Now, as a growing young adult, the hospital was administered by an all-voluntary community-based board of trustees. I smiled at his analogy.

Earl suddenly looked very serious. He gazed out the window for a moment and then back at me. "Dr. Larimore, I want to be honest with you. We've had a lot of doctors come and go, so we want you to see our town up close—the good, the bad, and the ugly. If you like it, if you feel called here, then we can definitely use another physician. But if it's not your style, I don't want you or Mrs. Larimore to be embarrassed to tell us so. We're not just looking for *a* doctor; we're looking for the *right* doctor. Someone we like, and someone who likes us."

This was definitely a unique approach. Most of the other hospital recruiters we'd met were intent on *selling* their community to us. They wanted us there—period, no matter what. This man seemed different, and I appreciated his candor and found it refreshing. For the next hour, he told us about the town. He explained the background and personality of each of the town's current four general practitioners and two general surgeons. He laid out the hospital's plans for expansion to a more modern facility and the board's desire to have new physicians who were well trained in family medicine—who could care for patients in the intensive care unit or the emergency room, who could care for children and families, who could deliver babies and provide surgical services. He explained that they were looking for well-trained generalists—not specialists.

This was music to my ears. Physicians who practice general medicine typically are entirely different creatures than those who specialize. They are trained differently, they think differently, and they practice differently. The specialist has to know everything about a narrow field of medicine—especially the rare and uncommon disorders within their area of focus. The generalist must know the common—the breadth, if you would, of medicine. The specialist cares for a single organ system, age-group, or gender—the generalist the entire family within his or her community. I recalled the observation of the famous internist Sir William Osler, who was reported to have said, "A well-trained, sensible family doctor is one of the most valuable assets in a community." The more Earl talked about what the local hospital was looking for, the more I knew that this town could be exactly what we were looking for.

Suddenly he stood, subtly indicating that our visit was over. "Well, I've kept you two far too long. We'll have plenty of time to visit tomorrow. You ought to get up to the inn. John and Ella Jo can't wait to meet you."

He then approached me and almost whispered, "John and Ella Jo have really been behind the move to bring some new young doctors into the area. Not everyone agrees with them, especially some of our older doctors. But they can tell you more about this."

As we said good-bye and got in the car, Barb expressed my thoughts. "Walt, *what* are we getting into?"

"I don't know, honey. I don't know."

chapter three

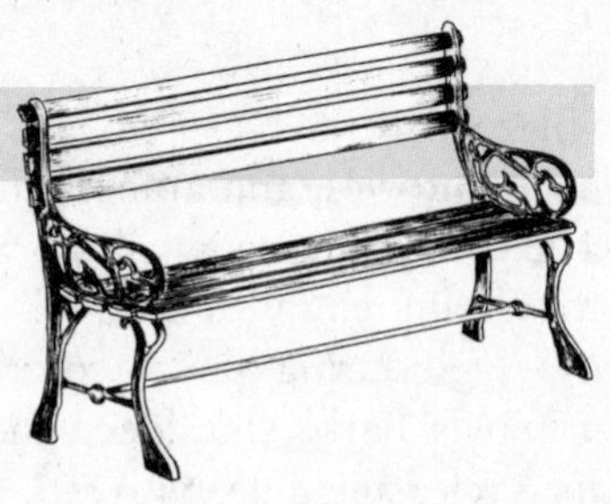

THE HEMLOCK INN

As we left the Douthit's driveway, we turned up Galbreath Creek Road. Less than a mile up was the entrance to the Hemlock Inn—almost hidden in a large grove of massive hemlock and Georgia pine trees. The driveway turned steeply up and around what was to us flatlanders a small mountain—but was to the locals "just a hill." At the top, the driveway opened into a clearing with several small sprawling buildings cast over the knob and looking out over the mountains.

We parked and followed the signs to the registration area. Opening a screen door, we entered a rustic lobby. Overstuffed sofas and wooden rockers were scattered comfortably around the room. A small crackling fire was burning in the stone fireplace, giving the room both a nice ambience and a pleasant aroma. Shelves of books ringed the room. Tables with puzzles partially constructed and newspapers partially read were scattered across the room.

We walked out onto a side porch, with woven-seat rocking chairs strewn across it, to look out at the hills that were literally ablaze with color—reds and yellows were painted across the promontories, and amber and orange hues speckled the bluffs. The spectacular view all the way to the peak of the distant Frye Mountain reminded us of why so many chose to visit this wilderness area during the fall color season. I found myself placing my arm over Barb's shoulders, and she leaned into me, taking in and then releasing a deep breath. I had come to learn that this was a sign of satisfaction—that she was feeling comfortable and safe. I looked down at her and she up at me. She gave me a squeeze. "I think this just might be *the* place."

I smiled. "Maybe so."

We looked back across the sensational expanse spread before us. We were indeed beginning to fall in love with this place.

"Well, well, well. Howdy, howdy, howdy," boomed a baritone voice, just before the sound of a slammed screen door greeted our ears. A tall, handsome man, in his fifties I would guess, was rapidly strolling toward us. His smile was pleasant and welcoming, and his right hand reached out, seeking a mate.

"You must be the Larimores. Welcome, welcome, welcome."

He seemed to enjoy treble phrases.

"I'm John Shell, the proprietor of the Hemlock Inn. We are *so* glad you're here."

After introductions were made and vigorous handshakes dispensed to us all, including Kate, we were ushered to the rocking chairs where we had a bit of pleasant discussion. Between subjects, I asked, "Mr. Shell, tell me a little bit about this area."

"John! Please call me John. Now, are you sure you want to talk about *that?*"

"You bet!" I exclaimed. "History is an interest of mine, Mr. Shell—uh, John."

"Well, first folks in this area were the Cherokee Indians," John began. "Their land holdings have long since been stolen from them, and many were forced to walk by foot to Oklahoma in what they called 'the Trail of Tears.' But many have returned, and the tribe has a strong pride that keeps the past alive through history and legends. The first white man known to walk these hills was William Bartram—who is described as having been an adventurous and courageous botanist. He came into this valley from the Nantahala Range in 1775. By that time there was an Indian village called Younaahqua, or Big Bear Springs. It was located on the present site of Bryson City. Later the village was called Tuckaleechy and later yet, Charleston."

"How do you remember all those dates and facts?" Barb asked.

"Oh, Barb, I just tell these stories so many times it's almost second nature," John chuckled. "But that's enough history for now. Let's go get you folks registered. You won't want to miss supper. Ella Jo is stirring up a right hearty dinner for you all."

In a second he was up and off. We followed him through the living room and the dining room, set with round tables, each with a lazy Susan at its center, and into the small office. Then, keys in hand, we were off to our room.

The inn's rooms, over thirty years old, showed their age—but the simple rustic character was appealing and relaxing. No TV or radio or phone—just the basics: an antique bed and chest of drawers, comfortable wing chairs, and a nice bathroom. The Hemlock Inn was *not* designed for guests to just stay put in their rooms. The days were for the hills.

I was unpacking our belongings and Barb was changing Kate's diaper when we heard the ringing of a bell. "Must be the dinner bell," Barb commented, almost to herself. She was humming and Kate was smiling. I sat down to wait for them to finish as the rays of the setting sun streamed in through the screen door, mixing with the evening breeze to rustle my wife's hair. My soul smiled.

The dining hall was packed. Each of the seven tables had eight chairs around it. John was at the door, greeting each arrival and directing them to their assigned table. Seating and eating was strictly family style—with John arranging and rearranging the inn's guests at each meal—guaranteeing a variety of conversation with people from all over the country. At our table alone were folks from New York, Atlanta, and Oregon—all escaping to the hills for rest and relaxation—some to read, some to think and meditate, some to hike. There was also a couple from Bryson City named R.P. and Sally Jenkins.

"Ella Jo's cooking is known far and wide," chimed R.P. "We like to come up here every chance we can—at least when John and Ella Jo have an opening at their table." He laughed, and John Shell beamed.

As we were gathering at our tables and meeting our meal mates, the young servers were bringing out a smorgasbord of delicacies on large platters and in large bowls. I was curious as to why no one was sitting—everybody was standing and greeting each other—it was almost like being at a family reunion. But I wasn't left to wonder for very long. At the ping of a small bell, everyone turned to Mr. Shell. At his side was a woman, about the same age but much shorter and rounder—and her smile was as radiant as an angel's.

When the crowd had quieted down a bit, John began, "Ella Jo and I want to welcome you newcomers to Hemlock Inn, which is known for having the most beautiful innkeeper's wife east of the Mississippi!"

He looked down at her and smiled, and her blush could have warmed the room. She grinned and whispered out loud, "Actually, east of California," and laughed easily and gracefully.

"I agree," he stated emphatically. "May we say grace?"

We all bowed our heads. Now I must tell you that this only made it easier to inhale the delicious aromas wafting up from the table. I was secretly hoping for a *very* short prayer—although surprised that there would be one at all. Not that I minded prayer—it was a regular part of my life, at least before meals. As a family we always said grace before a meal. It's just that doing so at a public dinner was a new and somewhat uncomfortable experience for me. However, after only a line or two, something happened.

"Our heavenly Father, we thank Thee for this beautiful day and this lovely location," John prayed earnestly. "We thank Thee for our health and for the activities of this day. And now we bow to thank Thee for this bountiful provision that Thou hast laid before us this evening. Bless the hands that prepared it for us. Bless it to our nourishment. And bless us to Thy service. May our sleep tonight be both sweet and restful. We ask these things in the wonderful name of Thy Son, Jesus Christ, our Lord."

During the prayer I had been instantly taken back to my paternal grandparents' home in Memphis, Tennessee. We held hands as we sat at the table, and my grandfather, a Pullman conductor for the Illinois Central railway's *La Louisiane*, would pray, "Father in heaven, we thank Thee . . ." In John's voice and words I could hear my grandfather—and the feelings of warmth and nostalgia were overwhelming. As he prayed, so did I—thanking God for the blessing of a family, chock-full of memories and traditions.

I was brought back to reality when the entire room chanted in unison: "Amen."

Before the amen's echo bounced back from the walls of the dining room, chairs were scraping on the wooden floor as the guests seemingly dove into their places and began to dig into the hearty and delicious Southern meal: fried chicken (of course!), perfectly seasoned with a thick, crunchy breading; green beans with ham hocks and just the right saltiness; ham that fell off the bone and could easily be cut with a fork; silky-smooth, creamy potatoes with brown and sawmill gravies; three types of salad with a variety of made-from-scratch salad dressings; candied carrots; at least three types of freshly baked bread, and a basketful of steaming-hot yeast rolls with local clover and wildflower honey butter and a wealth of other delectable homemade toppings and jams. Barb teased me that my eyes were as big as the countless platters.

During dinner we found out that R.P. and Sally were active in the leadership of Arlington Heights Baptist Church and that R.P was a past chairman of the hospital board of trustees. It finally dawned on me that this was not such a coincidence that the Jenkinses just happened to be here for dinner and seated at our table.

As Kate happily munched on a drumstick and mashed potatoes, we visited with a tableful of new friends. Most had been at the inn for one- or two-week visits, year after year, for many years. We learned that true newcomers, such as us, were uncommon—a rarity, in fact.

The dinner discussion was the typical talk of the day—where people went, what they did, what they discovered. Questions to the newcomers centered on who you were, where you were from, and why you had been so foolish as to never have visited the Hemlock Inn before. Upon discovering that we were considering this little hamlet as our home, a cacophony of oohs and aahs circled the table, peppered with comments like, "I'd sure move here if I could," and, "You sure are lucky to pick a place like this," or, "Honey, see what I told you? Young professionals *are* moving out here." These comments were an encouragement to us and increased our rapidly growing feelings of fondness for the area.

After we had finished dinner and Barb put Kate in bed, we joined the Shells and Jenkinses on the porch, pulling a group of rocking chairs into a semicircle. Dusk was beginning to fall over the valley, and as it did, the autumn colors of the trees underwent transformation through a cornucopia of colors. The hills almost seemed aflame. The wind was blowing gently.

Barb broke the companionable silence. "John and Ella Jo, what led you all to move to the area, or are you from here originally?"

"Oh no, we're not from here," John answered. "But we love this area. Moved up here from Atlanta to own and operate this lovely little inn in this beautiful locale." He paused to consider how best to articulate his thoughts. "There is so *very much* here that we like. The history of the area is a rich one. The people are wonderful. The weather's great, and there's plenty of fresh air and water. It's a safe community—a great place to raise your kids. The schools are good, and the teachers are top-notch. It's a religious community. The hunting and fishing and hiking are superb. And thanks to Mr. Douthit, our little hospital is just fabulous—given its size."

He paused again, looking troubled, almost confused about where to go next. R.P. Jenkins intervened, "Walt, our surgical services at the hospital are excellent. Dr. Mitchell and Dr. Cunningham bring in a lot of business and a lot of patients. They do a lot of surgery and do a good job. Our operating rooms are large and modern—they have all the best equipment. And our two nurse anesthetists are fabulous. People will travel here from quite a ways away."

John interjected, "And *some* of our medical services are good. We've got a new lab and a new emergency room. Our new X-ray equipment is state-of-the-art. Dr. Sale does an excellent job, but . . ."

There was a moment of silence. John and R.P. looked at each other. *What is going on?* I wondered.

"What the men are hesitant to say," interrupted Sally, "is that we have a number of physicians that are . . ." She paused. "How should I say this? They are, uh, getting older. Sometimes they can be moody or cantankerous. People around here get a little tired of that. So they leave and take their medical business elsewhere. That's not good for the hospital or the community."

"The older folks, the ones who have trouble traveling, don't seem to be leaving to see doctors in other towns," explained R.P. "But the younger families sure are."

"And," added John, "it doesn't help that none of the doctors deliver babies anymore. That's one of the reasons we're so excited about the possibility of you coming here. Your experience and training would be perfect for our little town."

"I wouldn't expect things to change overnight," warned R.P. "But as folks get to know you, they'll certainly stay and have their babies here."

"Just like they used to," Sally mused.

Quietness reigned for a few moments as we relished the cool air and the enveloping dusk.

"Well, folks," I said, "Barb and I are excited about finding a home for our family. We're eager to settle down and to build a practice somewhere. So tomorrow's going to be a special day for us. We're looking forward to seeing the hospital and the town and meeting the board members and the other doctors."

Both couples looked at each other. Then Ella Jo spoke her first words to me, "Dr. Larimore, I have to be honest with you. I'm not sure some of the doctors want to meet you."

This unsettled me. I was quiet.

"They've become so comfortable with the status quo. They've got plenty of patients and they make enough money. I'm worried that you might be a threat to them. There's not been a new doctor around here in quite a while. And those who come usually get shooed right away. It's downright shameful." She seemed almost angry.

"Ella Jo," her husband cautioned, "don't you think that type of talk's a bit severe for our new friend?"

"No, I do not!" she exclaimed—sitting up in her chair. "You board members"—she was pointing a finger at her husband and then at R.P.—"need to take back a little control from those medical deities. They've been running things just a little bit too long. It's hurting our hospital, and it's hurting our town. What we need around here is a well-timed funeral or two!" She sat back, obviously fuming, but done with her soliloquy.

"Well," Sally added, "I don't think that's true of Mitch and Ray. Mitch made Ray feel welcome and has brought him right into this community. And the other doctors have come to accept him. Goodness, I even think they like him."

"That's only because he's with Mitch," opined Ella Jo.

There was another moment of silence. "What we need to do," suggested John, "is see if Mitch and Ray would consider taking Walt under their wing. Their office is empty in the morning while they're in the operating room. One of them is off one afternoon a week. So there's room in their office at least seven half-days a week."

"That's a great idea, John!" exclaimed R.P. as he sat up in his rocking chair. "That could take care of everything."

I wasn't so sure. Barb gave me that "we need to go" look. "Ladies and gentlemen," I announced, "it's been a lovely evening. Ella Jo, the meal was above and beyond." Her smile ran ear to ear. "We've had a long day and have a longer one tomorrow. If it's OK, I think we'll turn in."

"Oh, you bet. You betcha," said John. He, Ella Jo, and the Jenkinses stood to say farewell.

"Tomorrow's the start of another day. A great day!" exclaimed R.P. as we turned to leave.

As we walked to our room, I thought, *Beautiful land. Warm and gracious people. Rich history. But the medical staff and the hospital—would I want to be a part of them? Or would they even want me to be a part of them?* My doubts were growing.

chapter four

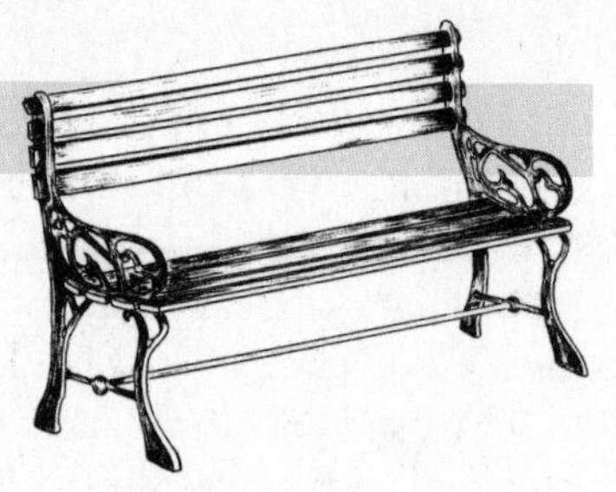

The Grand Tour

The next morning we were due to tour the hospital. We left the inn early so we'd have some time to drive around. The route from the Hemlock Inn to the Swain County General Hospital wound along Highway 19, which intersected Galbreath Creek Road at the edge of Fergusson's farm—the largest dairy farm in the county. Looking south across the farm, the mountains rose steeply to meet a brilliant-blue cloudless sky. We gazed at layer upon layer of misty clouds, slowly floating and drifting over the ridges and hollows—the namesake of the Smoky Mountains.

After turning on Highway 19 and skirting the farm, the road crossed the wide, shallow, but rapidly flowing Tuckaseigee River. The narrow two-lane bridge looked like a relic from the '30s or '40s—its handsome arches beginning to crumble a bit and its concrete walls scarred by many an encounter with wayward vehicles.

Just before entering Bryson City, right across the street from Shuler's Produce (the home of what would become our favorite boiled peanuts), we passed a barn. On the side, in peeling paint, was the injunction to

SEE 7 STATES FROM ROCK CITY
LOOKOUT MOUNTAIN—CHATTANOOGA, TN

Right after the barn, Highway 19 became Main Street. In a moment we were in the downtown business district—only three blocks long and one block wide—bookended by the only two traffic lights in town. We turned north onto Everett Street—named after the man who served as Bryson City's first mayor in the 1880s—and then crossed the river and followed the signs to Hospital Hill. As we turned toward the hospital, Barb pointed out a sign:

SWAIN SURGICAL ASSOCIATES
DR. WILLIAM E. MITCHELL AND DR. E. RAY CUNNINGHAM

We turned up Hospital Hill Road. At the top of the hill stood the Swain County General Hospital. The general practitioners' offices were across the road from the hospital. We passed their shingles—Harold Bacon, M.D., Eric Nordling, M.D., Paul Sale, M.D., and Ken Mathieson, D.O.—and pulled into the hospital parking lot.

"Walt," Barb commented, "the hospital is a whole lot larger than I expected." I agreed. The brick split-level building appeared well maintained and very nicely landscaped with flowers blooming alongside the entrance. With a mixture of apprehension and excitement, we entered through the front doors.

The receptionist was expecting us, and we were quickly escorted to Mr. Douthit's office.

After initial pleasantries, Mr. Douthit leaned forward purposely. "Walt and Barb, the hospital board has authorized me to aggressively recruit young physicians. Our current physicians are not getting any younger. With the exception of Dr. Cunningham, they range in age from fifty-two to eighty and have been here many, many years. They're excellent, but we must look to the future."

He paused for a moment. "Our first recruiting success was Dr. Ray Cunningham. He grew up here in Bryson City and then went away to college, medical school, and his surgical residency in Charleston, South Carolina. While away, he met and married a critical care nurse named Nancy. They've been in town for about two years. Ray is in practice with Bill Mitchell—we all call him Mitch—and Nancy is our infection control nurse here in the hospital."

Earl continued, "As surgeons, Mitch and Ray are available to do cesarean sections, but we have no nursery and no doctors interested in delivering and caring for newborns. So we're excited about the skills you could bring to our institution—especially with regard to pediatrics, obstetrics, and sports medicine."

"Sports medicine?" I asked. My interest must have been obvious. For the previous three years I had served the Duke University athletic department as a team physician. For a frustrated athlete such as myself, being able to receive sports medicine training at Duke was a dream come true.

"Well, we have some mighty fine sports programs here at Swain County High School. In fact, even though there's not a thousand folks in town, we'll have one to two thousand folks at home football games. Folks around here take their football real serious. But none of our doctors have been particularly interested in being the team physician. Only a couple, Dr. Mitchell and Dr. Bacon, will even go to some of the games. But they prefer to sit in the stands rather than work directly on the sidelines with the players and coaches. They'll come out of the stands to check out the more seriously hurt kids, but most of the time they leave the minor injuries to the coaches or paramedics."

He took a sip of coffee and glanced out the window. A gentle breeze was blowing through the trees. He continued, "We'll talk finances later, but first I want our head nurse, Eudora Gunn, to take you on a tour. Then I've got our board coming in to meet with you for lunch. Sound OK?"

There was a knock on the door and an ancient, petite, gray-haired nurse entered. Eudora Gunn had been a doctor's wife.

After he died, she continued in the profession and had retired to Bryson City. Earl had hired her early on to supervise the growing nursing staff when the original hospital building had expanded, offering more outpatient services and more beds.

Eudora took us on the grand tour and introduced us to *everyone*. We started in the three-bed emergency room, which was covered on a rotating basis by each of the town's six doctors, twenty-four hours a day, seven days a week. There we met Louise Thomas, who had run the ER for more years than most folks could remember. As Eudora continued to guide us around, conversations with the staff were warm and sincere, sprinkled with laughter. We were feeling more and more welcome.

"Ms. Gunn," Barb inquired, "has the hospital had trouble attracting new physicians?" (I knew Barb wanted to get an "in the trenches" perspective from a nurse.) Eudora told us stories about a number of young doctors who had come and gone. "In almost every case," she confided, "the spouse became unhappy with the small-town life—so eventually they left." We had the distinct and haunting feeling that this might be true but that it wasn't the whole truth!

The lab and X-ray facilities were small but more than adequate for a small hospital. Betty Carlson, the director of the lab, was a delightful woman who told us which lab results we could get immediately and which ones were sent to a reference lab and came back a day or two later. The pathologist in nearby Sylva helped supervise the lab and did all of the pathology studies. If frozen-section studies were necessary, the pathologist from Sylva would drive over to perform the study right in the hospital.

Carroll Stevenson headed the X-ray department. Not only did he provide all the basic X-ray services we would need, but a CT scanner came once a week on a trailer truck. This was big news, as CT scanners were fairly new technology. Also, although Bryson City had no radiologist in town, a consulting radiologist from a nearby city came in three days a week to read X-ray studies and to perform procedures like an upper gastrointestinal series or a barium enema. In an emergency, a radiologist could be called to travel the twenty-five or thirty miles to help us out.

The patient rooms were all semiprivate, although, since the hospital was seldom full, many patients enjoyed having a private room. An old four-bed ward next to the nurses' station was used as an intensive care unit—for the sickest of the hospital's patients.

All in all, we were increasingly impressed as we toured this small but more than adequate hospital. We liked the facility, and we liked the people. While not dazzled, we were well pleased.

Toward the end of the tour, Ms. Gunn said, "Let me show you a surprise." We exited from a side door and crossed the road to a small house sided with green cedar shingles. To us, the long narrow house looked like the shotgun houses we'd come to love while in medical school in New Orleans. As we walked up Eudora explained, "The hospital owns this home. They've allowed me to live here, but now that I'll be retiring I'll be moving out. The hospital would be willing to make this home available to you all, for as long as you might need it, at no cost."

Barb and I looked at each other with surprise etched in our eyes.

When we opened the screen door, we stepped into a fairly modern kitchen. The dining room's large picture window overlooked the rolling hills of the Swain County Recreation Park and the nearly endless vistas of the Deep Creek Valley and the Great Smoky Mountains National Park. As though in a spell, we were drawn to the window. "It's beautiful!" Barb gasped. Kate giggled contentedly.

At one end of the house was a master bedroom connected to a nursery. At the other end was a living room and a guest suite. There was a large basement and a root cellar. The root cellar was dug into the stone and lined with shelves full of canned fruits, vegetables, and meats. "People can stuff all the time and bring it to the staff at the hospital. I keep it down here because the temperature in the root cellar is sixty degrees year-round. You won't find yourself having to buy a lot of food, I suspect—just the staples."

Back outside the house I was drawn toward the fruit tree orchard behind the house. "That's Dr. Bacon's orchard. He tends it ever so carefully. You'll have all the apples, peaches, and pears you could ever eat. He lives right here behind the hospital. He's even older than me!" Eudora laughed out loud and continued, "Goodness, he's almost eighty and has been practicing here for nearly fifty years.

"Well, we better get back. You need to meet the board." Eudora took off in the direction of the hospital. We followed. Kate had fallen asleep in her stroller.

As the nurse led us down the driveway, Barb put her arm through mine, leaned toward me, and whispered, "Other than being right next to the hospital, I think it's perfect! I already know where all our furniture will go—and it will all fit!"

chapter five

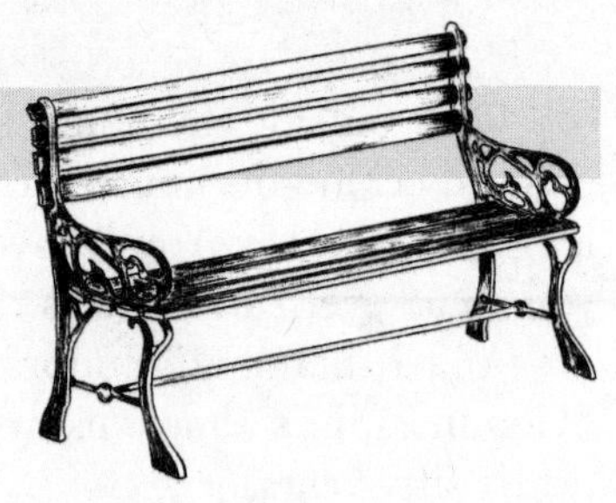

The Interview

When we returned to the hospital, we were escorted to Mr. Douthit's office. The conference room table was set for lunch; a group of men and women stood by the table talking. When we entered, everyone became very quiet and turned to stare at us.

Mr. Douthit broke the silence. "Ladies and gentlemen, this is Dr. and Mrs. Larimore and little Kate."

He introduced us around. We knew John Shell and R.P. Jenkins. We met Horace and Ruby DeHart, Jack Lyday, Fred Moody, and several other board members. We were seated for lunch, and Eloise Newman, the hospital's registered dietician, came with her staff to serve us.

Now, after having interviewed across the width and breadth of western North Carolina, we had eaten way too much hospital food. So our expectations for this event were very low indeed. But what was served us that day was a feast. The crispy, nicely spiced fried chicken, almond-covered rainbow trout, and garden-fresh green beans, carrots, and broccoli smelled glorious. The mouth-watering aroma of yeast rolls was accompanied by a collection of what I suspected were homemade jellies and jams nestled around a small pot of butter. And the food tasted even better than it smelled.

"Like Sunday dinner at my grandmom's," reminisced Fred Moody. Fred was a local attorney and the chairman of the board. He had graduated from one of the state's finest law schools, the University of North Carolina, and he had come to Swain County to practice law. He looked at me and said, "Dr. Larimore, this is one reason *not* to come to Swain County. The eating is just too good. I weighed only 160 pounds when I began my practice here. Now look at me." He was smiling and rubbing his tummy.

"Now, Fred, we're supposed to encourage the Larimores," chimed in Ruby DeHart. Mr. and Mrs. DeHart looked to be in their late seventies. They had lived in the county for decades and were active in local cultural affairs.

"Well, the Larimores are staying with the Shells out at the Hemlock Inn," added R.P., as John Shell began beaming. "So they've already been exposed to Ella Jo's culinary expertise. But I've got to tell you, Eloise, there's no better hospital food anywhere in this country."

"Here, here," exclaimed voices around the table as iced-tea glasses were raised in a salute.

Eloise, a tall, handsome woman, floated around the table serving her guests. She blushed, "Well, my lands! No need to fuss. It's just a little lunch."

"A *little* lunch!" exclaimed Jack Lyday. Jack was the county agricultural extension chairman. "If this is a *little* lunch, then the Titanic was a *little* rowboat." Everyone laughed.

"Seriously," began Earl Douthit, "the board has discussed Eloise's food before. It's one of the reasons we have trouble getting patients to leave the hospital after they're well. Most of them have never eaten so good."

Jack added, "That's why we got Fred to join the board."

"Why's that?" inquired the apparently perplexed attorney.

"To protect us from a lawsuit when some fool patient eats himself to death."

The laughter started again—at Fred's expense. We basked in the warmth of the group. They obviously liked each other and thought the world of their little hospital. We were feeling more and more like we were with family.

Eloise reentered the room with a homemade pie in each hand. One was pecan and one was apple—and both were piping hot, with steam rising off the flaky crusts. Behind her was a kitchen staff member with a container of homemade vanilla-bean ice cream. Behind them walked several men in white coats. It was like a parade—and it was time for us to meet the local doctors.

Introductions were made between us and the six physicians—Bacon, Mitchell, Cunningham, Mathieson, Nordling, and Sale. Harold Bacon, M.D., was the eldest of the county physicians. Although supposedly retired, he continued to see patients in the ER and in his small office next to the hospital. He had in the not too distant past lit up the gossip lines in a two-county area by marrying a decades-younger divorcée of one of the circuit judges. Mercedith Bacon was at the top of the social pecking order in town and very active in the local Democratic party.

William E. "Mitch" Mitchell, M.D., had served the United States as a Mobile Army Surgical Hospital (MASH) surgeon. He was a political and financial powerhouse in the county. A general surgeon and general practitioner, he had run the county medical proceedings for the twenty-five or so years of his practice and of late had run the local Republican party. After the death of his first wife, and not to be outdone by his senior competitor, he soon married a much younger woman from Asheville, North Carolina—Gay, whose name matched her propensity to laugh and socialize.

Ray Cunningham, M.D., the youngest doctor of the bunch, had begun his medical career in his hometown only two years before my arrival. He was in practice with Dr. Mitchell in the county's first and only "group practice," Swain Surgical Associates.

Kenneth Mathieson, D.O., had retired to Swain County after years of private practice elsewhere. Also in his late sixties, he found retirement to be unacceptable, and not too long after his arrival, he started practice.

Eric Nordling, M.D., and Paul Sale, M.D., were both general practitioners in their fifties. Both seemed to be loners; however, I learned that their approach to medicine was as different as night and day. Dr. Sale took care of nearly all of his patients' medical problems right in Bryson City—referring folks to the "big city" only if absolutely necessary. Dr. Nordling had the opposite approach: He referred as much as he could out-of-town. This conflict in practice and philosophy did not bode well for the future of their continuing to practice in the same town.

And yet that day of our first meeting all the doctors and board members seemed to hold genuinely warm feelings toward each other. The laughter was free-flowing. At one time I noticed R.P., Earl, and Dr. Mitchell enmeshed in a hushed and very serious discussion, which apparently ended in harmony—smiles and backslapping all around.

After dessert, the entire group, including the physicians, began to excuse themselves. Each of the nonphysicians seemed truly glad we were there. The physicians seemed a bit more reserved, but a few were friendly. Dr. Mathieson seemed irritated that I had come to town. Drs. Nordling and Sale also appeared reluctant to welcome me. But for the moment I wasn't discouraged.

Suddenly Barb and I were alone with Mr. Douthit. "Cathy," he called to his secretary, "would you bring me the folder with the offer?"

Here we go, I thought. *Down to business.*

Cathy brought in a manila folder that Earl carefully opened. He began to shuffle through the papers. "Ah, here we go." He pulled out a single sheet.

"Walt, we're not an affluent county or a rich hospital. Our physicians here are not paid even the national average. If you and Barb are looking to make a lot of money, we're not going to be the place for you all. But if you're looking for the type of environment and lifestyle that Swain County has to offer, then you'll be pleased here—and your income will be more than satisfactory." He paused.

"Go on," I encouraged.

He nodded. "First of all, we would pay for all of your relocation expenses. And we'd want the mover to do all your packing for you."

"That sounds very generous, Earl."

"To keep your expenses down, we'll cover all of your professional costs for the first year of practice. I've talked to Dr. Mitchell, and he will allow you to practice in his office, with himself and Dr. Cunningham. He will keep any monies collected for your work. We'll pay him your overhead and any money short on your salary. Any money collected above the cost of your salary and overhead will be split. One-half to Dr. Mitchell, one-quarter to the hospital, and one-quarter to you and Barb."

"OK," I stammered, trying to figure out the implications of such a complex arrangement.

"We're offering a first-year salary of $30,000."

I was *shocked*. This was less than the university paid their medical residents in training.

"Quite frankly, Mr. Douthit, I had expected a more generous offer. Most of the other counties are offering . . ." My voice trailed off. *Was I being selfish? NO! After thirteen years of primary and secondary school, four years of college, four years of medical school—all with no income other than Barb's teaching income, nine months per year—a teaching fellowship in England and three years of residency—not to mention school loans—NO, I was not being selfish. This offer just would not do!*

I glanced at my wife and saw that she was trying to hide her disappointment. "Now, I can tell by the looks on your faces that the salary *appears* inadequate. However, we feel the *entire* offer may be of interest to you." He paused and then continued. "On top of what I've mentioned, we will offer you, at no charge, the home that Mrs. Gunn showed you earlier—for as long as you wish to live there. The hospital will cover the cost of any and all repairs and of all utility bills and phone bills. In addition, you are both welcome to dine at the hospital at any time at no cost."

I looked at Barb again. She seemed a bit more interested.

"We will also pay for all of the costs incurred by you both when Dr. Larimore has to travel in order to obtain his continuing medical education. We would just ask that you preapprove these expenses with me prior to traveling.

"We will also provide for all your insurance needs—malpractice, car, home, medical, dental, life, and disability—which should save you considerable funds."

This was starting to sound better.

"In addition, we want to build a brand-new office building. Our current physician office facilities are not what we would like. So the board has had conversations with the North Carolina Office of Rural Health and with the Duke Endowment. We would like you to help us design a family medicine center, to be located within walking distance of the hospital. We'd like to begin recruiting other family doctors who could join you in this building as our older physicians begin to retire. This building will not cost you any money, but just the effort to help us design a wonderful facility for our clients—your patients."

This was starting to sound *much* better.

"Last, but not least, we want you to help us design our new in-hospital birthing center. We'd like to take the old delivery rooms and make them into two comfortable and attractive birthing suites that will be the envy of any hospital in the state."

He sat back and took a deep breath. "Walt and Barb, I don't expect you to decide overnight. Please take this information, think about it, and let me know your decision when you're ready." We agreed.

As we left the hospital, offer in hand, my mind was swirling. *There is so much that seems attractive, almost charming, about this town and its medical community. Yet neither Barb nor I have ever lived in such a small hamlet—so far from family and, Barb reminds me, a mall! We'll need time to talk, to debrief, and to pray.*

"Walt," pleaded Barb, "let's find a place to walk and talk." We decided to drive up the Deep Creek Valley. At the northern end of the valley was the border of the Great Smoky Mountains National Park. We parked and strolled up the wide walking path beside the creek—it was smooth enough to roll Kate in her stroller. During the summer the creek would be filled with the shrieks of kids tubing over the white-water rapids—but today it was peacefully quiet. Within a short time we were alone—just the rustling of the wide rushing creek, the singing of the birds in the thick overhead canopy, and the joyous sounds of Kate singing and humming.

Thick mountain laurel and rhododendron bushes hugged the path. We passed two waterfalls and sat, overlooking each, simply to discuss our impressions and concerns. Maybe it was the sheer beauty of the place—or the warmth of her people—or the hospital's overwhelming need for updated medical skills and technology. Maybe it was our need to feel needed—to make a difference. Whatever the reason, our hearts were in agreement. Barb leaned over to me as we sat by Indian Creek Falls and pronounced, "Walt, I think this *is* the place!" I smiled in agreement.

We left the park and drove west from town out to the Nantahala River, where we watched fly fishermen and kayakers at play. We soaked in the quiet, marveled at the lushness of the hills, and breathed in the clean mountain air. We spent the afternoon driving around the small town—and up the valleys and dales surrounding her—and into some of her larger hollows. It was a warm afternoon and the sky was a crystal blue. Our peace and confidence only grew. Eventually, as dusk began to descend, we drove back to town for our scheduled dinner with the partners of Swain Surgical Associates.

We parked and walked up to the gracious manor where we were to dine. What was then known as the Frye-Randolph House was originally a small Victorian lodge, built in 1895 by Captain Amos Frye. The captain later expanded it to an L-shaped plan, complete with lovely gables and a stone-pillared porch. Captain Frye and his wife, Lillian, lived in the house while the captain's palatial Fryemont Inn was being constructed just up the hill. After the captain's death, Lillian, by then the first practicing female attorney in western North Carolina, continued to practice law and run the inn until her death in 1957.

Dr. Mitchell and Dr. Cunningham were sitting outside with their wives, and they stood as we approached. Introductions were made all around. Gay Mitchell and Nancy Cunningham were the kind of sparkly people everyone instantly falls in love with. Their smiles were gracious and their laughter was infectious. We immediately liked them both—Gay the louder and more buoyant, effervescent, and outgoing; Nancy the more quiet and reserved. Unlike their husbands, both had been raised elsewhere, but they were quick to share with us their newfound love for the mountains and Bryson City.

The dinner bell rang, and we were escorted into what appeared to be a beautifully kept private home. Only the tourist brochures on one wall gave away the purpose of the Frye-Randolph house. We were shown into a private dining room where rich linens covered the table and candles glowed warmly. Our five-course meal was accompanied by light, friendly conversation. The proprietor and his wife, Bill and Ruth Adams, were in and out of the room—obviously great friends of our hosts and most hospitable to Barb, Kate, and me.

After dinner we were shown to the sitting room. A small fire was burning in the fireplace, and as Ray lit his pipe, the room's aromas were heady and warming.

"Walt," said Bill "Mitch" Mitchell, almost sounding stern, "Ray and I think you'd be a great addition to our medical staff. And we'd love for you to join us in our practice—at least until your new medical office can be built. But I've just got one concern I need to discuss with you."

"What's that?" I asked. My curiosity grew as Gay pulled out a folded sheaf of papers from her purse.

Mitch unfolded the papers, looked them over, and then handed them to me. "Is this the paperwork you sent to the hospital?"

I looked at the papers, instantly recognizing them. "Yes, this is the list of medical and surgical privileges I've asked for. I filled this out for Mr. Douthit before we made our trip out here. Is something wrong?"

"Sure is. Look at page 5."

I turned to page 5. It was a request for surgical privileges—cholecystectomy, appendectomy, fracture repair, hip replacement, upper gastrointestinal endoscopy, colonoscopy, breast biopsy, skin grafts, and a plethora of other surgical procedures. The page was blank. I had not checked any interest in applying for *any* of these privileges, because I had not been trained in any of these procedures.

"What's the problem, Dr. Mitchell?"

"Well, you didn't mark that you wanted any of those privileges."

"That's true, I don't. I'd plan to assist you and Ray with most of these. But I'm not trained to do them as the primary surgeon."

Mitch looked incredulous. Ray chimed in, "Told you!"

Mitch looked at him a bit sharply and then back at me. "You're a doctor, aren't you? You mean them boys at Duke didn't train you to be a doctor? How can you practice out here if you can't do these things?"

I smiled. Ray broke the silence, nicely expressing my sentiments. "Mitch, that's what I told you. I know that in your day doctors *were* trained to do it all. But not in *these* days. Family physicians like Walt, just like the ones I trained with at the Medical University of South Carolina in Charleston, are trained to take care of about 95 percent of all the problems they encounter. And they're trained to assist a general surgeon. But they're *not* general surgeons."

Mitch sighed. "Makes no sense to me. If you can't help us in the OR, then you're no more helpful than Sale, Mathieson, or Nordling."

"That's not true!" exclaimed Ray. "Walt's had *lots* more training than they've had. He's trained in obstetrics and delivering babies. He's trained to take care of infants and kids. He's forgotten a lot more dermatology, gynecology, psychology, and neurology than I ever learned. He knows intensive care. And he *can* help us in the OR. Furthermore, I'll bet he's willing to learn some of these procedures—aren't you, Walt?"

Ten eyes were suddenly fixed on me—including Barb's. "Well," I stammered, "sure . . . I'd be willing to learn anything that you'd be willing to teach me."

Mitch looked at me for a moment, then at Ray. Ray smiled at Mitch, and then they *both* looked at me.

"OK," Mitch said, standing up and extending his hand toward mine. "We have a deal." I shook his hand, not entirely taking in what had just occurred.

On the way back along the river toward the Hemlock Inn we were silent. As we crossed the Tuckaseigee River bridge, Barb spoke. "Walt . . ."

"Yes, honey?"

"Did we just agree to move to Bryson City?"

We were quiet for a few minutes. As we turned onto Galbreath Creek Road, I nodded. "I think so, honey. I think so."

"Me, too," she said.

"Me, too," piped Kate's voice from the backseat.

part two

Fast-Forward: Awkward Beginnings in the Smokies

chapter six

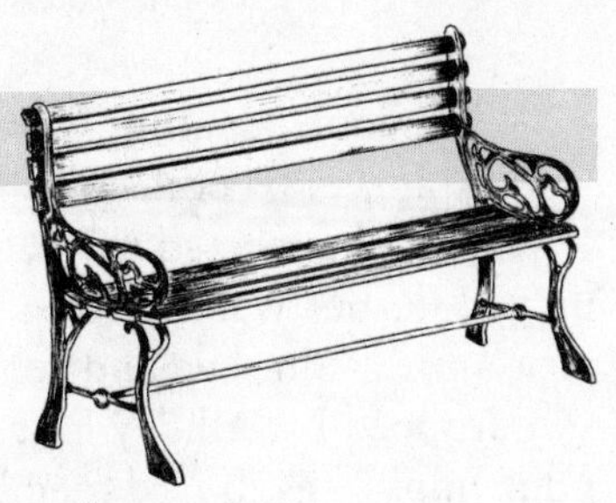

SETTLING IN

We arrived in Bryson City in September of the next year. Kate was nearly three, and after the many months Barb and I had devoted to doing physical therapy with her, she could stand and, with the help of special braces, even walk some.

We spent our first weekend moving into our little house by the hospital. One of my first duties was picking a location in which to place our newest possession—a wrought-iron park bench. The three of us sat in it together for the first time, gazing out over the Smoky Mountains.

I put my arm around Barb's shoulder and she snuggled close, with Kate tucked into the crook of her arm. "It fits the four of us just fine!"

For a second, Barb looked confused, and then she laughed as she rubbed her beautifully enlarged tummy. "Only five more months to go!" Barb was pregnant with our second child. We were excited about becoming parents again—and this child would be the second grandchild we would give to our families. Kate had been the first.

"You look beautiful," I whispered, as I pulled my wife close.

"This will be perfect," she whispered. "Perfect."

We had expected to spend the weekend alone, just getting moved in, but were in for a delightful surprise. We were both pleasantly astonished and genuinely warmed as person after person dropped by. All day long, on Saturday and on Sunday, hospital employees, board members, a few doctors, local political figures, and the newspaper editor—most of them accompanied by their families—dropped by to greet us, welcome us, and share housewarming gifts. Our root-cellar shelves were rapidly filling with their gifts of canned fruits, vegetables, jams, and stews.

"I'm not sure I'll *ever* have to go to the grocery," exclaimed Barb.

Sunday afternoon, Dr. Bacon was helping Barb organize the shelves in the cellar. "Well, honey, if you do run out, just let some of Walt's patients know—and they'll restock it all!" He chuckled. We were soon to realize that he was dead serious.

"Where's the new doc?" came a call from upstairs.

I bounded up the stairs to see a handsome young man who, when he saw me, stuck out his hand. "Howdy, Doc. I'm Gary Ayers, the morning deejay at WBHN. We're the local radio station—AM 1590." He paused. "In fact, we're not hard to find on the dial. We're the *only* radio station that can be heard in these parts," he observed with a chuckle. "Just wanted to come by and meet you—especially since you guys are a *great* source of information for the morning news!"

For a moment I thought he might be kidding. But he was not. Gary, as I was to learn, was *the* source to the county not only for world and national news, but he was also the mouthpiece for most of the better community gossip.

As Gary left, Dr. Bacon and Barb came up from the basement. "Be careful, son," warned Dr. Bacon. "If he likes ya, he can make life pleasant indeed. If he doesn't, look out!"

"What about the newspaper editor?" I asked.

"Oh, you mean Pete Lawson?"

"Yep. He was by earlier today."

"Nope. Not to worry. Pete's as good a newspaper journalist as there is. Plays his stories straight to the facts. I like Pete. A lot!"

And I liked Dr. Bacon. I asked him if he'd give me a personal tour of his orchard, located between our house and his.

"You bet!" he agreed. "Do you want to help with the harvest? I'd be glad to trade a few jars of canned apples, applesauce, and apple cider for your efforts."

"I'd be delighted." I smiled as I accompanied him outside, where we strolled through the rows of trees and eventually sat under the large fir tree in front of his house, gazing at the mountains. Dr. Bacon began to share a bit about his past and about the medical history of the county.

"Walt, I'm glad you're going to bring the babies back to our county. I was *so* disappointed when the younger docs and the hospital decided to let Sylva take away *our* babies."

"Did you attend births yourself?" I inquired.

He looked at me as though I had four eyes. "Did I attend births?" He chuckled. "Why, I've delivered hundreds and hundreds of babies in my time. I've even delivered scores of babies of girls I delivered. Now, *that's* when you know you're getting old—when you deliver your second generation. I've even delivered a few of what I call third-generation babies—where I delivered the baby, the mom, *and* the grandmom. Now you know for sure that I'm ancient." He threw his head back and laughed. I wondered if I would ever have the amazing privilege to attend the birth of a woman whose own birth I had attended.

"For years and years," Dr. Bacon continued, "before the hospital was built, why, I'd do all the deliveries at home. Remember taking the Model-T out into the hollows. Sometimes I'd have to push her across the creek bottoms, sometimes get stuck in mud. Would get to the house and stay until the baby was born. Sometimes that'd be hours and sometimes a day or two. Had some basic rules I'd always go by. First of all, I'd get all of the men out of the house. Something about men. They just seemed to get in the way and women always labored better without them."

"Wouldn't you allow a daddy to see his child be born?" I inquired.

"Oh my, yes. But he'd only be in the way during labor. He could come in for the birth—if *he* wanted and *if she* wanted. But if she didn't want him there, he'd just have to stay out. They seemed to understand—especially in those days.

"What I really wanted at the house was women—especially women who had had babies. Walt, there's not a man in the world that can care for a woman in labor like a woman who has gone through labor. I can't explain it, but a woman caring for a woman just seems to make the labor go faster. If there weren't any ladies present when I got there, I'd send the husband off to get some. It would give him something useful to do.

"I'd also always bring a bundle of fresh newspaper from town."

"Newspaper? For what?"

"Walt, newspaper is sterile. Perfectly sterile. I'd use the paper as drapes and to keep the bedsheets dry and clean. Also, once I knew the mom and baby were OK, it gave me a chance to sit back and catch up on the goings-on in town." He chuckled.

"Good obstetrics requires a good portion of patience. I've always said I needed a good cigar and a rocking chair to enjoy while I'm reading that paper. Just let things go their natural way. Almost always came out all right. In over forty years I only lost one baby—and that was from a knotted cord. And," he emphasized, "I never lost a mom. Not one."

"But, Dr. Bacon," I quizzed, "what if you got in trouble? Did you go to a hospital?"

"Nope. In those days we did what was called kitchen surgery."

"You did the C-sections at home?" I was incredulous.

"Of course. Why not?"

I paused. "Well, the lack of sterility could cause infection and death, and what about the lack of help and proper equipment?"

He laughed. "I guess you've never been exposed to 'kitchen surgery,' have you?"

"Nope, that's for sure!" I replied.

"Walt, in our kitchen-surgery days we had to be content to work with no luxuries. We had to learn what essentials we had to have and how to work quickly. This is more than most modern surgeons know. Our system involved small incisions and rapid surgery. I tell you, this minimizes more infection than all the modern face masks and head covers combined. We seldom had *any* wound infections in our kitchen surgeries. The most important factor was prompt surgery. Small incisions. Minimal unnecessary trauma to the tissues. Expert surgical technique. Minimal exposure of any internal tissue to the air. Rapid closure and good dressings. These were the tools and trade of the kitchen surgeon."

"Was lighting a problem?"

"It could be at times. Indeed. Lantern light is hard to use for surgery. The best light was a car headlight."

"What did you do—bring a car battery and light into the house?"

He laughed. "No, no. Just have someone drive the car up to the door or in front of a kitchen window and leave the headlights on—pointing into the kitchen. Then a family member would use a looking glass to reflect the light into the wound or onto the perineum. There was no better light than this—just as good as any operating room light!"

I was fascinated. "What about anesthesia?"

"That *was* a problem. Nothing worse than to have a patient half-asleep—or, worse yet, waking up during the surgery—or, even worse, to have your volunteer anesthetist go to sleep from the fumes! So I'd usually take my nurse or my wife, who knew how to administer the chloroform—in the early days—and ether more recently. Of course, in the last few years, portable masks of halothane were a godsend. If my wife or my nurse wasn't with me, I'd have to train a family member or friend. Actually, some of the country pastors who'd always show up during my sick calls got pretty good at helping me pass the gas."

I was quiet—feeling a bit uneducated in spite of having just come out of a prestigious medical school. I couldn't imagine the rush, the fear, the excitement of a kitchen C-section—or a kitchen *anything*.

Dr. Bacon continued, "Walt, some of my best surgery was done under these adverse conditions. It's hard to explain, but there was something much more exhilarating about driving through the elements to attend a woman delivering a baby at her home than there ever could be walking across the street to the hospital. Nothing stimulating in *that*."

I sensed our conversation was coming to a close. The apples were calling my new friend—some needing to be crushed for applesauce, some needing to be cooked, and some needing to be made into cider.

"The chief value, Walt, of the kitchen operations, over those done in the hospital, is that the young surgeon, the inexperienced physician, had no one to blame but himself for a poor result or an infection after surgery. You young guys, if any of these things happen, tend to blame the hospital or the staff or the nurses.

"The second value of the kitchen surgery is that it could be done immediately. Young surgeons don't understand that fear has an adverse influence on surgical recovery. You see, to most people hospitals are scary. They all seem to know people—friends and neighbors—who've gone to hospitals and died. Yet they know no one who's died on the kitchen table. So when the hospital was built and we quit doing most of our kitchen surgeries, we didn't realize the harm we were doing. Instead of seeing people early in their disease, they waited to come in for help. Patients would resist advice to go to the hospital and only come in when in severe distress.

"So, when the hospital first started doing surgery, our morbidity and mortality was unacceptably high. This caused more fear of the hospital and produced a vicious cycle. The more people who fared poorly at the hospital, the longer people waited to come to the hospital, and the worse they did when they got there. When we operated at home, we operated earlier in the course of the disease. The patient's fear factor was *much* lower. And they just did better.

"Walt, even today, I will *not* operate on someone who is deathly frightened. It doesn't matter what causes the fear—I will not operate on a frightened patient. I've seen more than one patient who, prior to surgery, said they had dreamed that they didn't recover—or who confessed that they thought they were going to die and not recuperate—who proceeded to make good on their prediction. Every old surgeon has similar stories to tell from his own experience. When we autopsied these cases, we did not find the cause of death in even one."

He took a slow, deep breath. "I believe they were literally scared to death."

He slowly stood. "Been a pleasure chatting with you, Walt, but I bet that lovely wife of yours has Sunday dinner about ready. You get on and I'll bring some cans over later this evening."

Later that evening Dr. Bacon did bring over dozens of jars and cans. Our root cellar was well stocked with candied apples, apple chips, applesauce, and apple cider—some of the best we've ever had. But the old physician's real gift that day was grounding me a bit in the history of my profession and my community. I may have known more *modern* medicine than he did, but not more medicine—and certainly not more *interesting* medicine!

chapter seven

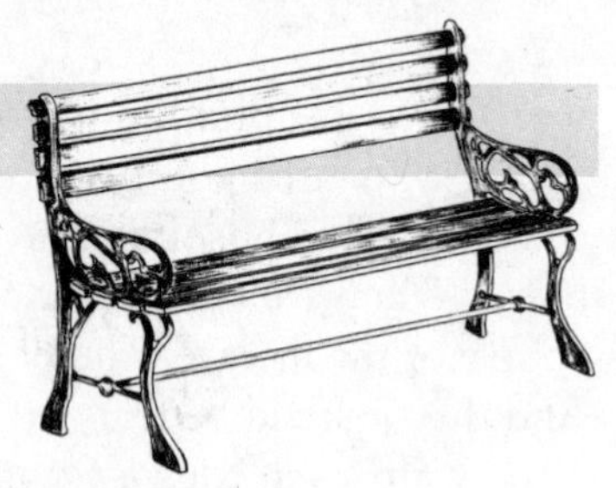

First-Day Jitters

Monday morning was my first official day of work as a family physician—the culmination of twenty-four years of education. I almost couldn't believe the big day had finally arrived. Today, I would just start making a living—almost eleven years after many of my high school friends had begun their careers.

I arrived at the hospital at 5:30 A.M., ready to meet Mitch for rounds. Mitch was, according to the evening supervisor, uncharacteristically late. I stood nervously at the nurses' station waiting for him. I didn't have to wait long. In he strode, confident and lively. As he entered the station, as though on cue all the nurses stood to attention and in unison said, "Good morning, Dr. Mitchell." I'm sure my mouth dropped open. Then a nurse appeared from nowhere with a pot of coffee and a clean cup and saucer. "Thank you, Verna," commented Mitch, without looking up from the pile of charts that had been carefully organized at his chair. This was *not* the way we made rounds at Duke. We were lucky if the nurses even noticed us when we entered the station—that is, unless they needed something.

As he quickly thumbed through each chart, he hummed to himself. Then Ray showed up. Same song, second verse. "Good morning, Dr. Cunningham!"

"Good morning, ladies."

Then another pot of coffee and cup with saucer appeared.

Then Mitch was up and walking. "Let's go see some folks, Walt." And we were off to visit the patients. I heard the rustling of charts. I looked back at the station as we headed down the corridor and saw Verna putting the charts into a rolling cart and then quickly pushing it as she tried to catch up with us.

As we saw each patient—each having been awakened by a nurse's aide who preceded us—Mitch asked a few questions, answered a few questions, did a brief exam, and, while doing so, dictated a note that was written in the chart by Verna. Then he would dictate some orders, which she would write on the order sheet—which he would sign—and then we were off to the next patient. The whole process took only a few moments with each patient.

We'd briefly discuss each case. He'd ask what I would do and then briskly criticize each answer. "Son, that's *not* the way we do it here." Attached to this oft-repeated phrase might be, "That would just cost too much money, and the folks here don't have much" or, "That's the hard way to do it. How about . . . ?" or, "You've got to be kidding! Didn't they teach you . . . ?" I was beginning to doubt the value of *any* of my last seven years of medical education—when suddenly we were done.

"Let's go get a bite to eat before surgery. We've got a full schedule today." We took the elevator—the first of only two in all of Swain County—to the basement and entered the small but comfortable hospital dining room, Eloise Newman's domain. Eloise, whose culinary expertise had so dazzled us the previous year, had been brought up in the "red meat and potatoes" school of food preparation. If it wasn't fried and fatty, it wasn't worth serving. The spread of available food was impressive. But no yogurt, no fruit, no muesli or granola, no whole-grain foods here! Rather, a veritable smorgasbord of yeast rolls and homemade biscuits, butter, homemade jams, eggs (scrambled or poached or fried), bacon, sausage (link or patty), grits, home fries, and pots and pots of strong coffee. This was a nutritional den of iniquity. But did it all ever taste good!

"Walt," barked Dr. Mitchell, "enough relaxation. Let's get to work!" With that, we were off to the OR, which was larger and more spacious than I had remembered from my tour when I'd interviewed here. The equipment was spotless and looked nearly new.

"Earl and the board keep us well equipped. You won't find a better OR suite in western North Carolina," Mitch boasted. He introduced me to the two nurse anesthetists, Alfred Jensen and Kim Hamrick. Kim's husband, Mike, was one of only two dentists in the county. Mitch also introduced me to the scrub and circulating nurses and the orderly. For a small hospital this was quite the setup. Ray and Mitch operated all morning, five to six days a week. Big-city surgeons often only operate two or three mornings a week!

That morning I assisted Mitch and Ray with eight surgeries—an elective gallbladder removal for gallstones, a hip replacement, an elective hernia repair, a breast biopsy, the placement of a set of ear tubes in a three-year-old, an upper gastrointestinal endoscopy, and the removal of a large tumor on a man's back. In some areas, general surgeons won't do this many cases in a week. But with a referral area of two counties, this OR was kept hopping.

My confidence in the hospital and in these two surgeons soared. They were good—*very* good. Mitch's hands were as fast and as skilled as any I had seen at any hospital in which I had scrubbed.

Throughout the morning Mitch invited me to do more and more. My adrenaline surged as I sensed the surgeons and the staff closely watching my every move. Did I know how to properly scrub, gown, and glove? Did I know how to assist—to help the surgeon operate more quickly and effectively? Could I sew—

and sew quickly? I answered question after question about anatomy, options, techniques, postoperative orders—sometimes almost nonstop. I felt like a medical student or an intern. It was an intense morning, yet I felt I did well, and I sensed Mitch's unspoken approval. He left the OR after the last operation, while Ray and I closed.

"Walt, don't feel bad about all these questions," Ray said. "Mitch did that to me for weeks. I wish I had done as well as you did."

I was pleased that Ray was satisfied. It had been a *very* good morning.

When we were finished, I walked over to the house for lunch.

"Honey, how'd it go?" shouted Barb from the basement.

"It went super. Great morning."

I sat at the dining room table and opened up the *Smoky Mountain Times*. This small but excellent paper would bring us the news and the printable gossip on a weekly basis.

I heard Barb running up the steps. When she got to the kitchen, she announced, "Honey, Eudora brought a mess of fresh vegetables and greens. She said that the nurses and staff always bring in extra from their gardens and leave it in the staff lounge so that those without gardens can enjoy the pickings."

This was our introduction into one of the major unreported industries of Swain County, namely, hunting and growing your own food. So Barb and I enjoyed our first lunch of local produce—remarking to one another that there was nothing tastier than fresh, homegrown food.

After lunch, we drove down Hospital Hill and into town for a visit to the Swain County courthouse, where we planned to register to vote. Its gold-painted dome, mounted with a weather vane, sat atop a neoclassical, octagonal cupola. Its whitewashed stucco walls and its pillared, ionic portico made for a very impressive courthouse for a small town.

Upstairs housed a beautiful courtroom, right out of *To Kill a Mockingbird*. Downstairs contained some of the county offices, including the voter registration area. There were only three ladies sitting at their desks when we arrived. One of them stood and approached us, "I'm Sarah Robinson. How may I help you?" Registration took only a few moments and went well until Sarah asked, "What party will you be registering with?"

In unison we answered, "Independent." We thought this would be wise, given the split politics of the medical staff and until we better knew the "lay of the land." Instantly we suspected we had made a mistake. Sarah gawked at us with a funny look. The other two women in the room nearly broke their necks snapping their heads up to stare at us, incredulously, as their collective jaws dropped.

Sarah recovered the quickest. "Independent?" she inquired.

"Yep," I said.

She repeated, "*Independent?*"

"Can't we register Independent?" queried Barb.

"Of course you *can,*" she responded, "it's just that *no one ever does.*" The other two women in the office acquiesced by solemnly shaking their heads no.

"OK," said Barb, "that's what we'd like to do."

The clerk bowed her head to stare at us over her glasses. She made one last effort. "Are you *sure?*"

"Yes, ma'am, we're sure," replied my less-than-sure-sounding wife.

We left the office with our new, but temporary, voting cards.

"That was weird!" we both agreed. We had no idea.

After dropping Barb off at the house, I drove to the offices of Swain Surgical Associates, looking forward with some trepidation to my first afternoon in private practice. I parked in the staff parking lot at the back of the building and entered the staff entrance. Shouts of "Surprise!" and "Welcome!" startled me and there on the table was a small cake that Sarah Crisp, the receptionist, had baked. The icing on the top spelled out the words, "Welcome, Dr. Walt." I'm sure I was beaming as I took in the scene—balloons and confetti blanketing the entire staff lounge.

Helen Gibson had been Mitch's nurse since before they invented dirt. Gay, Mitch's wife, was a trained medical assistant and had volunteered to assist Dr. Cunningham, and now me. Reva Blanton worked the front office with Sarah.

Helen spoke first. "Honey, we've got some cake here for you, but first the boss wants to see you. He's in his office." I suspected Mitch just wanted to personally welcome me to the practice. I suspected wrong. He was working on a chart, intently scrawling away.

"Sit down," he barked, pointing to an old chair with cracked leather upholstery. When he finished, he rocked back in his chair, looking not at me but at the ceiling. This did not look good. Then he rocked forward, placed his arms on the desktop and clasped his hands, looking down at them. This did not look good at all. Then he looked up at me.

"You stupid?" he asked.

"Am I what?" I wasn't sure I'd heard him right.

"You *stupid?*" he repeated.

"I . . . I don't think so," I stammered. "Why?"

"Well, son, you registered Independent at the courthouse. And I've got to tell you, in this county, *that's* stupid."

I slumped in the chair, stunned. "Most folks around here were born and bred Democrat. I consider that a form of ignorance at best, and a genetic disease at worst. But at least folks stand on their beliefs, even if they are wrong. Most of the rest of us, those with brains and the ability to think for ourselves, are Republican. And I tell you what, son; we're growing into a force around here. I suspect we'll take some of the elections coming up in a few weeks."

He rocked back, looking a bit more relaxed now that he had unleashed his verbal onslaught. He continued, "But, son, Independent is stupid. It says you stand for nothing, you believe nothing. It says you don't want to vote in the primaries. It says you're straddling the fence. Son, you need to make a decision. You need to either fish or cut bait."

Then he rocked forward again and opened up his desk drawer, taking out two small pieces of paper.

"Walt, I told the clerk's office you wanted to revoke your Independent status and change to the Republican party." He slid the two voter registration cards across the table.

I was in shock. It hadn't taken me more than ten minutes to get Barb home. Maybe another five to get to the office. In that time, Mitch had gotten the news from someone and had both the gumption and political clout to reregister us and get the cards sent to his office. I was outraged and didn't know whether to explode in righteous indignation or to laugh. I did neither. I guess I really *was* in shock.

He continued, "Son, if you want to change these to Democrat, that's fine with me, but you just can't be Independent—not around here. It's stupid. Go on now. The girls have a little party planned for you. I'll be out in a few minutes."

I picked up the voter registration cards. I wasn't sure what I would do with them. I turned to leave.

"Please close the door after you." I did.

Everyone was busy now. The waiting room was packed. The exam rooms were filled. The office buzzed.

Helen came up to me with her first of many, many orders. "Your first patient is in room 2. The patient just has a cold but is as mad as a hornet that he can't see Mitch. I tried to calm him down a bit for you. Let me know if you need any help."

I looked over the chart, then knocked and entered the room.

The patient took one look at me and exclaimed, "You've got to be kidding me. You're *too young to be a doctor*, aren't you? HELEN, WHERE'S MY DOCTOR? HELEN?!?!"

I thought to myself, with some dismay, *Welcome to rural private practice!*

chapter eight

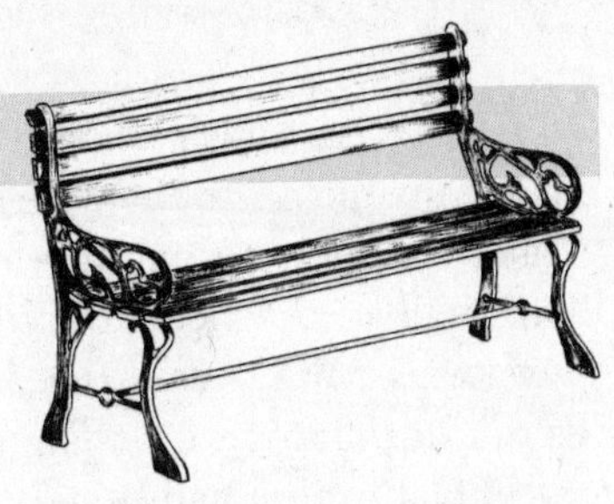

Emergency!

Somehow I survived my first week of practice, including my first experience as the county coroner. So far I hadn't made any major mistakes or caused any fatalities. The sixth commandment of Moses parallels the first commandment of medicine. This is often publicly quoted as "First, do no harm." However, any first-year medical student knows that behind the lines what is really taught them is this: "First, do not kill the patient"—always wise advice.

At 6:00 A.M. the clock radio went off to initiate both our day and the broadcast day of WBHN, AM 1590. Each weekday morning, Barb and I would awaken with WBHN and morning deejay Gary Ayers's country crooning and conservative views about local gossip—uh, news and politics. I immediately grew fond of his broadcasting style and later would come to appreciate his friendship.

Today I was to be the on-call doctor once again. Each of the seven of us had four or five twenty-four-hour cycles each month in which we were on call for the county. Since the hospital had no emergency physicians and the county had no coroner, the on-call doctor was responsible for every kind of medical need that came up on his shift. Although the variety of this type of responsibility was brand-new to me, it was the way general practitioners in America had practiced for scores of decades. My fellow six local physicians, with over 170 years of combined practice experience, were not planning on changing the way things had been done since the hospital had been built decades before.

Depending on the time of year, the day of the week, whether it was a payday or not, being on call could be leisurely, slow, and relaxing, or it could be gruesome, grimy, and laborious. Tourist season, running from Memorial Day weekend through Labor Day weekend, as well as the "color season" of October, was usually fraught with the medical consequences of the foolishness or carelessness of visiting tourists. Being September—the summer tourist rush over and the annual color season yet to come—things were lighter now, both in the office I shared with Mitch and Ray and in the hospital ER. So by the time I'd seen the last patient of the day at the office, I was still wondering when I'd face my first on-call emergency.

I drove home from the office, parked in the old garage behind our home, and enjoyed walking around a bit on the path that ran along the ridge of Hospital Hill. All of the windows in our house were open, and I could see the curtains gently wafting in the evening breeze. I could hear Barb singing in the kitchen. I could feel the stress of the day melting away. I loved to hear Barb sing or hum—it was one of the ways by which I could tell that her day had gone well. Our little Kate was standing as usual at the screen door—waiting for her daddy. This was always the highlight of my day. I loved my daughter dearly, and I loved being a daddy.

Because of Kate's cerebral palsy, Barb's current pregnancy, prior to our move, had been handled at Duke by our family physician as a high-risk pregnancy. Three ultrasound examinations had revealed that the developing child, a little girl, was healthy and growing normally. We had named her Erin Elizabeth. We were looking forward to Kate having a sister.

I had never wanted to be my family's physician but was willing to serve as Barb's maternity caregiver until Rick Pyeritz, M.D., my partner-to-be, arrived later in the fall. Rick and I had been residents at Duke and had decided to practice in Bryson City together. Initially we would share space with Ray and Mitch, but we'd begin our group practice within a year in the new building soon to be constructed. Barb was not due to deliver baby Erin until late January, so my job as Barb and Erin's doctor, pending Rick's arrival, should be fairly easy. I was absolutely thrilled with our hospital's new state-of-the-art, two-bed, LDRP birthing center—a center I had helped design during my senior resident year at Duke. LDRP centers had large, comfortable birthing suites where a family could Labor, Deliver, Recover, and receive Postpartum care all in one room. We laughingly called our center "the smallest LDRP birthing center in the world." I particularly anticipated having my own child born there.

Kate's disability and the hours of therapy she required each day were often draining on Barb and Kate. On top of that, there were still boxes to be unpacked. Nevertheless, as I walked toward our little home that cool September evening, Barb's singing meant that her heart was light. So was mine. My step quickened. I thought, *Maybe this small, old, creaky house in this tiny mountain town will become more than just a little house by the hospital. Maybe it will really become a home*—our *home.*

As I walked up to the door, Kate squealed. I picked her up to give her a big hug and then went inside to help Barb with the dinner preparations. Although I kept my ear cocked toward the phone, no call came for the new doctor in town. All was quiet throughout the evening, and Barb and I wrapped up the long day by sitting outside on the bench, watching the moonless sky sparkle over Deep Creek. When we got in bed that night, I promptly fell fast asleep. Then the call came.

"You the new doc?" twanged the voice on the other end of a phone that had shattered my serene slumber.

"Yes, I am. I'm Dr. Larimore." Before the next words came out, I smiled and thought of my internal medicine professor at

Duke, Dr. Gene Stead. He taught us, "Never, never, never ask a patient, 'Can I help you?' Of course you can help the patient! If you can't help them, you're in the wrong business. Instead ask, 'How may I help you?' That's what a physician is there for—and that's what your patient needs—a physician." So, almost sensing Dr. Stead sitting on the bed next to me, I asked, "How may I help you?"

"This here's Clem Monteith. You better get up here to my place—and I mean now!" exclaimed the distressed voice.

"Get up where?" I inquired, now fully awake.

"Doc, I'm not kidding. She's about to deliver. You better get up here!"

Now the picture was clearer. Because the physicians in Bryson City often made home visits and because almost all the county's residents had been delivered at home—at least prior to 1950, when the hospital opened, and some still did so—a few of the long-established families still desired and expected home care. However, being a well-trained, highly technical birth attendant, I shared the delusion of many of my obstetrical colleagues that deliveries were best performed in the hospital setting.

Nevertheless, I was a trained professional and knew how to defuse a tense situation. So, now sitting up on the side of the bed, I took control. "Sir, it might be best for you to bring her to the hospital now. I'll meet you there." Furthermore, not unaware of the abject poverty in the county and the fact that many residents did not have transportation, I added, "Do you have a car?"

His answer was peppered with colorful language, not fit to repeat word for word, but he said something like this: "No, I don't have no blasted car, son." He paused to take a deep breath, then exclaimed, "I got a truck! But I'll tell you what, there ain't no blasted way I'm gonna get her in that blasted truck!! Now listen here, she's about to deliver and you better get up here—quick!"

I knew I needed to get up there. At least I could calm him down and assess the situation. Furthermore, I could have the paramedics from the Swain County Rescue Squad meet me at the house.

They would have any of the equipment I might need, I thought altruistically. A selfish thought also entered my mind. I mean, if the paramedics could see me do a great home delivery—*only* if necessary, of course—I thought, humbly, *that* would be superb.

The reputations of the older physicians in town—at least the ones who were respected—had been made in their first few heroic cases, now ingrained in the nearly legendary and historic mythology that exists in any medical staff. *Ah*, I thought modestly, *tonight the Larimore epoch begins!*

While I was fantasizing, Clem Monteith's anxious voice erupted into my ear. "She's gonna deliver and you better get up here! The front-porch light is on." He paused, then exclaimed, "Oh my, I can hear her pushing. Get here quick! I don't want to lose her!" Then the line went dead.

That pretty much settled things. I would just have to go to his house, where I could calm him down and assess the situation. But, *Oh no*! I thought. I hadn't asked him how to get to his place. And that meant calling Millie, the courteous and helpful dispatcher. Surely she'd know the way. I quickly called dispatch and heard a snarl, "Swain County Dispatch."

"Millie, this is Dr. Larimore."

After a pause, she responded with her condescending, "Yes, I know."

Now was the time to let the cat out of the bag. I cringed as I pleaded, "Millie, where is Clem Monteith's place?"

Millie heaved a big sigh into the phone. "Son, you thought about investing in a map? They're not that expensive, and on a doctor's salary you might could even afford a case."

Cute, I thought. "Yes, I'll try to remember to get one, but I need to get up there—now."

She paused again, then snarled, "Yes. *I know.*"

Thankfully it wasn't long before I was informed that Clem lived up in a hollow near town, and Millie promised she'd call the rescue squad—who also took calls at their homes—to meet me at the house.

I quickly pulled on some scrubs, threw on a coat, and grabbed my traditional physician's black bag. As I started the car, I felt myself shudder. *Instead of being the hero, would I lose my first patient?* Imagine the scorn. Imagine the gossip—uh, news—coming from the local radio at 6:00 A.M. tomorrow. I could hear Gary Ayers's voice. "Well, the new doctor in town, Doc Larimore, lost a patient last night. He was doing an ill-advised home delivery at Clem's place . . ." I felt my pulse rise with the RPMs of the small engine as I raced down the hill behind the hospital—never thinking of stopping by the ER to ask the ER nurse, Louise, to come along with me.

I wiped the sweat from my brow as I raced across the Tuckaseigee River bridge and through the town's two stoplights. My thoughts were racing faster than the engine. *I wasn't sure exactly what was in my black bag.* It had been given to me at the beginning of my clinical rotations at the LSU School of Medicine in New Orleans—which I called "Harvard on the Bayou"—in 1975. The bag had been a gift to each medical student from the Eli Lilly Pharmaceutical Company.

So, I thought, *what's in the bag?* And, *Will it be of any help?* And, *What if the ambulance doesn't get there?* All I could think of was getting *someone* to boil some water. I had no idea why you boiled water before a home delivery. I just knew I had seen it done on one of the medical shows on TV. I just didn't know why.

As I rounded the curve leading into the hollow, I pressed the Toyota, and the frantic search began. Which house was it? I found myself saying a little prayer for divine guidance. Driving past a number of homes with no porch light on, I drove around two bends and through what appeared to be a field. Then I spotted a small farmhouse—and, sure enough, the porch light was on. *Lord,* I quickly prayed, *grant me wisdom and calmness.* I turned up the driveway.

As I pulled in by the front of the house, I was surprised to see a middle-aged man sitting, rather calmly, in a rocking chair on his front porch. He stood up as I rushed from the car, forgetting the black bag. He tossed aside the straw on which he'd been chewing, and as he reached the bottom step, stopping only long enough to spit out a small stream of chewing tobacco, he proclaimed, "She's in the barn." He then turned and began to walk toward the barn. "Let's get going, son."

I stopped—stunned. As he approached the barn, I stood, mouth agape, thinking, *He's gotten his daughter pregnant!* This first perverse thought was followed by others even more nefarious. *He's gotten her pregnant, and now I must complete the dirty deed!*

I could just hear Gary Ayers proclaim on the morning news, "The new doc, who we *thought* was well trained and qualified, actually delivered an illegitimate child last night on School House Hill—the result of perverted incest—under the attempted cover of a moonless night. In the dark and in secret, he attempted to cover up this most heinous of sins. Now incarcerated in Swain County jail, he is expected to be quickly tried and, after permanently losing his license to practice medicine, will be transported to the state prison in Statesville to serve his life term."

The farmer turned to shout, "Hurry up, son. She's gonna deliver!"

As I began to follow quickly in the farmer's steps, I heard a sound that chilled my blood.

Could it be?

It was.

It was a long, low-toned, painful, pleading—"Moooooooooo."

It couldn't be. It *couldn't* be.

As I ran into the barn, I saw my first full-term maternity-care patient in private practice. I had delivered several hundred babies in medical school and residency, but never a baby like this—a white-faced heifer locked in breech—with the farmer placing the mom-to-be in a headlock device.

chapter nine

The Delivery

"It's a bull!" I shrieked. "You called me all the way up here to take care of a bull?" exclaimed the inexperienced people-doctor.

The farmer turned to look at me. Now it was his turn to be shocked. "Son," he exclaimed, "this ain't no blasted bull." (Never had a truer statement been uttered—pun intended.) "This here's a yearling heifer. She's a she, not a he, and *she's* in trouble. And, she and I *really* need your help. *Now!*"

"But I'm not a vet." I made this obvious statement innocently enough. I did not know that the county had no veterinarian. I did not know that the physicians in town were expected to treat *all* the county's residents—human and otherwise. I did not know that, during my career in Swain County, I would learn to sew up pig-gored hunting dogs, to do an ultrasound on dogs and cats during pregnancy so that the owners could know how many young ones would be available for sale, and to X-ray and bandage animals of every sort that had been hit by automobiles. At *that* moment of medical crisis in Clem Monteith's barn, I simply blurted out helplessly, "But I'm not a vet."

He looked incredulous. "You're a *doctor*, aren't you? Son, let's just get to work. Even *you* can do this." It was clear that the respect usually accorded to physicians was rapidly eroding in this particular case. Obviously the profession's reputation needed to be protected—and maybe, in this case, resurrected.

"Tell me what to do, and I'll do the best I can," I announced.

Clem looked at me like a coach knowing that, if the game's going to be won, he'd have to encourage his freshman quarterback. Calmly he reassured me, "I know you will, Doc. She's real special to me. I need help. That's why I called you. Let's get to it."

He patted the mom on her rump, lifting her tail. I could see two tiny hooves protruding from the genital area. On the floor, between the north end of the south-facing cow and the wall, was a chain connected to a "come-along." A come-along is a device used to pull a chain connected to a load, and it was most frequently utilized in the county for pulling logs up inclines to the logging roads above.

Now the plan was becoming clear—even to this rookie.

After gently wrapping a towel around the calf's rear legs, Clem reached down to grab his end of the chain and then wrapped it slowly around the now-padded legs. As he did this, I picked up my end of the come-along and inserted its hook into an eyebolt attached to a pole at the edge of the pen.

"Begin to tighten her up," he shouted to me.

I could feel the sweat trickling down my brow—even though the evening was cool—and my palms were sweating. As I slowly ratcheted the come-along handle, the chain rose from the floor between us and began to tighten.

The mom-to-be tried to look back at us. Her big brown eyes seemed to plead with us to be gentle.

"Doc, be careful. Try not to go too fast or too tight. Let's don't hurt this little one."

I could sense his caring and compassion. I suddenly realized that his fondness for his "patient" was not really different from mine. There was at once, and very suddenly, a connection between this farmer and me. Two birth attendants working together—attending the entry of a new life into the crisp mountain air. Without us, this little one—and maybe its mom—likely wouldn't make it. With us they just might. And the odds depended on one very caring and experienced farmer and one very nervous and green, young physician.

As the chain began to pull the calf's little legs, the farmer took off his shirt, threw it to the side, and bent over a bucket of water. He pulled out a bar of soap that was floating in the bucket and began to lather up his right hand and arm. At first I thought, *Why in the world is he scrubbing up?* And then, *Why in the world is he scrubbing only one arm?* Then it became clear. He gently placed his right hand and then his right arm up the heifer's birth canal.

"I'll see if I can help you out a bit, darling." Her body tensed as she sensed him working. I cranked, she pushed and bellowed, and he manipulated the little one out of the birth canal. Slowly the body began to ease out of the canal. As I was tightening the come-along and sensing its progress, I looked at the come-along and then at the calf being slowly delivered. I began to imagine this device in the hospital delivery room. I could hear Gary Ayers announcing, "The newest doctor in town, Dr. Larimore, has become nationally renowned for his introduction of the 'birthing come-along' that he uses in the Swain County General Hospital birthing suites. This specialized and sterilized come-along, similar to the come-alongs used by loggers, has helped the young physician through many difficult deliveries—literally pulling the doctor and newborn out of trouble." My thoughts were interrupted.

"Back off, Doc!" Clem shouted. "Back off and get over here!"

I loosened the come-along and ran to his side.

"Here," he said, as he gently guided my hands under the calf's warm and slimy body. "Help me hold her up!" I placed my arms under the "baby." Then Clem sensitively and carefully loosened the chain from the hooves.

He looked at me. "You go ahead and deliver her," he said, smiling. My mind flashed back six years earlier to the moment when the chief resident in obstetrics at Charity Hospital in New Orleans allowed me to perform my first delivery. "Here, Walt," Dr. Warren Lombard gently instructed, "come here. You go ahead and deliver her. You can do it. I'll be right here with you." And then this gentle man, this expert obstetrician and superb teacher, had guided my hands with his as I attended my first human birth.

"Careful, son, careful," the farmer counseled, as I was transported from New Orleans back to the barn. I began to pull gently. I looked up at the farmer. His eyes were saying, "You can do it, son, you *can*." Even the mom-to-be, now looking at me quietly, seemed to be confident. So I began to pull, and ever so gently the calf began to come out. First the shoulders. Then the neck. Before I knew it, the head emerged.

I guess I was expecting a baby the weight of those I had delivered while in residency, not the eighty-pounder I was now delivering. When she was born, I either weakened or couldn't bear the weight alone—and she and I and the farmer all collapsed to the hay-covered floor.

The calf immediately began to breathe. The farmer got up to release the mom from the headlock. All I could do was stare in disbelief. There she was—half in my lap and half on the floor—my first full-term delivery in private practice. My first complicated delivery. My first vaginal breech delivery. Sure it was a heifer, but what a beautiful calf she was! She had lived. Her mom had lived. I had lived. The sudden rush of emotion surprised me. I felt tears stinging my eyes.

The mom turned and began to nuzzle and lick her baby. With this stimulation, the calf began to struggle to get to her feet. I released her and she wobbled to her mom. As they touched noses and the mom cleaned the newborn, I could only sit and watch with admiration the circle of life, once again completed. I felt so fortunate to be there to witness once again—up close and personal—the continuation of life, the miracle of life. *Dear Lord,* I silently prayed, *thank you for guiding my hands. Thank you for this special experience.*

Unknown to me, during the delivery the paramedics had arrived. After getting to the barn, all they could do was watch a new, young physician they had never met attend his first delivery. They stood quietly by, probably not knowing whether to laugh or groan.

They watched the farmer as he offered me his calloused, hardened hand and I took it. He pulled me to my feet. And with an uncalloused and soft heart he gave me a hug. "Thanks, Doc. Thanks. You helped me save the calf."

When he released me I could see that his eyes were a bit misty. "You did good. Real good."

I was taken aback by the moistness in his eyes. Then it struck me. This was not just an animal to him. This yearling heifer was something more special than that. It was my first inkling of a mountain reality—that a man's herd was an extension of his family, especially if he had only a few animals. His life revolved around his animals and his sustenance depended on them. He grew to love each one of them, to name them, to learn their peculiarities and their habits. He could read them—and the weather—better than you or I could read the newspaper. My admiration and respect for the farmer grew immensely in just a few microseconds.

"No," I told him, "thank *you*. I appreciate the opportunity and the teaching."

He smiled. As I turned toward the door, for the first time I saw the paramedics. They too were smiling from ear to ear. As I approached I heard the mountain drawl of one I would come to know so very well over the years. "You the new doc?" asked the shorter and slightly more portly of the two.

"Yes, I am. I'm Walt Larimore. Thanks for coming."

"I'm Don Grissom, and this here's Billy." I turned back to be sure the farmer, the mom, and the baby were OK. Being assured that all was well, we bade them good-bye and left the barn. As we stepped outside, I continued, "I hope this was no trouble. I didn't know it was a cow."

Don put his hand on my shoulder. "Not to worry, Doc, we've had lots stranger calls than this. And . . . well, the outcome was pretty good, wasn't it?"

Billy, trying to heap more encouragement on me than I deserved, continued, "Besides, Doc, we'd rather be called when we're not needed than not be called when we are needed."

I sheepishly thanked them again, told them I looked forward to getting to know them, and walked over to my Toyota and hopped in. Only then did I realize that the front of my scrubs was soaking wet, as were my hands—wet and sticky. Fortunately, there was a rag in the glove compartment with which I could wipe my hands and the steering wheel.

During the short drive down School House Hill and back up Hospital Hill, I found myself overflowing with relief and gratitude—not unlike what most physicians feel after an emergency situation where the work is done well and the results are satisfying.

As I arrived home it was nearly 3:00 A.M. Not much time to sleep before another day of practice would begin. Walking to the house, I could see that a new moon had risen—on our small community, on its newest member, and on a new career.

Gary Ayers woke us up at 6:00 A.M. Barb nudged me awake, begging me to "turn that thing off." But, half-asleep, I smiled and felt a warm comfort when Gary announced, "The new doc in town, Dr. Walt Larimore, delivered his first baby in the middle of the night last night—a white-faced heifer up at Clem Monteith's place. Word is the cow and calf are fine. No word on the doc . . ."

By late that morning, the news was all over town. The reviews, according to those who talked to "Doc" John, the town's gregarious pharmacist at Super Swain Drug Store, were "generally good." I was later to learn that, coming from "Doc" John, this was a high compliment indeed—rarely extended to an "outsider." During evening rounds at the hospital, nurses and doctors were offering their congratulations and smiles.

I was sitting at the nurses' station, writing a progress note on a patient's chart, when I heard: "Heck of a way to start your career." The statement was followed by a chuckle from Dr. Bacon. The octogenarian smiled. "I'm proud of you, son. Didn't know they taught much animal medicine up there in the ivory tower of Duke." He chuckled again as he took off down the hall at a brisk pace—his hallmark. I presumed, perhaps mistakenly, that this was a compliment—and thus considered the praise of a respected colleague to be sweet.

Mitch chimed in from across the nurses' station. "Tell you what, son, when we get an afternoon free, I'm gonna teach you all about cattle. Why, I'll even teach you how to conceive those things!" Before I could ask him to explain what he was talking about, he had left the station and was heading down the hall.

The next day Helen asked me if I had a minute to speak to a patient in the lobby. Mitch's nurse had a devilish smile on her face.

"What's going on, Helen?"

The smile quickly left as she perceived me to be questioning her authority. "Just come with me to the waiting room, young man. *Now!*" I didn't argue.

As I entered the lobby, it took me a minute to recognize Clem. He was cleaned up—but then so was I. He had his left arm around a homely woman, seemingly dressed in her Sunday best. He walked over with an ear-to-ear smile, missing a few teeth, and began to enthusiastically pump my hand.

"Doc, just came by to say thanks once again for what you done the other night for me and my family. This here's my wife, Doris." I was to learn that they had no children. Indeed, Clem's herd and his wife *were* his family.

"Well, it's good to see you again, Mr. Monteith, and it's good to meet you, Mrs. Monteith."

"Clem and Doris will work just fine for us." Clem smiled and then dropped his head for a moment, seemingly gathering his words. (I was to learn that this is a common behavior in the area. It gives the speaker time to think and builds the drama of the moment.)

"Doc, we're just here to say that we know you're new in these parts and we know you haven't done lots of animal work, but we think you done real good and we want you to know we appreciate it."

"You're more than welcome," I stammered, more embarrassed than thankful.

"Doc," he said falteringly, "we don't have any way to pay you back for your service just yet. But we'll pay you when we can."

"That's OK," I replied. After all, I hadn't even considered charging for my services. No one had ever taught me how to provide medical services to cows, much less how to charge for those services.

He paused for just a moment. I wasn't quite sure what to do—or what to say.

"Go ahead," Doris spoke up. "Go ahead and tell him, honey."

"Well, Doc, we want you to know that we named the calf after you."

Wow, I thought. *Possibly a prize-winning hybrid white-faced heifer. And furthermore, named "Dr. Walt Larimore" or "Professor Larimore" or just "The Doc." Man-o-man!* I was beginning to feel a bit of pride welling up, only to be overcome by curiosity. "What did you name her?" I asked.

"We named her 'Walter.'"

I could hear Helen trying to swallow her laughter.

Clem and Doris were beaming as they left the office.

I went back to work—after all, there were patients waiting to be seen.

As far as I know, my first full-term delivery is still alive. She's delivered a bunch of her own calves over the last two decades. But I bet she's never experienced a birth like her own. And even though I've delivered over 1,500 newborns in my career, few of those deliveries are as memorable as the birth of Walter.

chapter ten

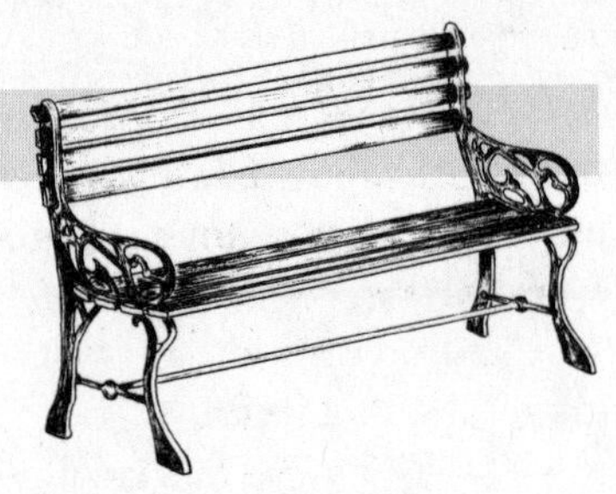

The "Expert"

A few weeks passed. I was starting to feel like I just *might* fit in here, alongside townspeople and patients and doctors whose ways were clearly different from where I'd cut my medical teeth. Then I received a call from Marcellus "Buck" Buchanan. Mr. Buchanan had been the Superior Court solicitor (the district attorney) over the seven counties of western North Carolina since 1967—after serving three terms as a state representative in the North Carolina legislature in the 1950s. His offices were in Sylva.

"Sorry to have to call you, son. I'd love to come over there and meet you in person. But duty calls."

For some reason I can't explain, I just didn't like his tone. So I kept our exchange professional. "How can I help you, sir?"

"Well, son, I just got your coroner's report."

Time seemed to stop. My mind raced back to the night just a few weeks before when I had been called to my first murder case. The scene of the house flooded with police car lights and the memory of the headless body and the brain-covered walls washed over me from head to toe. Moreover, the feelings of inadequacy on the evening of the murder and the uncertainty of whether moving to Bryson City had been wise or not—coupled with Mitch's subsequent and frequent questioning of my competence ("Are you stupid?")—left me suddenly feeling shaken and unsure.

The DA continued, "Son, your report looks good—real good—and it sure enough agrees with the autopsy."

I felt a bit of pride rising in my chest—after all, I had been well trained in both England and in a world-class medical center in the latest science and techniques. But even though I had been well trained in the science of medicine, I was feeling less prepared for the *practice* of medicine—at least in Bryson City. Yet when it came to the murder investigation, I thought, *It really isn't brain surgery.* I mean, after all, the man had his head blown off. What else could the cause of death be? I relaxed and decided to stay cool. "Thank you, sir."

He then asked several questions about the crime scene investigation report. Finally he concluded again, "You did a terrific job, son. Just terrific."

I wasn't sure where this was going. I had pronounced a man dead and determined that his head was missing and splattered all across the wall of a small bedroom. This was not a major forensic coup.

He went on, "You just did a superlative job, son, exceptional." The syrup was getting a bit too sweet and was being poured on a little too thickly. "In fact," he said, lowering his voice to a near whisper, "your report is a whole lot better than most. I'm used to receiving documents with far less quality and completeness from your neck of the woods—if you know what I mean."

Again I felt proud. I should have known better. Only a moment later he smashed my good feelings with his next pronouncement. "Son, we're going for murder one for this insect. I would like to see him fry—to a crisp. Squishing an insect like this is too quick, too painless. I want him to fry." To me this was a *most* unpleasant thought. The Wild West philosophy and practice of inflicting torment on the already condemned seemed to be alive and well—at least in Sylva.

"Here's what I'm planning," the DA continued. "I want to call you as my first witness in the trial. I suspect it will be one of the bigger trials in our area this year. I'm expecting plenty of media coverage and interviews. I'm expecting that young attorneys from all over the western part of the state will come to see this trial. And, son, I don't want to let them down—and I don't want *you* to let me down."

Oh, great! A puffed-up, egotistical, self-centered media hog. Just what I need. I couldn't believe it. All I could say was, "Yes, sir."

He kept on talking, in his slow southern drawl. "But don't worry, son. Don't worry. My boys will come over there and work with you a bit. We'll get you shaped up in no time at all. There's one thing I can promise you: I'll make you look really good, son." He paused. Must have been for drama. Maybe he was just practicing. "Any questions?"

Yeah, where can I go throw up? I thought. But I continued to keep my cool, "No, sir, none at all."

"Well then, you have a good day, you hear?" He hung up and I felt hung out. *Testify in court? I had never been in court. What would I do? What would I be asked? How would I prepare?* I was in a bit of a panic—until I thought of Fred Moody, the good-natured attorney and chairman of the hospital board, whom I'd met during my interview over Eloise Newman's delicious and welcoming lunch. I picked up the phone to call Fred.

He had heard about the case. "In fact, Walt, I'll be representing the accused. Judge Leatherwood wanted the best!" he said as he chuckled. I enjoyed Fred's humor—dry and to the point, disarming and endearing. Fred always enjoyed working to help the underdog—a fact that attracted business from the entire region to his small downtown office next to Bennett's Drug

Store. "Why don't you drop by the office today after work, and we'll chat."

When I arrived at his office—its walls covered with bookshelves crammed with law books and diplomas—he immediately put me at ease. "Walt, your part will be the easiest part of the entire trial. First, the district attorney will qualify you as an expert. Walt, by now everyone in town knows about your training and expertise. Even I won't be able to fight that motion."

He smiled, then continued. "Once the judge certifies you as an expert, then the DA will question you about your investigation—what you saw and what you concluded. The main fact to which he'll want you to attest is the cause of death. Since both you and the pathologist who did the autopsy have certified that the cause of death was a gunshot wound to the head, that should be easy."

"Is that all?"

"Well, then I'll get a chance to cross-examine you, Walt."

I felt my eyes narrow. "What will that be like?"

"Well, I expect I'll be brutal. The questions will be tough and medically demanding. I'll put you to the test, for sure." He paused—his face serious but his eyes smiling.

"Are you kidding?"

Then he broke into a smile. "Yeah."

He became serious again. "Actually, I'll have a lot of *other* work ahead of me before and during this trial. I can't imagine that I'll have *any* cross-examination of you at all." He smiled again. My mistake was assuming it was the smile of someone who was actually on my side.

"Now, some of my predecessors, they would have grilled you. No doubt about it."

"Who are you talking about, Fred?"

"Walt, I'm just the tail end of a line of simple attorneys here in Swain County. But I tell you, there have been some mighty good ones. The older folks around the courthouse all talk about Fred Fisher. He tutored a fellow named A. J. Franklin, who was licensed to practice law in 1899. R. L. Leatherwood and A. M. Frye, who built the Fryemont Inn, had excellent reputations. Another fellow who tutored here in town before obtaining his law license was S. W. Black, who was educated by T. K. Bryson himself—who was kin to Colonel Thaddeus Dillard Bryson, the namesake of our fair village."

I was impressed by Fred's command of local history.

"So, Walt, I'm just carrying on the proud tradition of country lawyers. We don't know a whole lot, but we try to do a whole lot of good." He laughed. I liked Fred.

Several weeks before the trial, two young attorneys from the district attorney's office called. They wanted to visit me to prepare me for trial. They covered the basics of being a witness for the state. They covered what I should wear to the trial—professional suit, not showy or gaudy or loud. They covered how I should address the jury—as a teacher and as an expert, never defensive or aloof. They instructed me in how to answer questions and how to swear in—they actually taught me how to stand and place my right hand on the Bible and how to hold my left hand and how to look the jurors in the eye as I say, "I do." My goodness, I didn't get this much preparation for marriage or for performing surgery.

They spent nearly two hours rehearsing questions and answers, examination and cross-examination. They reviewed every trick question in the book, except one—one they and I should have expected but did not.

For what seemed like an eternity, they covered detail after detail. Then, to cap off the day, they spent time reviewing the many mistakes made by other doctors in my position. Toward the end of the meeting, something came to the forefront that turned my stomach.

"Doctor," intoned one of the DA's staff, "are you aware that the DA is planning to run for the state senate?"

"No, I didn't know that."

"Well, he is considering it. And, Doctor, we're planning this trial to be one of his showpieces for the year. It's real important to the DA that he look good. Real good. We want to help you help him. Understand?"

I nodded my head affirmatively, although not really sure what I might do or say in a small-town murder trial that could have anything at all to do with a race for the senate. Silly me, I thought this trial might be about justice and truth—about proving the facts. After all, one man was dead and another was on trial for his life.

Then I found myself getting angry. Finally I lost my cool. "Gentlemen, I don't really give a hoot about your boss's political career. I don't really care how he looks at this trial. I will testify honestly and forthrightly that it is my personal and professional opinion that this was a crime of passion, but not premeditated murder—certainly not worthy of the death penalty. I'll testify about the little bit of investigation I did and I'll testify as to the cause of death. But my role ends there. That you would even begin to think that my testimony might swing the senate race seems grandiose at best—or ludicrous at the very least. I find it highly insulting."

I stood to leave. They seemed stunned. "Good day."

I left the room. I was angry and disillusioned. I was nervous about participating in this trial, but I was determined to be prepared and do my job. If only I had known that I'd end up looking like a fool . . .

chapter eleven

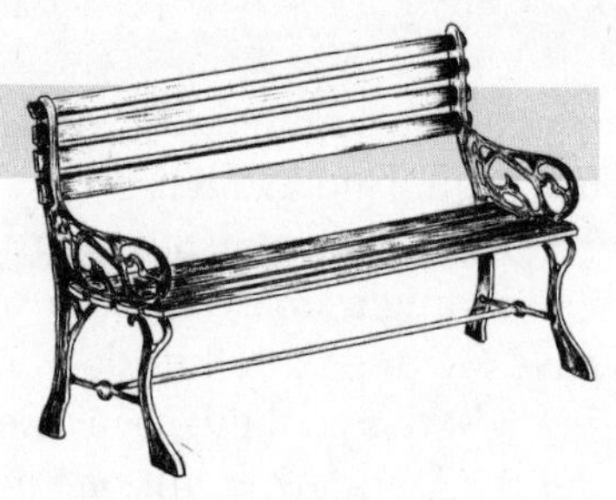

THE TRIAL

The day of the trial dawned; yet I had been awake for hours, wondering, *What is really going to happen today? Will I seem credible and professional? Will this be one of my reputation-building moments?* By 3:00 A.M. I was wide-awake. I tossed and turned for another hour, trying to rid my mind of the flurry of thoughts and concerns. Finally I just went ahead and got up.

I had come to believe that waking up like this was just God's special way of nudging me for a private meeting time. I had a soft reading chair that served as the repository of my derriere for these quiet times—time to read the Scriptures (listen to God's words) and to pray (to talk to him). I had grown fond of this time and soon found it essential to my day-to-day well-being. It's just that these times were not usually so early in the morning.

At 6:00 A.M. it was time to take a shower and get dressed. Barb had picked out my best suit for my "day in court." After breakfast, I crossed the street to make rounds at the hospital. Several of the nurses and Dr. Mitchell whistled when they saw me. Mitch commented, "You shore are gussied up." Louise, never one to mince words, asked, "Someone die?" I smiled—so did she. At about 8:30, I headed to the county courthouse for the 9:00 A.M. start of court.

The scene at the courthouse was a bit outrageous. As I drove up, my first clue that this was not the usual case in Swain County was the TV vans and the satellite truck set up in the parking lot. There was a line forming at the front door. I ducked past the line and the reporters to the side entrance used by the attorneys and staff. My new friend, Deputy Rogers, let me in the door.

Once inside the courtroom, I saw Fred Moody sitting alone at the defendant's desk. He was reviewing a small mountain of papers. At the prosecutor's table was a crew of men and women in what appeared to be their Sunday-best suits—they actually looked more like stockbrokers than country attorneys. In the middle, dressed in a crisp but slightly off-white three-piece suit, was the silver-haired district attorney and senator-wanna-be. I felt like I was walking into a theater where preparations for a high-stakes performance were under way.

One of the DA's young staff members saw me and announced to him my arrival. Mr. Buchanan flashed his pearly white, near-perfect smile and passed through the gate in the bar to come meet me. "Welcome, Doctor, welcome. Are you ready to become a star? Son, I'm going to make you a star!" he proclaimed as he brusquely swatted me across the back. "Let me show you where I want you to sit."

He walked me up to a bench just behind the bar where we chatted for a few minutes. He cocked his head over to a row of seats behind the defense table, to a group of well-dressed young men, chatting together and laughing. "Know who they are?"

"Not really."

"That's a group of young attorneys from all over—Robbinsville, Murphy, Andrews, Franklin, Sylva, and Waynesville. Why, there's even a couple from Asheville. They're all here to watch the old dog at work. Let's give them a good show, son."

He swatted my back again as the door to the chamber opened to allow the waiting crowd to enter. Quickly he was off to socialize with potential voters.

A moment later the accused and the members of the jury entered the courtroom. The bailiff announced the entry of the judge, and we all stood as he entered. He sat down and gaveled the court to order. During the attorneys' opening statements I found myself daydreaming a bit, feeling the lack of sleep, and then nearly nodding off several times. I was startled back to reality when I heard the DA's booming voice declare, "Your Honor, we call as the People's first witness Dr. Walter L. Larimore."

In one instant it seemed as though all of the eyes in the courtroom were on me. For a brief moment, I felt the nausea and cold sweat I'd felt the night of the murder. I stood, feeling my legs shaking a bit. As Deputy Rogers opened the gate, I passed the bar and walked briskly to the witness-box. The bailiff approached with a Bible in his hand. I swore to tell the truth, the whole truth, and nothing but the truth, so help me God. Of course, I did this while obediently eyeing the members of the jury. I then made myself comfortable in the leather-covered witness chair.

The DA slowly stood, smiling at the jury as he approached the witness stand. "Can you tell the jury your name?" Mr. Buchanan almost crooned.

"Walt Larimore."

"And you are a medical doctor, an M.D. Is that correct?"

"Yes, sir."

"And is it correct that you received your M.D. degree at the Louisiana State University School of Medicine in New Orleans, Louisiana, finishing in the top five in your class?"

"Yes, sir. That is true."

"And is it true that after completing a general practice teaching fellowship at the Queen's Medical Center in Nottingham, England, you entered and completed your family medicine residency training at the Duke University Medical Center in Durham, North Carolina? Is that true?"

"Yes, sir."

"*The* Duke University, the *world-famous* Duke University Medical Center?"

I paused. *Isn't this going a bit overboard?* I thought. Nevertheless, I responded, "Yes, sir."

Turning to the jury, he flashed his famous smile, then turned toward the spectators in the courtroom, continuing, "The medical university that trains some of the best physicians in the world—*that* Duke University?"

Well, although this was a bit over the top, I was beginning to enjoy him. Here was a dashing and charismatic attorney informing the attorneys of western North Carolina, the news media, and scores of curious locals about my training and qualifications. I couldn't pay for this type of advertising. This was, I presumed, a new doctor's dream come true.

The DA, smiling from ear to ear, now approached the jury. "And, Dr. Larimore, is it true that you are authorized by this great state of North Carolina as a certified coroner?"

I furrowed my brow. "Uh, no, sir, that's not true, sir."

He immediately corrected his error. "Um, yes. Why yes. But is it not true that you are certified by the state of North Carolina as a medical examiner?"

"*That* is correct, sir," I replied.

"Your Honor," came the sharp retort from my friend, Mr. Moody, as he slowly stood to his feet.

"Mr. Moody?" replied the somewhat startled judge.

Fred slowly straightened his lanky frame, not nearly as expensively clad as his opponent. "Your Honor, the defense is *well* aware of Dr. Larimore's copious CV. We are aware of his superlative training and his *extensive* experience."

Wow, I thought to myself, *my man Fred!* I basked in the sunshine of this unexpected bravado. But then, I should not have been surprised. Fred was a friend—a supporter. Why wouldn't he want the new doctor in his hometown to look good?

"I am aware that Mr. Buchanan desires to qualify Dr. Larimore as an expert in this case," Fred continued. "Your Honor,

I may have been born at night, but sir, I was not born last night." He paused as the gallery chuckled. Both reporters and young attorneys were scribbling notes. And I was relishing the moment.

"The defense not only has no objection to qualifying Dr. Larimore as an expert, sir, but it is *our* view that Dr. Larimore, based on his clearly documented and independently certified training and experience, may be the *singularly most qualified* expert to have ever appeared in this court."

I was so grateful for a friend so willing to brag a bit on me. It's one thing for the DA from another town to sing your praises, but then to have those praises expanded and trumped by a well-respected native—well, could it get any better that that?

So for the next twenty minutes I was in my element. I was prepared for all the questions and performed for the jury my role as professor. Photographs and charts, records and certifications were all expertly identified and explained. I could almost feel the jury in the palm of my hand. I was imagining that most of these folks and virtually the entire gallery would be leaving the courtroom to call the office for new patient appointments that afternoon—or, at the very latest, tomorrow morning. I was imagining the need to call the phone company at the first morning break of the trial just to have them install another phone line or two. I was even wondering if people might not travel from other towns just to see such an expert as myself.

Then it was over—or so I thought. Mr. Buchanan, smiling at me, the jury, and then the judge, proclaimed, "No more questions, Your Honor."

The judge looked at Fred, who was still studying his mountain of papers. Mr. Moody didn't move.

"Mr. Moody!" exclaimed the judge. Fred looked up a bit. He seemed to be perplexed. Almost surprised.

"Do you have any cross-examination, Mr. Moody?" queried the judge. Once again Fred raised himself up, shaking down his rather baggy pants. He picked up a folder of papers as he approached the witness-box. I saw a twinkle in his eye as our eyes momentarily locked. He placed the folder on the railing in front of the jury, reading something and slowly shaking his head from side to side.

"Ladies and gentlemen of the jury," he announced, "I must tell you that in *all* my years as an attorney and in all my years of law school and as a law clerk, I don't think I've ever seen a more brilliant display of medical expertise and knowledge." Now I *really* couldn't believe what I was hearing. The DA already had me both looking and feeling pretty good. Now my friend Fred was putting some extremely sweet icing on the cake. I could begin to imagine the news headlines: "World-famous medical expert provides stellar testimony in Bryson City courtroom."

He went on. "Not only will I *never* be able to object to his qualifications as a medical expert in this court, I hope to never have to oppose his outstanding expertise or testimony ever again. To do so might well end my career." He smiled at the jury and then at me as he turned to the gallery. Now my suspicious juices began to boil. Something suddenly seemed wrong. Really wrong.

"Ladies and gentlemen of the jury, for an attorney to venture even *one* question after such complete and compelling testimony might seem both pretentious and egotistic. Nevertheless, I feel compelled, even at the risk of ridicule or embarrassment, to ask Dr. Larimore one small question—if you will allow me." Now not only were my suspicions up, but so were the hairs on the back of my neck. I was beginning to feel nauseated.

Mr. Moody slowly turned toward me. The twinkle was still in his eye, but now it looked more like the eye of a tiger. "Dr. Larimore, would you be so kind as to tell the jury just how many medical examiner's cases you've performed in your long, illustrious, celebrated, acclaimed, and fabled career?"

I thought I heard the audible hiss of air escaping from my rapidly deflating ego as I felt the blood rushing from my head to my feet. As Mr. Moody, head down, reading his sheaf of papers, slowly walked back to the defense table, I replied, "This is my first case."

He jerked to a stop, and his folder dropped to the floor, slapping the hardwood with a sound that caused those eyes not yet glued to him to so glue. A bunch of loose papers—all amazingly white, with no writing or typing or drawing or marking of any kind on them—flew in all directions around his feet. The eyes of the young attorneys and the spectators were wide with trepidation. Gasps echoed throughout the room.

As the gasps and the papers quietly settled down, Fred slowly turned toward me with the most amazing look of shock I had ever seen. Even to this day I still don't know how he did it, but his face was white and his hands were trembling. He *knew* this was my first case. Yet no one in sight, except me, knew that he knew. He pulled a handkerchief out of his pocket, wiping his forehead as he approached the jury.

"Ladies and gentlemen, I must offer you my most sincere apology. As you know, my client's life is on the line. Yet, even so, I have made one of the most grievous mistakes of my career. I have, without objection, allowed our esteemed district attorney to qualify to you, as a supposed expert, an extremely young man with no experience as a coroner or a medical examiner. He has, it appears, never, ever, been part of a coroner's case. He, it appears, has never, ever, investigated a petty crime—much less a capital crime."

The DA was quiet. Where was the objection? My reputation was going down like the Hindenburg. I needed help—and fast!

"So, ladies and gentlemen, please forgive my certification of this man as an expert. I can't take that back now. But now we all know the truth. He's never done this before! And this is a mistake I will never make again. But, ladies and gentlemen, please, I implore you, don't hold my inexperience and poor judgment against the man I represent."

By now I was resigned to my fate. A shrewd country lawyer—experienced in the substance of law and the art of the theater, had trumped both my inexperience and the DA's bravado. "I have no further questions, Your Honor."

My admiration for my friend soared as he walked back to his chair. I had observed an Oscar-level performance—the demonstration of a remarkable skill. Here was a simple man, pulling out every trick he could in order to do the best job he could for his client. He would continue applying his various and copious skills for the rest of the week—and I dropped by on several occasions to sit in the back of the courtroom and observe his expertise. He would be paid very little for his work—apart from the immense admiration of the young attorneys and one young physician, who were blessed to have seen both his amazing performance and his consummate skill.

Fred's legacy lives on in those he taught—by word and deed—that success in life is not defined as just being excellent at what you do, but as doing the excellent in an excellent way, even when there is no obvious reward for doing so. Fred taught me early in my career that the difference between extraordinary and ordinary is the "extra." And I was able, in the end, to get beyond the fact that this important lesson was learned at my expense!

I was new to this small town. But the town and its ways were certainly not new. I had so much yet to learn.

chapter twelve

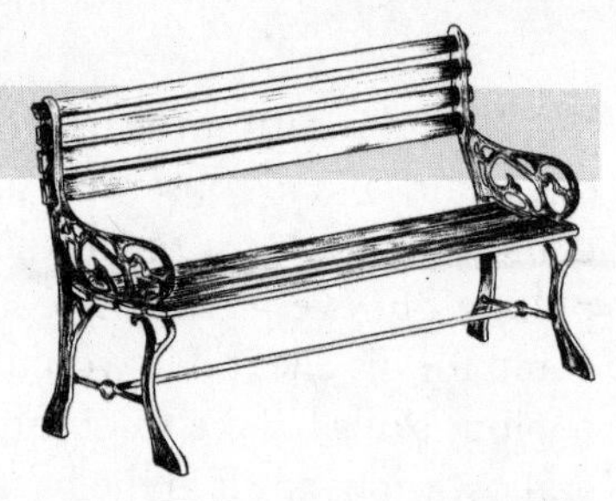

Shitake Sam

Sam was one of the entrepreneurs in town. Oh, he would never use such a term. But when it came to trying new ideas, he was the man. His dad had farmed the end of a small hollow near Bryson City—mostly corn and burley leaf tobacco. In those days the tobacco brought in more money, but the corn was useful as a supplement crop and to feed the livestock during the cold, gray winters. However, the crops could only be grown on the valley floor and the more gentle slopes, which left a fair amount of steep forestland.

Now, the forest could be logged every few years, but that didn't provide for the year-to-year needs of the farm or the family. With tobacco prices dropping, and with an upsurge of out-of-towners demanding more exotic menus in the local inns and in the finer restaurants in Asheville, Sam took a hankering to learning how to grow mushrooms.

He had talked first to Mr. Lyday, the county agriculture agent, who didn't have a clue about mushrooms or how to grow them, or even if they *could* be grown in our part of the country. But a call to Raleigh resulted in a small bundle of information. Indeed, a particular brand of mushroom, the Shitake mushroom, loved a hot, humid summer and a cool to cold but damp winter. They did not do well in the direct sunlight, but it was said they would flourish in the relative shade of a forest floor. Furthermore, the ideal growth medium for this particular type of mushroom was a dying oak tree, and our oaks in the Great Smokies seemed to be one of the oaks they loved the most.

So Sam learned how to drill a one-inch hole all across the top of the oak logs, pack a plug of sphagnum moss into the hole, and sprinkle the mushroom spores on top. He ordered the spores all the way from Japan, and while waiting for them to arrive he rigged up a sprinkler system using the crystal-clear, ice-cold water flowing from one of the several small branches (or creeks) on the property.

It wasn't too many years before Sam's entire forested cove was covered with logs growing the newest cash crop of that century. Others in Swain County had smaller patches of Shitake, and before too long, trucks from Knoxville, Asheville, Waynesville, and even Sylva were dropping by Bryson City once a week to pick up the luscious, fresh Shitakes. Why, Sam even gave a talk at Rotary Club about his Shitakes—and that's where we first met.

Our second meeting was in the emergency room. I was there, sewing up a minor hand laceration, when the call came over the radio.

"Louise, this is Rescue One."

Now since there was no Rescue Two, I was frequently amused by this type of call. I guess the Swain County Rescue Squad was just planning for the inevitable future growth.

"Go ahead, Rescue One," Louise responded.

I threw and tied the last stitch, which was admired by its new owner, and then began dressing the wound while Louise learned about our next guest.

"Louise, this is Don. I've got Shitake Sam with me."

I hadn't heard this nickname before but knew immediately to whom the paramedic was referring.

"He's busted up his ankle pretty bad. We've put an air splint on it. His vitals are OK. But he's already taken a fair amount of anesthesia."

His anesthesia, I suspected, was crystal clear, drunk from a Mason jar, and nearly 150 proof. I suspected we'd smell Sam well before we saw him.

"Ten-four, Rescue One. What's your twenty?"

"We'll be there in ten, Louie."

"Louie" was their nickname for Louise. I could call her Louise but never Louie—at least not yet. Only a few of the locals could call her Louie and get away with it.

"Doc!" Louise exclaimed. "What you doing making a dressing here? Don't you know that's my job?!"

She continued to fuss as she completely redressed my patient's wound. I thought I'd done a pretty good job, but I was continuing to learn my proper place in the scheme of things. And dressing wounds was *not* the doctor's place.

While Louise wrapped and fussed, I finished my paperwork and wrote a proper prescription for a pain reliever and an antibiotic. At Duke I would have seen my patient back in twelve to fourteen days to remove the stitches. However, here he'd see Louise for the suture remove. I'd learned that this was just the way it was in Bryson City.

I heard the beeping of the ambulance as it backed up to the emergency room entrance, and in a few moments Don and Billy walked in with Sam and his stretcher in tow.

After quickly transferring Sam onto the emergency room gurney, Don turned to me. "You may not remember me, Doc. Don Grissom. Billy and I met you up at Clem's place," and he quickly thrust out his hand to grasp mine. His hand was rough, calloused, huge, and strong. It enveloped mine, yet almost gently gave it one pump.

"Sure, I remember you," I said. "Good to see you." I remembered that night only *too* well.

The smell of Sam's alcohol-induced "anesthesia" and the deep snores indicating its effectiveness inundated the emergency room.

"Doc, his pulses and sensation in his feet are fine," Louise reported. "I'm gonna take him on over to Carroll in X ray."

In most ERs the doctor does a history and an exam. But the scheme of things here was that those were part of the nurse's duties. The doctors in town—in order to preserve their sanity and to try to spend some time at home when on call—leaned quite heavily, as they did in those days in many small rural ERs, on the eyes, the ears, the skills, and the experience of the ER nurse. In a few minutes, Sam, his snores and smell, and his X rays were back.

"A trimalleolar fracture," Louise announced confidently. "I'll get him ready to cast."

Before I could catch myself, I blurted out, "Cast? Are you crazy?"

Sam and his gurney ground to an immediate halt.

Louise, looking half-incredulous and half-incensed, cocked her head and said, "Dr. Larimore, I am *not* crazy, and I'd suggest that you *never* speak to me in that tone again."

I could feel the blood rising in my face. "I'm sorry, Louise," I apologized. "But at Duke ..." She didn't even let me finish my statement. I was going to tell her about the studies showing how well these fractures do with an operative technique called ORIF (Open Reduction and Internal Fixation), which means that we surgically open the fracture site, wash out the blood, and then use wires or screws or other hardware to hold the bones together while they heal. I wanted to tell her how I was experienced in assisting the orthopedic surgeons in doing this operation and how quickly we could expect Shitake Sam to be back on his feet. In fact, with the newfangled fiberglass cast, he could even be tending his mushrooms soon. But I wasn't able to finish my lecture.

"Young man," she almost snarled, "you're *not* at Duke, you're in *my* ER. I'd recommend you *not* forget it!"

I stood aside, chastised and befuddled. I'd been around a lot of strong-willed ER nurses, but never one like Louise.

"I'll shave his leg, prep for a hematoma block, and get the plaster ready."

Now she was talking heresy—at least to a Duke-trained physician. Hematoma blocks were injections of an anesthetic agent, such as lidocaine, through the skin and into the fracture itself. They were used before a closed reduction and casting—not before an ORIF, which would have been, in my opinion, the correct treatment. Sam could be kept comfortable until he sobered up and then taken to the operating room for the recommended and modern ORIF. I was befuddled at her brashness.

She went on, seemingly not noticing my deepening befuddlement.

"After you get him numb, I'll help you with the skintight cast."

Now I was at the absolute height of bewilderment. "Skintight cast?" I stammered.

She stopped, straightened up to her full five-foot four-inch frame, and stared straight up into my eyes, now on a slumping six-foot two-inch frame. "Doctor, you do know how to put on a skintight cast, don't you?"

How was I to say no? I had never even heard of such a thing. And what's more, all of my training in casting, most of it from the fabulous cast technicians at Womack Army Hospital in Fort Bragg, North Carolina, had emphasized the use of proper padding to prevent the cast from pressing against the skin—which could cause sores or ulcers.

My bafflement must now have been unmistakable. "Dr. Mitchell is your backup," she muttered as she turned to roll Sam and his gurney into the ER bay and I turned to the phone. Surely Mitch could help me make some sense of this.

"Hello," the obviously sleepy voice rasped.

"Mitch, this is Walt. I've got Shitake Sam here in the ER. He's got a displaced, closed, trimalleolar fracture of the ankle with normal vascular and neural function, but he's pretty loaded up with moonshine. I was thinking of putting him in a splint and then to bed. Can I put him on the OR schedule for you in the morning for an ORIF?"

"Does he have any abrasions or lacerations?"

"No," I responded slowly. "If he had, I wouldn't have wanted to put him on the schedule." In cases where there are cuts or scrapes we'll try to put off surgery if we can, to reduce the risk of infection when we finally do operate.

"Well, son, why not go ahead and place him in a skintight cast? Then admit him to keep the leg elevated and have the nurses check his foot circulation and sensation every fifteen to twenty minutes, and we can discharge him as soon as he's sober and feeling well enough."

I couldn't believe my ears. I would later learn that this early twentieth-century technique had been almost completely replaced by surgical procedures—at least outside of this county. I must have been stone-silent or muttering to myself. Either way, Mitch picked up on my response.

"Son," he slowly queried, "you do know how to do a skintight cast, don't you?"

"Well, sir, I've got to tell you, we always operated on these types of fractures."

"Son, this ain't Duke."

This was something I was quickly coming to recognize! Dr. Mitchell continued. "I bet I've been using this skintight cast technique for nearly twenty-five years. A whole lot longer than most of your professors have practiced."

Well, in fact, that wasn't true. A number of my professors at Duke had been practicing their craft for nearly four decades, but bringing that up at this particular moment didn't seem appropriate.

"Now let me tell you," Dr. Mitchell barked, "no one, and I mean *no one*, likes to operate more than me. I love being in the OR, just *love* it! But for this type of fracture, I think this approach works just fine. What's more, I've only ever had to remove *one* cast because of swelling. It just plain works. That's just the way it is."

Again I remained silent. "Walt, you've got lots of book knowledge—great training, great education—but I'm here to tell you, the folks in the ivory tower of academics don't have a monopoly on medical knowledge. There's still lots of good old-fashioned medicine that works just fine. And it can be a whole lot cheaper to boot!

"Tell you what, son. Get Louise to show you how to do it. If you have any problems, give me a call." Before I could respond, he hung up.

I followed the fumes into Sam's ER bay. Louise had shaved his now splintless leg from the ankle to the thigh.

"Louise, I don't think he's gonna need a hematoma block. Would you mind helping me with the cast?"

She smiled. I think it was the first smile I ever saw from Louise. It wouldn't be the last.

"Why, I'd be delighted to teach you what little I know, Doctor."

The humility seemed both false and a tad bit out-of-place. But for the next twenty minutes this experienced nurse guided a novice in the task of very carefully wrapping and shaping his first skintight cast. We rolled Sam down to the four-bed intensive care unit, and I watched as the nurses deftly slung his casted leg from an orthopedic bed frame. His foot was practically pointing toward the ceiling. I left Sam, his snores, and his skintight cast in the capable care of the floor nurses. They assured me that they were used to caring for this type of thing. I was just hoping his foot wouldn't fall off, should his ankle swell and the foot lose circulation. I could hear Gary Ayers on the morning news: "Last night, the town's newest physician ..."

chapter thirteen

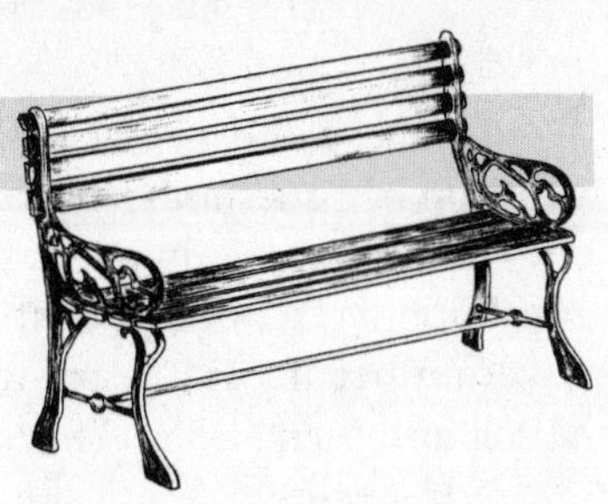

Wet behind the Ears

A few days later Dr. Mitchell and I were discussing several of the patients I had seen in the office the day before—as well as looking at some of the plans for the new office building. I was growing to appreciate Mitch's wisdom, experience, and common sense. Suddenly Helen came in to tell me, "Walt, your first patient is ready and in the procedure room."

"Whatcha doing, Walt?" inquired Mitch.

"I don't know," I answered. I looked up to the nurse. "Helen, *what* am I doing?"

"Well, I'm no doctor . . . ," she began, with her usual and somewhat sarcastic disclaimer, "but it looks like a small noninfected sebaceous cyst." She paused for a second and then inquired, "You gonna use the iodine?"

At first I thought she was discussing the substance I would use to clean the skin prior to making an incision to remove the cyst. I thought, *Doctors haven't used iodine for operative prep for years. Most doctors use Betadine.* My mind quickly reviewed our protocols at the hospital. *Dr. Mitchell uses Betadine in the OR.*

Wouldn't he use the same thing here in the office? So I decided to question her question—not necessarily a wise decision.

"Helen, I usually use Betadine. Don't you have that?"

Initially she looked confused. And then she began to laugh, covering her mouth to try to hide her laughter. She looked at Mitch and then at me.

"Dr. Larimore . . . ," she giggled.

I looked at Mitch. *What was so funny?* I wondered.

"Walt, didn't they teach you about removing sebaceous cysts with iodine crystals at that fancy medical center?" Mitch chided.

Now it was my turn to look confused. "What in the world are you two talking about?"

Mitch stood there chuckling. "Helen, let's teach this wet-behind-the-ears youngin' an old dog's trick, whatcha say?"

"Sounds good to me, Doctor," she replied. She looked down her nose at me and turned to leave, while Mitch got ready to give me another lesson on how medicine had been practiced in these parts for the past fifty years. Mitch sat on the front edge of his desk, arms crossed across his chest. It was lecture time. "Actually, Walt, I didn't learn this technique in school or in the service. Dr. Bacon taught me this, and he picked it up from the guys that were here before him."

He thought for a moment, then continued, "Gosh, I guess I've been using this technique for over thirty years, but I don't think I've ever seen it in a medical article or a textbook."

"Mitch, you've got my curiosity up. Tell me about it."

"Well, Walt, you can only use this technique to remove an *uninfected* sebaceous cyst. And you can only use the technique in areas where the skin is fairly thin. Just won't work if the skin's real thick or if there's *any* infection or inflammation. In those cases it's best to just cut it out by using the standard surgical technique. But in the right cases it works like a dream and is great for most of the local folks because they don't have to come back to the doctor for follow-up or to have stitches removed. All you do is numb up the skin over the cyst with a little bleb of lidocaine.

Then make a two- or three-millimeter stab wound, using a #11-blade scalpel, down into the cyst. Take one or two iodine crystals—we get them from Doc John at the drugstore—and place 'em deep into the center of the cyst after you've made the incision. Put on a Band-Aid, and that's all there is to it."

I was dumbfounded. "How does that get rid of the cyst?"

"Well, son, it doesn't." Mitch was quiet, but his eyes were laughing. *Was he pulling my leg? Was this a joke?* He continued, "Apparently the iodine desiccates the cheesy sebum in the cyst. Causes it to shrink, blacken, and harden into a rock-hard little stone. This takes several days. While that painless chemical reaction takes place, there is just enough drainage to keep your stab wound open. After, say, five to seven days, the patient or a family member can just squeeze on the cyst, and out it will pop—like a pea out of a pod."

"I've gotta see this," I exclaimed.

"Won't take but a minute for me to show you. Come on."

I followed him down the hall to the procedure room where Helen already had the patient settled onto the operating table.

"How you doing, Jimmy?" asked Dr. Mitchell as he washed his hands and put on a pair of gloves. "Let's take a look at that thing."

There was a half-inch lump on the young man's scalp, just behind the ear. "How long's this thing been there?" Mitch asked.

"Don't rightly know, Doc. Don't rightly know. But it's sure getting bigger. And it bugs the dickens out of me when I try to brush my hair. Sure would like it out."

"No problem, Jimmy. Let me numb it up a bit. I want to show our new doc how we do this around here. Jimmy, this here's Dr. Walt Larimore." Mitch nodded in my direction. "He's just joined us. Did his training down at Duke. But they didn't teach him everything down there, did they, Walt?"

"Nope, guess not. Good to meet you, Jimmy."

"Good to meet you, Doc. You're learning from the best here. He's took care of all our folks. My daddy and my daddy's daddy. Won't find better. Nope, you won't."

"I'm sure you're right, Jimmy."

"Jimmy, you hold tight. I'm gonna numb this a bit." In only a second or two, Mitch applied a bleb of lidocaine and then Helen took the syringe and handed him a scalpel. He quickly and deftly made the stab and squeezed out just a bit of the malodorous and cheesy-looking sebum from the cyst.

"Walt, that confirms the diagnosis. Nothing but nothing looks or smells like the contents of a sebaceous cyst. The body has millions and millions of microscopic sebaceous glands. There's one or two in each pore of the skin. The sebaceous oil from these glands is one of the body's natural oils. But if the gland gets plugged up, it just keeps making the oil and it builds and builds until a pronounced cyst forms. I sure like seeing them when they're not infected. One whole heck of a lot easier to treat."

By now Helen had fetched a small black bottle and a pair of forceps. "Walt, you just take one or two small iodine crystals ..." He reached into the bottle with the forceps, withdrawing a small black crystal, " ... and jam it into the middle of the cyst." Which he did. Jimmy didn't flinch.

"That's it, Jimmy. This thing will be ready to squeeze out in about a week. I'll have Helen here explain to you how to do that and how to care for it until then. If you have any trouble, you let us know, ya hear?"

"Yes, sir. I hear ya. Thank you, Dr. Mitchell."

Then I heard, for the first time, a statement for which Mitch was famous. It made the patient feel good about coming in for the visit and magnified the doctor's reputation throughout the region. "Jimmy, you got to me just in time with this thing. If you had waited much longer, it probably would have gotten infected, and I tell you, that's a mess, son. But I believe we got it just in time."

"Thanks, Dr. Mitchell. Sure appreciate you."

"You bet, Jimmy. No problem at all." Mitch paused just a moment, and I could see an idea dawn in his head. "Tell you what. Instead of me having Helen tell you how to pop this cyst out in a week, how about you drop by the office and let me show young Dr. Larimore how this works? That sound OK? I know you work just down the road. We could see you on your lunch break, and there'll be no charge for that visit. Sound OK?"

"You bet, Doc. No problem at all. Always enjoy those free visits. After all, you don't do *that* very often."

Mitch smiled. "Gotta pay those bills, Jimmy. Gotta pay those bills." He looked at Helen and me. "Jimmy, you wouldn't believe what it costs to hire good help these days." We smiled.

"Jimmy, you be sure to tell your dad and mom hi for me, you hear?"

"Be glad to."

Mitch signaled me with his eyes and a nod of his head. We stepped out of the room.

"What do you think of this old mountain technique?" Mitch asked me.

"I'll have to admit it's pretty neat. Does it really work?"

"Nearly every time. Piece of cake, son, piece of cake."

He paused for a moment as though reminiscing, then continued, "Nothing like the practice of medicine, son. Nothing like this profession. I've got to have the best job on earth." He turned to head into the next examining room. As he closed the door I heard him saying, "Good thing you got here to see me, Sammy. Let me look at that thing."

I smiled.

The next week, I saw Jimmy's name on my schedule and greeted him as Helen and I entered the room.

"How you doing, Jimmy?"

"Just fine, Doc, just fine. I'll be glad to get this thing out. The black drainage has messed up the collar of a shirt or two—at least until I figured out how to stick a cotton ball over it."

"Sounds like a good idea. Let me have a look at that thing."

The cyst had indeed shrunk to at least fifty percent of its previous size and looked like a dark black stone just under the skin.

"Want me to show you how Dr. Mitchell does it?" asked Helen.

"You bet." I took a couple of steps back.

Helen washed her hands and put on a pair of gloves. She placed a pointer finger on each side of the lump.

"Jimmy, hold on now. Shouldn't hurt much."

Then she pressed her fingertips toward each other and the iodizing remnant of the cyst popped out with the help of the compression on each side of the wound.

I smiled. "Wow, that looked easy. Jimmy, did that hurt?"

"Not a bit, Doc. Not even a little bit."

Helen smiled as she placed a dab of Neosporin and a Band-Aid over the wound. "Piece of cake, Jimmy. Just put a dab of antibiotic ointment on this four times a day. It should be healed in just a few days."

As Jimmy was leaving, Helen commented, "Usually I just teach a family member to do this at home. Saves the patient some time, some money, and, for many of them, a trip to town."

I figured this was only one of many old tricks this new dog was going to need to learn in rural private practice.

At the end of each day in the office, Mitch, Ray, and I would usually sit for a few minutes and chat about the day. A topic of recurring concern to me was Drs. Mathieson and Nordling. Both seemed constantly irritated by my presence. Whenever I'd enter a nurses' station, they would leave. Mitch and Ray tried to reassure me, and they encouraged me to just give them some time. We also talked about problem patients and practice management issues. Having had training in practice management while in residency, I assumed I had some expertise, albeit no experience.

Because my schedule as a new doctor in town was less crowded than Mitch's or Ray's, I offered to help them develop and improve some of their office procedures and policies. One of the most noticeable deficiencies was the billing and collection system. Mitch had some unpaid bills that were decades old. He would send out a bill four times a year—and would keep doing it, sometimes for many years.

We had been taught in our practice management classes that this way of billing was fairly useless. If within the span of about four months the average person had either not paid their bill or made arrangements to pay it off, our teachers said, there was virtually no chance that it would ever be paid. So we were taught that if the patient didn't respond to the fourth or fifth monthly bill, then he or she should be sent a stern letter—return receipt requested—telling them to either pay the bill within thirty days or call the office to arrange to make payments on the bill within thirty days. If they didn't do so, they would be dismissed from the practice within thirty days and their bill would be sent to a collection agency.

When I suggested this mode of operation to Mitch and Ray one evening, Mitch's response was swift and stern. "You stupid, son? *That* won't work here. First of all, folks pay when they can—and *not* before. Very few folks 'round these parts leave a bill unpaid unless they're in tight straits. Second of all, if I throw them out of the practice, they'll tell everyone they know. That's no good for them, for me, or for you boys. Might work in the big city. But not here, not with our folks."

I looked at Ray. He shrugged. I felt I shouldn't push.

Mitch left to do evening rounds at the hospital. Ray looked at me. "You were wise not to press the issue. I've only been here two years, but I'm still learning a lot. Mitch knows his medicine and he knows this community. I'm learning to trust his gut. Let's just see what happens."

"Sounds good to me, Ray."

"But, Walt, don't stop making suggestions. You've made some great ones. Glad you're here."

Later that week, I was doing a well-baby exam when there was a knock on the door. Without waiting for my response, Mitch entered. He greeted the patient, "Howdy, Tammy. My oh my, little Libby sure is growing. Mind if I borrow your doctor for just a moment?"

We stepped into the hall. "Got a second?" Mitch asked. "Want you to meet someone."

He headed down the hall to his office. I followed. Reva was chatting with a young couple. Sitting on the woman's lap was a three- or four-year-old child. The way they were dressed indicated that they were not well-off. The man's calloused hands and his tanned and wrinkled skin—making him look older than his age—indicated that he probably worked outdoors.

"Bobby and Jennie Sue, this here is our new doctor—Dr. Walt Larimore. He's just joined us. I wanted him to hear what you had to say."

The couple looked embarrassed.

"Go ahead," Mitch encouraged, "he'll be as proud of you as I am."

Bobby began to speak—hesitantly and in low tones. "Well, me and Jennie Sue had Faye Marie here nearly three years ago over in Sylva. We come home from the hospital, and when she was six weeks old, I tripped while carryin' Faye Marie out to the car. We was heading out to church. Anyway, we took a tumble and little Faye Marie banged the tip-top of her head on the car door. It wasn't a real big cut, but she bled like a stuck pig. 'Bout scared me to death, and Jennie Sue here was near hysterical. I stopped the bleeding with my kerchief and we ran up here to the hospital. Louise called Dr. Mitchell, and he come and sewed her up."

He paused and looked at the floor. "Frankly, we didn't have the $60 to pay the bill, what with the baby doctor bills and all. My lumberin's been a bit on the downside—prices not that good—and gas and oil's been up. So I just couldn't pay the bill. I called up Dr. Mitchell's office, and Reva here just said pay when I could. Dr. Mitchell hasn't even sent me a bill since then."

He took a deep breath, then continued. "Well, we begun savin' a bit, whenever we could. Cut back a bit on some things. And today we come in to pay our bill. To make it right."

He looked up at Dr. Mitchell, admiringly. "Want to see your work?" He smiled and turned toward his daughter. Separating the hair on her forehead, he said, "Looky here. Can't hardly see the scar."

Mitch and I leaned forward. Indeed there was a barely discernable line, just a bit lighter in color than her skin color. I wasn't even sure I would have been able to see it if her father's calloused finger hadn't pointed it out.

"She's healed mighty fine, Bobby."

"I think she had a good doctor and that's why she healed so good."

"Well," replied Mitch, "you brought her to the right place, and just in time too! That made all the difference." I smiled at hearing this classic Mitchism again.

"We're much obliged to you, Dr. Mitchell." Bobby held out his hand, offering three crisp $20 bills.

"Thank you," Mitch said.

"No, thank *you*, Doctor. We best be off now."

"Bobby, you be sure to tell your daddy and momma hello for me, you hear?"

"Yes, sir, I will," he replied as he left. Jennie Sue politely smiled and turned to follow her husband down the hall, little Faye Marie in tow.

I sat in silence.

Mitch turned to Reva. "Tell our young Dr. Larimore, will you, Reva? How often does that happen?"

"Oh my gosh, Dr. Mitchell. Several times a week. We've even had family members come settle a bill after a patient has passed on. Folks around here take care of their bills. May take a while, but you can depend on them."

"Reva," Mitch asked, "what's the oldest bill that has ever been paid?"

Reva thought for a minute. "I suspect it was the Balls. You delivered their last child about seventeen years ago. They came and paid the bill just this summer. Said they didn't want their daughter graduating from high school with any bills left unpaid."

"Thanks, Reva." He smiled as she stood up to leave the room.

Mitch looked at me. "Those big-city practice management experts, they ever tell you about this?"

Now it was my turn to be embarrassed. "No, sir, I don't think they've ever heard about this sort of thing."

"Wouldn't look very good if I had thrown them out of the practice, would it? Or if I had sicced a collection agency on them, now would it?"

"No, sir, I don't think it would either look good or be very wise."

"Me neither, son." He turned to leave. "Let's get back to work. Lots of folks to see and lots left to learn."

At first I thought he was referring to my ineptitude. But then I realized that wasn't the case. He was referring to our profession—one in which we continue to learn right up to the day we stop practicing.

I smiled. Indeed, this new dog had a lot to learn from this old dog. In many ways Mitch reminded me of Fred Moody. Both not only knew their profession, but they also knew the people and they knew the community's ways. I found myself wanting to have their skill and their insight—neither of which was learned in their schooling but was forged on the anvil of time.

Mitch would often tell me, "Son, good judgment comes from experience, and experience comes from bad judgment." I didn't enjoy the mistakes I was making—the deficits in my knowledge base that were continually being revealed—but I was learning that the local doctors' "backward ways" were often more helpful and fruitful than my book knowledge, which I had thought would be much more valuable than it was turning out to be. I was especially learning to trust Dr. Mitchell's gut instincts and his vast experience. More important than that, I decided, I was *willing* to learn—no matter how difficult or humbling Mitch might make that process for me. I was discovering that, in the practice of medicine, the learning never stops. And, like it or not, I had a long, long way to go—and to grow.

chapter fourteen

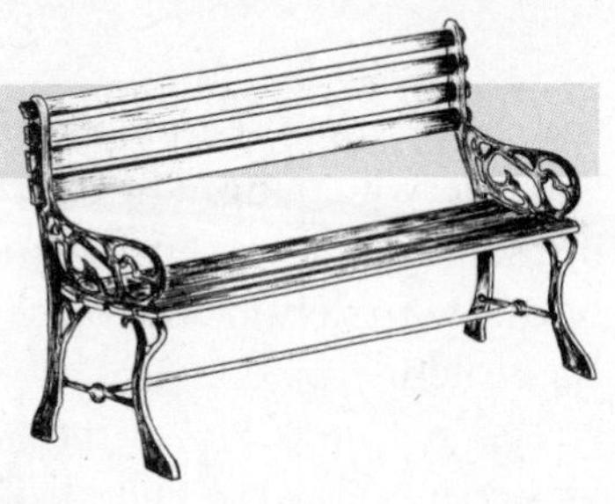

Lessons in Daily Practice

It was Hal Fergusson's third visit to the office in less than a month. For a local, that was tantamount to a medical emergency. I was beginning to learn that diseases in these parts usually presented late and well developed. Family physicians in more affluent areas had the opposite dilemma, where running to the physician at the first sniffle or hint of discomfort was nearly a national obsession—almost as rampant as the universal demand for a prescription for maladies that would heal just with the passing of time.

Hal was a handyman, as had been his dad. Hal was known as a no-nonsense kind of guy who could perform any sort of home repair. Honest and straight shooting. Ray had treated him after a couple of accidents and had indicated that Hal's pain threshold was fairly high. He had suffered a mean second-degree burn on the top of his hand when a propane torch he was using to solder some copper pipes together slipped. He only came to the office when the pain from a secondary bacterial infection was overwhelming. The delay in treatment cost him a few days in the hospital for intravenous antibiotics and surgery on the burn site to debride the eschar. "He could have lost that hand," Ray told me.

So here was Hal in the office for the third time. Something was up, and it wasn't good. The previous two visits had been for rectal pain and bright-red bleeding with each bowel movement. The diagnosis had been simple and straightforward—an anal fissure, which is a small tear through the thin and delicate skin overlying the anus and the lower rectum. These tears can be slow to heal—especially if the victim is as chronically constipated as Hal, who refused to eat anything with fiber in it and was habitually dehydrated. "Doc, can't be drinkin' water all day. Elsewise I'd be peein' all day. In my work, bathrooms are always available but not always functional. That's why *I'm* in 'em."

During my first visit with Hal, he shared one of his favorite stories about Dr. Mitchell. "I was called over here to the office on an 'emergency.' One of the toilets in the office was leakin' at the floor and makin' a mess. I came over and found the problem pretty quick. All I needed to do was tighten a couple of nuts where the toilet was attached to the floor. My bill for this urgent call was $25. Mitch nearly went through the roof. 'That's more than three times what I charge,' he yelled at me. Then he hollered, 'And I'm a doctor!'

"I tell ya, Doc, he was red in the face. So I just looked him straight in the eye and told him, 'Yeah, I didn't make this much money when I was a doctor either.' Well, Helen started a'snickerin'—which I hear got her in hot water for several days. But then Doc started laughin'. He paid the bill. We been friends ever since."

During Hal's first visit I simply prescribed a stool softener—which he refused to take—and petroleum jelly to be applied before and after each bowel movement. Unfortunately for Hal, his eliminations were too infrequent to allow the utilization of enough jelly for positive effect. The wound dried and cracked, and the pain and bleeding began again.

At his second visit I insisted that he try a tablet form of stool softener and a prescription antibacterial ointment. He was very compliant with both orders. We doctors know that pain increases a patient's motivation to follow the doctor's recommendations. Unfortunately, even though Hal's elimination frequency increased, so did his pain.

On exam today, the fissure looked wider and longer. The area of indurated (hard) tissue around it was larger than at the previous two visits—although there was no sign of abscess. The rule of thumb at Duke had been that if the anal fissure didn't heal, a surgical operation should be considered to cut out the offending tissue and allow the fresh, uninfected tissue to heal more quickly. Being in the office with two surgeons made such consultations easy and relatively painless.

While Hal was dressing after the exam, I stepped into the hallway to wait for one of my colleagues to emerge from an exam room. Fortunately for me and for Hal, Mitch was the first one out—as Ray and I would have gladly, but unknowingly and unnecessarily, taken Hal to the operating room for this malady.

"Son," Mitch said, "he's only had this three weeks. Can take months to heal. I don't hardly ever take them to the OR before the fissure's been there three months—less'n there's an abscess. But come to think of it, bet I haven't had one in OR in a dozen years since Dr. Bacon taught me the ol' nitroglycerin trick."

The ol' nitroglycerin trick? My mind was racing through mental medical file after medical file but coming up empty. Fortunately, Dr. Mitchell didn't ask me to reveal my ignorance. This was to be yet another case where my first professors in the world of real-life medicine would teach me something that wouldn't be published in the medical literature for another dozen years or more.

"It's really simple," Mitch explained. "The older docs have been using this technique forever. It used to be more difficult to formulate, because Doc John had to keep the nitroglycerin in a cool, dark corner of the pharmacy. But when they came out with the premixed nitroglycerin ointment a few years back, it sure made things easier."

"How in the world does it work? *Does* it work?"

"Like I said, son, I haven't taken a chronic anal fissure to the OR since I started using the stuff. I suspect the nitroglycerin increases the blood flow to the area, same way it increases blood flow to the heart during an attack of angina. That helps the healing. But it also seems to have a pain-relieving effect. Not rightly sure how it does that, but folks claim it works. It's sure cheaper and easier than surgery."

"So how do you prescribe it?"

"Simple, son, simple. Just prescribe anal nitroglycerin, and Doc John'll mix it up for ya. He'll fill a four-ounce tub with the stuff, and then instruct the patient to apply a pea-sized dab to the sore area four times a day and after each bowel movement. When Hal's feeling better, he can decrease to three times a day, and, when better yet, he can decrease to twice a day. Let him know it can take up to eight weeks for the fissure to heal completely. Now if it's not healed in eight weeks, then we can consider operating."

"Anal nitroglycerin!" I mused. "Why, I never . . ."

"Yep." Mitch got that glint in his eye and the wry smile that preceded some sort of quip or joke. "I call this condition 'anal angina.'"

Great name! I thought, as he went chuckling into an exam room to see his next patient.

Hal was delighted with the suggestion. "Actually, Doc," he asserted, "done heard of that from ol' Calvin Johnson when I was up fixin' some pipes at his place. Said it worked like a charm for him. Don't know why we didn't think of that before."

Then he leaned toward me a bit, almost whispering, "Calvin said he'd get the prescription and use it for his manly duties."

"*Manly duties?*" I must have looked confused.

"You know, Doc," his voice lowered, "it helped his potency."

"His potency?"

"Yep," nodded Mr. Fergusson, continuing to whisper. "He said he'd take a small dab of that nitroglycerin ointment the doctor prescribed and rub it on the end of his thing."

"His thing?"

"Doc, you kidding me? You know, his . . . uh, . . ." He seemed to be searching for just the right word.

"You mean he put the nitroglycerin on his . . . ?"

"That's what he said. Sure as shooting. So, Doc, I'd be wondering . . . ," he paused and looked at the floor for a moment, then continued, "if you might consider either doubling the prescription size or maybe making it refillable."

I decided to comply with the request, but warned, "Hal, topical nitroglycerin can cause a headache or a flushed feeling if you use too much."

Hal smiled—looking almost frisky. "Side effects would sure be worth it, Doc!"

We both chuckled.

I saw Hal in town a few weeks later. "How is everything?" I inquired.

"Haven't seen me back, have you?" He smiled. "Anyway, the prescription you gave me worked on *both* the north and south end of me."

I'm sure everyone within hearing distance of our guffaws wondered what Mr. Fergusson and the new doctor found so exceedingly funny.

My next patient that day was Leonard, a ninety-eight-year-old man who came to the office for, of all things, a premarital exam. Too embarrassed to tell the staff that it was a premarital exam—for reasons that became fabulously famous during the subsequent months—he simply scheduled a routine heart exam.

In those days doctors were still doing premarital exams and the state required a blood test for syphilis. (We had only four or five sexually transmitted diseases to be concerned about then; these days it's approaching fifty.) Anyway, Leonard's previous *three* wives had all succumbed to cancer. His impotence problems with wife number three had been "healed" by Mitch's prescription of topical nitroglycerin.

During his exam, this brittle elder, who suffered from labile congestive heart failure secondary to several heart attacks, as well as very unpredictable chest pain secondary to a severe case of coronary artery disease, confided to me that he was marrying a young barmaid.

"Why?" I queried.

"Because," he replied, smiling, "I wanted to marry someone who would outlive me!"

"Are you gonna consummate this thing?" I asked.

"Of course!" he exclaimed. "But *not* until we're married!"

"But," I protested, "you must be very, very careful. Too strenuous of a honeymoon could mean a heart attack or even death!"

He looked me straight in the eye and said, "Well, Doc, if she dies, she dies!"

I think I must have looked, for a moment, utterly bewildered. Then he smiled and began to laugh. I realized I'd been snookered. He confessed that he was actually marrying a "proper" woman, although she was twenty years his junior. I began to chuckle, both at myself and then with him. We both began to laugh and laugh until we had tears running down our faces. Helen barged in to shush us up. We continued to do some shushed-up giggling.

One of the many truisms of medicine is that the doctor-patient relationship is foundational to the healing process. I have found that this involves each party learning how to teach the other. Many of the pearls of wisdom and the practical tips I've gleaned over two decades were discovered by my patients and taught to me. Some have subsequently been evaluated scientifically—while others remain anecdotal observations only.

Delores Smith was one of those patients who taught me. This elderly woman suffered from recurrent nosebleeds that occasionally required a trip to the office for an anterior nasal pack or a cauterization. I had tried all of our standard treatments, but topical steroids, nasal saline, topical petroleum jelly, topical Neosporin, and room humidification didn't help at all. I was befuddled. Finally I decided to try a new trick that I had picked up at a medical conference.

"Delores, here's a prescription for an antibiotic ointment. You just take a dab and rub it on the inside of each nostril—once in the morning and once in the evening. Then you kind of give your nose a pinch to spread the ointment a bit. If you use this every day, and keep using a humidifier, I think this'll do the trick."

I didn't see her for many months, and I was sure my therapy was the distinct reason she wasn't coming in with any more nosebleeds. She next appeared in the office for her annual exam that spring. During the exam I commented, "Delores, I see from your chart that you've not been in for any more nosebleeds. I guess the ointment I prescribed must have worked for you."

"Well . . . ," she started, then blushed, looking away. "A prescription ointment *did* do the trick."

There was an uncomfortable pause in the conversation. "Was it the ointment I prescribed?" I asked.

Another pause—her eyes still turned away from mine. She shook her head no.

"Whose then?" I asked.

"Well, Doctor, it was a prescription from Canada."

Trying not to act *too* defensive, I inquired, "What type of prescription?" Actually, I was a bit curious. A family doctor can never have too many tools in his black bag. Maybe I would learn about a new one today.

"Fortunately for me, Dr. Larimore, my sister Dianna, who lives in Nova Scotia, inherited the same family predisposition to these types of nosebleeds. Her general practitioner, an ancient man, explained to her that the rosiness of her ruddy Irish cheeks had just migrated into her nostrils. He explained that this seemed to happen in only the most sensitive and exquisite of the grand dames. My sister found this medical assessment charming—especially when this gentleman explained that even Queen Victoria herself suffered this malady."

What a cunning old codger, I thought to myself of my Canadian colleague. *A master of the bedside technique!*

She continued, "He explained to her that as a woman matures . . ."

Matures! What a great expression! My interest in and admiration for this fellow was increasing by the moment.

". . . the skin can thin a bit—become a tad more fragile, dainty, and delicate. This can be true inside the nostril as well as among other parts."

"So what did he recommend?" I wasn't even remotely prepared for the answer.

"Premarin cream," Delores stated matter-of-factly.

I couldn't contain my surprise. "Premarin *vaginal* cream?" This common preparation of topical estrogen was often prescribed to women after menopause to thicken the walls of the vagina if vaginal dryness or pain during intercourse was a problem.

Delores looked at me as though I was daft. "But of course! He said that the lining of a woman's private parts and the lining of her nostrils contained the same type of skin. Didn't you know that?"

"Well," I stammered, "of course I knew that. I've just never heard of using this cream in the nose."

"He told my sister that most doctors had never bothered to think this through, but that since the skin of both areas is the same, then the same treatment could be used for both. He told her he had been prescribing it for years."

"Well, quite frankly, Delores, it makes a bit of sense, I must admit. How did he say to use it?"

Her smile radiated as she became the professor, I the pupil. She was fairly gloating in the experience. "This is what he told my sister to do, and it's what I did too. I applied a BB-sized drop of the Premarin cream to the inside of each nostril with a Q-tip—twice a day for thirty days, then daily for thirty days, then three times a week for another month, and then one or two times per week until the weather began to get a bit warmer."

"How long did it take to work?"

"I had no more nosebleeds after using the cream for just a few weeks."

"Mind if I take a look?"

"Of course not."

The inside of her nostrils looked nice and pink. None of the unsightly little spider veins I had seen last fall.

"Delores, your nasal mucosae look almost as beautiful as you do."

She blushed. *I can pick up a thing or two,* I thought—*even across international borders!*

"Thanks for the teaching," I said.

She looked at me, cocking her head as though in disbelief. I could almost read her mind: *A doctor—thanking* me *for teaching* him?

"Thank *you,*" Delores answered, "for being such an attentive pupil." She smiled. So did I.

The office calls during my first year in practice continually gave me a chance both to teach and to be taught. Ray approached me in the hall one afternoon about a patient with a skin problem—chronic urticaria, which is doctor-talk for hives. Ray had done the extensive laboratory tests recommended by an Asheville dermatologist he had called—and the lab tests were entirely normal. The medications he'd prescribed had either caused side effects or had had no effect. He and the patient were frustrated, and he was considering sending the fellow off for further treatment. But before doing so, he asked for a second opinion.

I wasn't sure I had a single thing to offer, but I did see the patient and spent some time taking an elaborate history—just like a detective looking for the perpetrator. But none was found. For some reason, toward the end of the interview, I remembered Terry Kane, M.D., my chief while I was in training at Duke University, who used to say, "You can take all the history you want, but when all is said and done, you gotta take their clothes off and look!"

Although the young man was already clad in his briefs, and although his skin, hair, and nails appeared normal, I had him pull down first his briefs and then his socks. And there, underneath the socks that had never been removed before, at least in our office, was a rip-roaring case of tinea pedis and onychomycosis—doctor-talk for athlete's foot and athlete's toenails. Ray and I exchanged knowing glances. We both realized, instantly, that this was a likely cause for the hives, since a fungal infection of the skin can result in recurrent hives in a susceptible person.

"Jim, you ever notice this rash before?" I asked.

"Oh yeah, Doc. Been there off and on most of my life."

I took an ophthalmoscope off the wall and turned it on. The ophthalmoscope is designed to help a doctor look into the eye—especially at the retina. However, because its light is bright and because it magnifies the view manyfold, it can be an excellent tool for examining the skin.

"Yep," I commented. "I thought so."

"What is it, Doc?" asked a now worried Jim.

"Infection looks deep, Jim. I'm suspecting it and the hives are connected. Tell you what, if you're willing to take a little pill four times a day for the next three months, I believe we might just whip this thing."

"Don't know if I can remember."

"Don't worry about it, Jim. You just have your lovely wife, Elaine, do the remembering for you."

He smiled, "That she can do, Doc. That she can do."

That wasn't the last time that day I used the ophthalmoscope trick. In fact, the next patient was a little girl who had suffered an insect bite on her wrist while working in the garden the previous weekend. The girl's severe pain caused her mom to bring the little one to the emergency department twice—each time for an injection for pain.

To the naked eye, the skin looked almost normal, except for a small red line. However, under ophthalmoscopic magnification I could see two tiny parallel rows of red raised lesions—almost like two dotted lines lying together like a railroad track. I knew instantly what it was—a classic case of "caterpillar dermatitis." Once I knew what it was, treating the pain required merely removing the tiny toxin-containing stingers embedded in the little girl's skin.

I had Gay get me a piece of ordinary Scotch tape. As the mom gently held her daughter's arm in place, I stuck the tape to the lesions, rubbing the tape onto the skin. Then I carefully removed the tape, which had all of the little caterpillar hairs stuck to it. The pain relief for my little patient was almost immediate.

This is one of those treatments that always makes the doctor look wise—instantly. I, for one, was glad that the tape worked in this prickly situation.

One of the lifelong joys of family practice is that we family physicians can fill in our basic training with a day-to-day training that continues for the rest of our professional lives. For instance, one morning a six-year-old patient who had shingles came to the office for a follow-up. I had done the original exam and had made the diagnosis, even before the rash broke out. Today the mother and child were seeing Mitch for the follow-up. Apparently the mother had told him about my "hitting the nail on the head by using the Kleenex test."

A few days earlier she'd brought in her child, who was complaining of having "funny-feeling skin" that felt like it was burning, even though there was no rash whatsoever. I had learned the Kleenex test from cardiologist E. Harvey Estes during my residency. All the doctor had to do was gently pull a tissue, hanging loosely from his or her fingers, over the affected skin. If the sensation was painful to the patient, it served to predict the characteristic shingles rash that would follow. Mitch had never heard of such a thing and continued to brag about my lesson all afternoon. I, of course, was elated to be the one who earned his praise.

Toward the end of the day he had a chance to return the favor. A lumberman came in for a last-minute visit to have his hand sewed together with Dr. Mitchell's "cut glue." I examined the man's hands and fingers, which were thickly calloused from his daily labor. It was not unusual, he said, for these calluses to crack open at the beginning of autumn when the air became cooler and drier. Needless to say, these cracks, as they tried to scab and then were broken open again and again, resulted in a fair amount of pain. The problem was apparent, but I had no idea what he meant by the "cut glue" treatment.

I left the room to find the maestro. "Walt," explained Mitch, "this is a fairly recent trick of mine. You just fill the cracks with Super Glue."

"Super Glue?" I half-asked and half-repeated—with more than a trace of doubt in my voice.

"Yep. Although application of the glue will sting like the dickens for a few minutes, the stinging stops quickly and the wound seems to heal faster than on its own. Not only will the Super Glue hold the cracks shut, it's the only 'bandage' I've found that will stick to a sweaty palm. Then you just have the patient use a file or a pumice stone every night to keep those calluses a bit thinner. That will prevent further cracking."

The lumberman hated the actual cut-glue treatment but loved the result—his cracked fingers and palms were sealed and pain free.

Just down the street from Swain Surgical Associates was Super Swain Drug Store. After seeing the rest of my afternoon patients, I decided to walk down to make the acquaintance of the infamous "Doc John"—John Mattox, Registered Pharmacist. Doc

John was one of the old-timers, able not only to bottle up the most recent prescription medications but also to take raw ingredients and compound them into pills or potions or ointments or poultices or extracts or teas or powders. You name it, he could mix it—whether for oral, rectal, or topical application. Doc John was a generalist in the best sense of the term. He did it all. Not only that, he was known far and wide for his home remedies. Uncommon was the patient I saw in the office who had not first tried one of "Doc John's Tried-and-True Home Remedies." What came to surprise me over the years was just how many of them actually worked.

I stepped into the store and was immediately swept up in feelings of nostalgia. The store looked almost identical to the Rexall Drug Store that my family frequented when I was growing up. I had precious memories of my dad occasionally taking me before school to the soda fountain for biscuits and bacon. I can remember us sharing a cup of coffee—mine mixed as café au lait—and my feeling *very* grown-up.

At the back of the store was Doc John—aging, balding, and laughing with a customer, a deep roaring laugh accompanied by an affectionate swat on the customer's back. You could sense his joie de vivre and understand why his customers liked him so much.

As the customer turned to leave, Doc John turned to me. "How can I help you, son?"

"Hi. Are you John Mattox?"

He looked a bit suspicious. "Am," he replied.

"I'm Walt Larimore. I just wanted to come by and meet you."

He immediately broke into a wide grin, pumped my hand in a vigorous and prolonged handshake, and commented, "My, oh my. I imagined someone *much* older. They all say you look young, but I never dreamed. Come, sit over here. Got a moment?" He ushered me to one of the booths near the soda bar. "How about a milk shake—on the house?"

"Sure, I'd love one. Vanilla will be fine."

"Malt?"

"No thanks."

"Becky," he hollered to his wife, who was behind the soda bar. "This here's the new doc. Can you get him and me a vanilla shake, honey?"

He turned his attention back to me. "Doc, where'd you go to medical school?" Before I could answer, he continued. "Because I thought they taught you guys how *not* to write—you know, how to scribble."

I looked at him—more than a little mystified.

"In fact," he continued, "I heard that when you fellows graduate from medical school, they make you sign your name on a ledger. And if they can read your name, you fail! They don't give you your diploma!" He began to laugh and laugh. I smiled. "Anyway, I figured you must have failed out—at least once—because I can actually *read* your handwriting on your prescriptions." His laughter burst forth yet again.

As I headed for home that evening, I could feel my confidence in my skills beginning to increase. My "book" knowledge and my "practical" knowledge were now starting to work together. After supper Barb laughed as she came across an advertisement in a magazine. She read it to me. "If it creaks, cramps, cries, eats, stings, smarts, swells, twists, twinges, burps, burns, aches, sticks, twitches, crumbles, or hurts, we've got just the doctor for you."

She paused. I asked, "Is that it?"

She laughed again. "Nope. The answer is . . . the family physician." She gave my arm a reassuring squeeze. My confidence soared even higher.

That evening I sat out back on my bench. My thoughts returned to Barb's encouragement. I found myself musing about general family practice—my growing forte. To my way of thinking, general practice is both unique and difficult—not so much in terms of the breadth of expertise required but in the complexity of providing medical care in the patients' real world. The focus of family docs like me is to combine the *science* of medicine with the *art* of medicine—in the real-life context of the community in which our patients live. A general practitioner has to be ready at any moment to switch between different perspectives—biomedical, psychological, relational, and spiritual.

I smiled to myself as I gazed out over the valley. *A generalist,* I mused. *Not what everyone in medicine wants to be, but certainly what I sense I'm called to be. And maybe I'm beginning to get there. I'm not yet the family doctor I want to be, but it's coming. Slowly, ever so slowly, it's coming.*

chapter fifteen

White Lies

One day after lunch I walked over to the hospital for afternoon rounds. I saw Louise coming down the hall. Ever since the case of the skintight cast, I had felt uncomfortable being around the ER nurse. I wasn't sure why. Perhaps I was still wrestling with the fact that her clinical and practical experience so vastly outweighed mine. Perhaps it was the reality that she knew these people and their ways so much more intimately than I did. Although she was nice enough, around her I just felt uneducated. And what was even more painful, I felt unappreciated.

Louise was heading toward the ER with a syringe in her hand. I was trying to think of something to say, but she beat me to the punch.

"Dr. Larimore, you got a moment? I need a hand." She continued on to the ER without comment. I followed like an obedient pup. As we walked toward the ER, I saw Louise place the syringe in her pocket. An elderly man was coming out of the ER, holding his paperwork and struggling into his plaid coat.

"Louise, the sugar worked like a charm. The hiccups are completely gone. You may never see me again in this place!" He smiled and turned to leave.

Louise smiled and glanced my way. "I'll explain later."

We entered the ER, and I could hear the whimpering of a child, which increased in volume as we approached the cubicle. We went in, and I saw a small woman with a four- or five-year-old boy.

"Mae Bell, Dr. Sales says it's the strep throat and that some penicillin should clear it up pretty quickly."

I suspected Dr. Sale was on call for the ER. For some reason, Louise always called him Dr. Sales.

Louise went on. "The best way to get the medicine into him is to put it into a muscle." She paused and pointed to her hip. The mother's eyes widened a bit as she recognized the "shotlike" gesture. "Is that OK?" asked Louise. The mother began to nod her head yes. Louise continued, "And the best way to get the medicine into the muscle is to have your little one lie down on his stomach. OK?"

The mother continued to nod. The young tot had no idea what was coming. The fully informed verbal consents often administered these days to the very young and their parents were just not a part of medical practice back then—certainly not in Bryson City.

"Henry . . ." Louise now directed her comments at the unsuspecting lad. "I want you to get up on the bed and lay on your tummy so that Miss Louise can check your backside." Louise wasn't just "checking his backside," she was getting ready to give him a shot. *Was this lying?* I wondered, making a mental note to ask her about this later.

Henry was eyeing Louise with an impressive degree of distrust, especially since a white-coat-clad, doctor-looking type of guy was standing next to her. But he allowed his mom to help him up and lay on his tummy—glancing back over his shoulder with grave suspicion.

As Louise moved closer, she instructed, "Mae Bell, can you give Henry a little back massage while I look at his back? And Dr. Larimore, I want you to take Henry's feet and turn them so that the toes are pointing toward each other and hold them there for a moment."

I'm sure I looked at her with a furrowed brow. *What in the world was she thinking?* I had never seen such a thing. But obediently I gently grabbed Henry's ankles and turned the toes so they were facing each other while his mom rubbed his back. Louise very quickly pulled down one corner of his pants, took an alcohol sponge from her pocket and rubbed it across the skin, gently pinched Henry's unsuspecting upper buttock between her left thumb and index finger, and with her right hand reached into her pocket, single-handedly unsheathed the needle, and drove it into his flesh. Before he knew it, the syringe was empty and the deed done.

As we all released our grip, the full implication of the dirty deed traveled up Henry's gluteal nerve and spinal column to the pain center of his young developing brain. This resulted in neural impulses that both instantly widened his eyes and tightened his perioral muscles, which caused his diaphragm to contract and draw in a full breath of air. His intercostal muscles then contracted with such force that the subsequent yell was heard clear out in the waiting room. The embrace of a loving mother muffled the crying as Louise and I stepped out of the cubicle.

"Thank you for the help, Dr. Larimore," said the nurse as she resheathed the needle and jotted a note on the patient's chart.

"Louise, two questions," I said. "One, what's this about sugar and hiccups? Two, what's the deal about the toes?"

Louise smiled and then slyly asked, "Why, Dr. Larimore, didn't they teach these things to you all at the big Duke University?"

"Don't believe so, Louise. We were too busy learning how to save lives."

My hint of humor was obviously not received well as Louise glared at me over her spectacles. "Actually, Louise, I wasn't taught either technique. What's the deal?"

"What *were* you taught to do if someone comes into the ER with a bad case of hiccups that had been going on for hours or days?" Louise quizzed me.

"We usually used intravenous Thorazine. That seemed to work pretty well—at least in the two or three cases I've seen."

"We've used Thorazine here, but I can't even remember the last time. The sugar seems to work just fine. It's sure a lot cheaper. Just like with Shitake Sam when he broke his ankle, we try to do things the least expensive way we can. Many of these folks don't have no medical insurance. 'Nother thing 'bout the sugar is that it has none of the side effects that meds like Thorazine can have."

"How do you administer it?"

She looked confused. "The Thorazine?"

I chuckled. "No, no. The sugar."

"Oh, well, it's real simple. Just take a heaping tablespoon of granulated sugar—I get it from the staff lounge—and have the patient swallow it down."

"That's it?"

"Yep, that's it. Usually works in ten to fifteen minutes."

"How does it work?"

"Dr. Larimore, I don't have a clue," she answered bluntly. "I just know it does."

"OK. So what's the deal with the toes?"

Louise perked up. "I do know how that one works. Let me show you. Dr. Larimore, stand facing the counter."

I did, but asked, "Louise, you're not going to give me a shot, are you?"

She laughed, "No sir. No shot. Just a demonstration. Here, I'll do it with you."

She stood and faced the counter beside me. "Now turn your toes in so they're pointing toward each other," she instructed.

We both turned our toes in. *It's a good thing no one's watching this!* I thought.

"Now," she continued, "try to tighten up your buttock muscles."

I tried, but my gluteal muscles just wouldn't contract—at least not very much.

"Wow," I commented. "That's really great!"

"You see, pointing those old toes pigeonlike keeps the buttocks from tightening up. You can do this standing or lying down. By preventing the tightening of the gluteal muscles, you can relieve some of the pain for the patient. That's just the way it is."

By now there was no more whimpering from the cubicle. Mae Bell and Henry appeared from behind the curtain—no worse for wear. As they left the ER, I turned to Louise.

"Louise, just one more quick question. You really lied to that little boy, didn't you?"

"Say what?"

"You told him you were just going to check his backside—when you knew all along you were going to give him a shot. Isn't that lying?"

"Well, Dr. Larimore, I've learned that misleading statements made for the benefit of the patient or the family are sometimes appropriate. They're just white lies."

I furrowed my brow. "Louise, isn't a lie a lie? I mean, is there really any difference between a white lie and a lie? Aren't they both really just the same thing?"

She paused to rub her chin and then explained, "Not really, Dr. Larimore. One intends to deceive and one intends, in a caring way, to help."

"But," I persisted, "both of them are still lies. How can a lie help a situation?"

Louise smiled kindly, if perhaps a bit condescendingly. "Dr. Larimore, after President Carter was elected, I heard a story 'bout his momma, who had a home in Plains, Georgia. She hated to do press interviews. She resented the way the reporters mischaracterized her son and what he stood for—especially his spiritual beliefs.

"So after her son's election, his staff persuaded her to do an interview with a well-known national magazine. Miss Lillian did *not* want to do the interview, but she agreed—as long as it was done in her home on her home turf and the interview was limited to thirty minutes or less."

I was wondering where this was going but continued to listen.

"On the appointed day the reporter drove up to the house, walked past the Secret Service agents and up to the front porch. She knocked on the screen door. Miss Lillian greeted her and took her into the parlor, where they both sat down. Miss Lillian offered her no refreshments, which would be highly unusual, even rude, in that area of the South.

"The reporter tried to make small talk. Miss Lillian's response was to look at her wristwatch and say, 'You have twenty-seven minutes.'

"The reporter began her interview with what was to Miss Lillian one of the most offensive questions she could be asked: 'The president has been quoted as saying that his religious beliefs would compel him to never knowingly tell a lie. You raised the president from the time he was a baby. You saw him grow up. During that time did you know him to ever tell a lie?'

"Miss Lillian's cheeks flushed, but she remained cool on the outside. 'When you say "lie," asked Miss Lillian, 'do you mean a white lie or a black lie?'

"It was the reporter's turn to flush. 'What's the difference?' she asked indignantly. 'Isn't a lie a lie? I mean, just what is a white lie?'

"Miss Lillian stared right at that reporter lady and said, 'A white lie is like . . . ,' she thought for a moment and then continued on, 'a white lie is like when I met you at the door and said, "'It's so good to meet you."'"

Louise threw her head back and laughed. I laughed with her. She had made her point.

From that moment on I began to feel comfortable around Louise. Maybe it was because I relaxed about not being the know-it-all that doctors are often led to believe they should strive to be. Perhaps I was becoming more accepting of the fact that as long as I was to practice medicine, I would need to continue to learn and be taught—by my patients and by my colleagues.

Louise and I developed a special relationship. Sure, it was a bit bumpy at the start—but, like a fine wine, it mellowed and matured into something very valuable to me. No lie. Not even a white one!

chapter sixteen

The Epiphany

One day during morning rounds the call came over the hospital intercom. "Dr. Larimore, stat to the ER." I was in the EKG reading room, on the other end from the ER. I quickly ran the couple of hundred feet.

The patient appeared whiter than the sheets on which she lay, and she was gasping for breath with very rapid, shallow breaths. Even more ominous was a rapidly expanding pool of bright-red blood on the floor under her gurney—at least four or five feet in diameter. Worse yet, there were several waterfalls of blood actively dripping from the edge of the sheet covering the patient.

"Dr. Larimore, get over here!" Louise shouted. "She's hemorrhaging from the vagina." I ran over as Louise continued her history. "She had a positive pregnancy test last week, and her last period was about three or four months ago," yelled the ER nurse, who was cutting off the woman's clothes, while Betty, the lab director, was starting an IV and drawing blood for lab samples. Nancy Cunningham had run in to help us and was starting oxygen.

"Let's set up for an exam, *now!*" I ordered. "Louise, get the Gyn tray!" In moments the stirrups were set up and the patient pulled down to the end of the bed, flat on her back, legs spread—we call it the dorsal lithotomy position. I quickly gloved and turned my attention to the woman's perineum, which had blood coming from the vagina at a remarkable pace. "What's your name?" I asked her. She didn't answer but just stared at the ceiling. We were losing her.

Louise, who knew everyone in town, filled in some of the details. "Her name's Doreen, she's eighteen, been married about six months. Just out of Swain High last May. Works down at the plant."

"Doreen, I'm going to do a quick exam. I'll be as gentle as I can. I suspect you're losing your baby. We'll do everything we can to help you." In my heart I was thinking, *I don't want to lose you, Doreen. Fight for me. Lord*, I prayed, *help Doreen. Help me!*

I went to work, quickly inserting a sterile speculum, and discovered what I was expecting to discover. Doreen's cervix, the opening to her womb, was about three-quarters of an inch dilated, and hung up in it was a dark clot of material—what medical professionals usually called "the products of conception," what I called a preborn child who was miscarrying. Around the tiny baby and placenta the uterus was hemorrhaging—and hemorrhaging big-time. The cure would be to remove the little body and placenta as quickly as possible.

"Ring forceps!" I asked Louise for an instrument I could use to gently extract the fragile mass. It came out intact and I examined it. All I could see was the placenta. This was not unusual, as the tiny preborn child could often pass without being noticed—or sometimes could be absorbed by the womb before the miscarriage.

"Nancy, let's give five units of Pitocin IM and add twenty units to the fullest IV bag and slow the flow of that bag to 125 cc's per hour." The Pitocin, normally used to induce labor, would hopefully stimulate the uterus to contract, and the contraction of the muscles should then slow or even stop the bleeding.

"Walt," Betty said, "I'll run the usual labs and get some blood set up. Looks like you'll need it."

"Thanks, Betty," I called out as she headed toward the lab.

I placed the mass in a formaldehyde container that Louise had opened. Then I quickly removed the speculum. Louise was working in tandem with me as though we had done this many times together. Obviously, for once I was doing what the older physicians would have done in the same circumstances. It felt good.

Louise squeezed some sterile K-Y Jelly onto my outstretched fingers. "Doreen, we've gotten the miscarriage out safely. Now I need to examine you on the inside. Can you take some deep breaths?" She still seemed dazed and incommunicado but did begin to breathe deeply. I did a rapid manual exam. I could feel no other products inside the uterus. Then with my inside fingers I lifted the uterus up toward the abdominal wall. With my outside fingers, I began to push and massage. "Doreen, this may be uncomfortable, but it will help the Pitocin stop the bleeding. Can you bear with me a moment?" She nodded. As I massaged the uterus I could feel it shrinking and hardening. *Thank you, Lord*, I prayed.

Nancy asked, "How about a second line?"

"Great idea. Will do. It needs to be a large bore needle and normal saline. We'll use that line to transfuse her."

"Done." Nancy had the IV inserted in seconds. This nurse was good, real good!

The uterus was continuing to contract, and very little blood was now flowing. "Vaginal pack," I said.

"Yes, sir," responded Louise. She turned to get one from a nearby cabinet. I slowly inserted the pack, which is a roll of narrow sterile gauze. *Whew,* I thought to myself, *I think we're going to make it!*

"Good job, Dr. Larimore," Louise whispered. She fairly glowed.

"Hematocrit is ten," announced Betty as she rushed back into the emergency room. "Blood is O negative. I'm cross matching for six units."

Each transfusion of packed red blood cells would increase Doreen's hematocrit by about three points. A hematocrit of forty would be normal, but if we could transfuse her to twenty-five or thirty, she could build her blood count from there just by taking some oral iron.

"Betty, bet we won't need more than four or five units, but let's do get started as soon as the units are ready."

"Yes, sir," she said, and headed back to the lab.

I took off my gloves and went to stand at Doreen's side. I took her hand in mine. "You OK?"

She turned her head away, tears now flowing freely. She shook her head no.

"Are you having any pain?"

"It just feels like menstrual cramps."

"Doreen, I'm sorry we had to work so quickly. But we had to stop the bleeding. I'm expecting you to make a full recovery, but we'll need to give you some blood to replace all that you've lost. I'm hoping you'll be able to go home in a day or two."

That evening, I dropped by Doreen's room. She had received fluids and had tolerated the transfusions without reaction. Her hematocrit was twenty-four, and her color and temperament were both improving. She was sitting up in bed and sipping water. A young man was beside her.

"Hi, Dr. Larimore," exclaimed an almost chipper patient. "This is my husband, Harold."

"Pleased to meet you," Harold said as he offered his hand. "Thanks for saving my wife's life."

"I'm just glad she got over here in time," I commented—feeling almost Mitchlike.

He went on. "We were at the plant, working. I got called to the nurse's office. Found Doreen layin' on the bed. Her pants were soaked with blood. I 'bout fainted. Ambulance came to get her."

"I suspect that was pretty scary, wasn't it?" They both nodded their heads in agreement. I was quiet for a moment, and so were they.

"Doreen, I need to pull out the packing. That will make you feel a whole lot better. Harold, do you want to step out for a moment while I do this?"

"No sir!" he replied. "If it's all the same to you, I'd just as soon stay with Doreen."

"OK with me if it's OK with your wife." She nodded, and I pulled on sterile gloves as Louise got the patient into position. "Doreen, as I pull out the gauze, you should feel some pressure but no pain." Harold was watching intently. Knowing that people sometimes swoon when watching a medical procedure, I said, "You may want to sit down on the chair there. Sometimes there's some blood, and that can make a fellow feel a tad bit weak."

Harold sat down but didn't let go of his wife's hand. As I pulled on the gauze, it slid out without difficulty. But, to my astonishment, attached to the end of the gauze was a three-inch-long fetus. Looking just like a miniature baby, its eyes, arms, legs, hands, and even the nubs of fingers were all discernible. I gently picked up the little one and placed him in my palm. Their eyes were as big as saucers. So were mine. The word *fetus* seemed so cold, so inhuman. So I said, "Doreen and Harold, this is your little baby."

They seemed much more curious than sad or shocked. They looked and asked question after question.

Harold asked, "Can you tell if it's a boy or girl?"

"It's hard to tell at this stage, but he sure looks normal."

"He looks kind of like a real baby," Doreen commented.

I smiled and nodded. She *was* right. "He *is* a real baby, Doreen. Just real small and real fragile." I paused for a second, feeling the tears forming in my eyes. I looked at the young couple and felt the first tear fall on my cheek. "I'm sorry he didn't make it."

Their eyes met, and then they grasped each other's hands even more firmly. Doreen turned back to me, her lower lip quivering and tears beginning to stream down her cheeks. "Can we bury our baby?" she asked.

I looked to Louise for help—having never encountered this question before. The nurse nodded her head yes. So did I. As Doreen's tears continued to flow, she reached out to touch her little one and then gently stroked his head. "He's so soft and fragile." Then she pulled her hand back and began to weep aloud. Harold moved closer to her on the bed, placing his arm around her and gently patting her back. His eyes were filled with tears. "Now, now, Doreen. It's going to be OK, honey." Then he collapsed and they wept in each other's arms.

I sat quietly, feeling honored to be able to share this intimate moment with this couple. After they had composed themselves, I suggested, "If you feel like naming the baby, I think it would be a good thing to do." They nodded affirmatively.

I wasn't sure how to phrase my thoughts—I wasn't even sure if my request was professional or appropriate—but I felt compelled to ask. "Harold and Doreen, your baby is the first baby I've delivered here in Bryson City. He's also the first baby I've lost." I felt more tears streaming down my cheeks. The words were hard to get out, but I stumbled on. "If you don't mind, and if it wouldn't be an imposition to you, I'd sure appreciate being able to come to his funeral."

Harold and Doreen both nodded. Then as they wept and hugged, I placed the baby on a small 4 x 4-inch gauze and handed it to Louise—whose cheeks were also tearstained. She left the room.

I was quiet—trying to compose myself. I pulled out my handkerchief and blew my nose. Finally I said, "Doreen and Harold, I was wondering, would you mind if we said a little prayer?"

This was a new experience for me. In medical school and residency we were never taught to pray with patients. In fact, many of my professors thought that bringing religion into medical care was unethical. But I had long ago come to see my patients as consisting of mind, body, and spirit. I knew a loss like this could affect all three.

They nodded. "Lord," I began, not at all sure that what I was doing was appropriate or correct, "thank you for Doreen's health. We could have lost her today, but did not. Harold and I both thank you for this." I paused, not sure what to say next. "Lord, thank you for this little baby. I know that he's now in your arms. We ask you to care for him and love him. And I ask that Harold and Doreen would heal quickly and, if it is in your will, that you would allow them to experience the gift of another child—one they can love and raise. Amen."

They continued to hug and cry in each other's arms. I just sat by, in silence. As they composed themselves, Harold was the first to speak. "Doc, that was very special for us. Thanks."

I was relieved to realize that my spiritual treatment could be as, or maybe even more, effective than my medical treatment—certainly that they could complement each other. I offered to call their pastor, and they thought that'd be a good idea. Then I left to make the call and to finish my rounds.

After dinner at home, the phone was quiet, but my spirit was not. Although I was still on call, I decided to go out to the bench and sit for a spell. The view of the mountains and the cool evening air were both refreshing. I knew that the experience of the loss of a child was as old as the hills around me—and I knew it would never hurt less. And yet I recognized the blessing I had experienced—the blessing of being invited into a young family's emergency and into their loss and grief, to have been summoned into their intimacy, having never even met them before, just by the nature of my profession. I think it was the first time I realized, at the very core of my soul, the wonderful opportunity that had been given me as a physician.

I thought of all the things a patient allows a doctor—even one they've never met—to do or say. They would, without challenge, disrobe at my request; they would tell me things they wouldn't tell anyone else; they would put their very lives in my hands; they'd even make major lifestyle changes based on my recommendations.

Then I realized something that truly gave me pause. *These men and women who honor me truly honor me by allowing me to care for them. Most of them were granting me credibility before I had even earned it. In essence, they trusted me before I had earned their trust.*

As I gazed on the moonlit, misty vistas, I was filled with a sense of expectancy—a realization that God was whispering to me through every clinical encounter, as well as through every moment spent on this bench. A yearning welled up inside of me: I wanted to hear more. And then I had the most powerful realization of my career: *I am meeting people in whose lives the God of the universe is working—working in profoundly powerful ways.* It was, for me, an epiphany that would forever change me, my marriage, my life, and my practice.

part three

Play: Making Bryson City Home

chapter seventeen

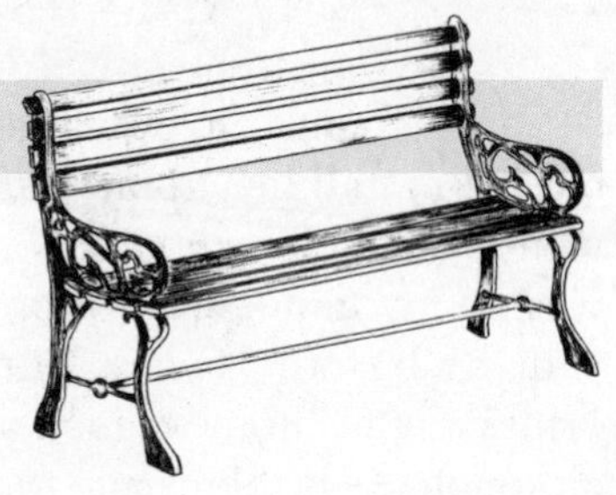

BECOMING PART OF THE TEAM

I had just finished seeing the last patient on a Monday morning when Dr. Mitchell walked by, reading a chart. He suddenly stopped and whirled around. "Hey, Walt. You going to the game this week?"

"What game?"

He looked astonished and then began to smile. It was a smile I was growing to recognize and despise—a near-sneer of amazement that I was so ignorant as to not know a basic fact of medicine or of town history or of life itself. "You're kidding me, aren't you?" he would always ask, adding his classic, "You stupid?"—sometimes verbally, sometimes just implied.

"No, sir," I would always reply with a sigh. "I'm not," meaning but not audibly saying, I'm *not* kidding and I'm *not* stupid.

Then he'd shrug his shoulders, resigning himself to the fact that his young protégé was indeed, as he called it, "city stupid."

"Well, son," he began, as he did with all of his lectures to me, "I'm talking about *the* football game." He paused. I waited. There was *no way* I was going to ask the question that was on my mind: *What football game?* Fortunately he continued the lesson. "Swain County's going to be playing Sylva Friday night. 'Bout as good a rivalry as there is around here—although the Robbinsville game is always a battle too. Anyway, 'bout ev'ryone in town goes."

My mind flashed back in an instant to the impact that football had had on my life. The peak of my personal football career was my sophomore year in high school. I started as a defensive cornerback on the Robert E. Lee High School junior varsity team. The other cornerback, Chris Stuart, and I could read each other's mind just by looking at each other. We were, in my opinion, a great team. I loved playing alongside him and being his friend. It was my best year.

The last two years of high school ball saw me on the sidelines, insisting on trying to be a star wide receiver when in fact I had no offensive talent whatsoever. My pride overshadowed the simple fact that if I ever wanted to see time on the field, I needed to return to the defensive side of the ball. To my permanent chagrin, I simply never swallowed my pride on this matter.

So it only made sense to me, as it does to most physicians who are somewhat pathologically frustrated athletes, to become involved in sports medicine—as I had done during my training at Duke. Suddenly my mind flashed back to a discussion I'd had with Mr. Douthit almost exactly one year before: "Folks around here take their football real serious. But none of our doctors have been particularly interested in being the team physician. Only a couple, Dr. Mitchell and Dr. Bacon, will even go to some of the games. But they prefer to sit in the stands. . . ." *Sit in the stands?* I thought. That was anathema.

Mitch broke into my reverie. "Anyway, if you and Barb want to go to the game with me and Gay, we'd love to take you."

"Mitch, Barb doesn't enjoy football very much, and sitting on a cold bench this far along in her pregnancy would be uncomfortable, so I doubt she'd want to come along. But how would you feel if I went up to the school and talked to the coaches about becoming the team physician?"

He furrowed his brow, looking a bit shocked. "Why, son, *I'm* the team physician—have been for years."

Oops, I thought. *I didn't know that. What to do? What to say?* Suddenly I had an idea. "What I meant, Mitch, was the team's *sideline* physician. I've been told you like to sit in the stands with your wife. I'd kind of like to be on the field. You know, check any injuries when they're fresh. Get to know the kids and the coaches a bit."

His look softened. Maybe I was overcoming the offense I had unknowingly inflicted. After all, he had known most of these kids since birth. I did not. But there was a problem.

"Son, the coaches can do that. They know when to call me."

"I suspect you're right," I answered, my mind racing for options. "But perhaps I could handle some of the routine injuries and then I'd only have to call you for the more serious ones." I knew, and I suspect he knew, that I was posturing. But he nodded anyway.

"May want to go over to practice and talk to the coach," he suggested. "Name's Dietz—Boyce Dietz. He's *not* local. Lives over in Sylva. Actually, I suspect if he had his way, he'd be coachin' over there. But he's here, and he does a pretty dern good job. Anyway, go up there and talk to him about it."

I couldn't wait.

I was almost giddy throughout the afternoon, at times excited about the prospect of being the team's sideline physician, at times nervous, thinking I might be rejected—being new to the town and all. I was aching for a stronger sense of belonging here in Bryson City. And I really wanted to make my mark in some way, to make a difference in the end.

After seeing my last patient for the day, I drove up to the "temple" for local football—the Swain County stadium. For a small town this stadium was magnificent. I suspect there are many junior colleges lusting for such a venue. It was carved into the side of a small mountain. The visitors' metal bleachers could hold nearly 1,000 fans, but the concrete home stands, running from 25-yard line to 25-yard line and climbing over thirty rows high, could easily seat 2,500 fans—with another 2,000 or so being accommodated on the adjoining hillside. At the peak of the stadium was a spacious press box. At the north end of the stadium was a field house that was more suited for a small college than a high school.

I parked outside the chain-link fence and walked toward the immaculately groomed field. I felt strangely at home. Several dozen spectators occupied the lower row of the stadium, and lining the fence at the edge of the field were another couple dozen men. I came to find out that they, along with many others, attended nearly every practice. Some had kids playing, but most did not. They just loved football and they loved this team. It had become part of their life, part of their family. Earl Douthit was right—the team played a vital role in this community's life.

As I walked up to the fence, one man turned toward me. He looked slightly familiar and obviously recognized me. "Hey, Doc. How ya doing?" He was a large man with a friendly smile. He stuck out his hand to give mine a shaking. "Preston Tuttle's the name. Met you at Dr. Mitchell's office."

Now I remembered. Mr. Tuttle had come in with a bad cold or something. "Good to see you again, Mr. Tuttle."

"Preston's fine with me, Doc, if it's all the same to you."

"OK, Preston. And, uh, Walt works for me."

"Sounds good to me, Doc." He couldn't bring himself to call me Walt. Never did.

"Doc, this here's Joe Benny Shuler."

I shook hands with Joe Benny, who had been standing next to Preston.

"He's your mailman."

"Yep," Joe Benny said. "Been bringing your mail up to the Gunn house. Man, you shore do git a buncha magazines, and them thangs are some kind of heavy."

Preston's eyebrows rose. I suspected he was wondering exactly what kind of magazines I was getting. I was to learn that in the economy of mountain gossip, one was guilty only until proven innocent.

Joe Benny chuckled. "Preston, Doc here gets a mess of medical magazines. He don't get any of them brown-paper-wrapped magazines like you."

Preston swatted him on the head and turned to me. "There's one sure way you can tell that ol' Joe Benny's a lyin' to ya."

"How's that?" asked Joe Benny.

Preston continued looking at me and said, "His lips are movin'."

Both men laughed. They clearly liked each other.

"Preston, I'm surprised to see so many folks out here watching practice," I commented.

He chuckled. "Actually, the crowd's a bit sparse just now. When the plant lets out, then the crowd will really grow. Folks 'round here love this team. Most of these folks either played on this team or had kids who played. A few, like me, have kids playing now."

"Where's Coach Dietz?" I asked.

"That's him over there." Preston pointed to a man standing on the line of scrimmage, just watching—allowing his junior coaches to coach. "One mighty fine head coach we've got there. Hasn't had a losing season since his first year. In fact, he's won over 80 percent of his games. Took us to the state championship in '79. Nearly got us there last year. He's put together the best staff in the state. Over there," he pointed to a man in the middle of the defensive team huddle, "is Bob Marr. He was the head coach over at Cherokee. Man, Cherokee is one of our bitterest rivals. Yet ol' Boyce Dietz done stole him away from Cherokee. Best line coach in the state. Colleges are always trying to recruit him. But he loves it here too much."

Preston went through each of the staff, highlighting their résumé, their strengths and their weaknesses, their families and their pedigree. Then he proceeded to inform me about the team members and their biographies. His knowledge was truly impressive. "I've been coaching most of these boys since their youth league days. Watched 'em grow up. It's a joy to watch 'em now. We're gonna have a great team this year. A great team."

I explained to Preston my desire to work with the team.

He looked worried. "Have you talked to Doc Mitchell? He kinda thinks of hisself as the team physician, although he's never been out to a practice and only comes down from the stands if he's called. Seems to like the glory he gets when the whole town hears his name called over the loudspeakers. You best talk this over with him."

"Preston, I have."

He looked shocked. "You *have?* What'd he say?"

"Well, he encouraged me to come talk to the coach about it."

"I'm surprised. Real surprised. When did you talk to him?"

"Well, I'm working with him in his office, so we talked just this afternoon."

Preston nodded knowingly.

"What?" I asked.

"You're working for him. That explains it," Preston announced matter-of-factly. "You see, that man wants to either control everything or know about everything. So maybe he thinks he'll still be able to control things and still get the glory even if you're on the field."

Preston motioned for me to follow him, and we headed over to Coach Dietz.

"Coach, this here's the town's new doc. Dr. Larimore, this here's the finest high school football coach in the great state of North Carolina, Boyce Dietz."

"Good to meet you, Doc."

"You too, Coach."

"Coach, Doc here wants to help the team."

"Need all the help we can get, Doc. Whatcha got in mind?"

"Well, for the last three years of my residency I studied sports medicine under Dr. Frank Bassett, the team physician for

Duke University athletics for many years. If you'd be interested, I'd be willing to pitch in and help you with any sports medicine needs you might have. I'd be pleased to come and check the kids at practice once or twice a week and to be on the sidelines during the games."

His eyes widened a bit.

"Of course, I don't mean to intrude if you've already got some folks working with you. Just want to help out if you need me."

He remained silent, looking real serious.

Preston broke in. "Doc here's working with Docs Mitchell and Cunningham—down in their office. He done talked with Doc Mitchell and Doc done give him the OK to come talk to you."

Now the coach's expression relaxed. He smiled and turned his head to spit out some dip. "This town can be a bit political," he confided. *The understatement of the century,* I thought. "Can't be too careful. But if it's OK with Mitchell, I'd be right glad to have you with us." He stuck out his hand to seal the deal.

I was thrilled. To me there was nowhere better to be during football season than on the sidelines with your favorite team. Number one, you had the best seat in the house. Two, you got to know the coaches and the ballplayers and their families. Three, for a would-be or over-the-hill athlete, there was the ongoing and vicarious thrill of reliving past hopes and dreams. I couldn't believe my good fortune. I couldn't believe that no other doctor wanted this honor—this joy.

I whistled all the way home. I was a team physician. Well, . . . sideline physician. This was big—really big!

chapter eighteen

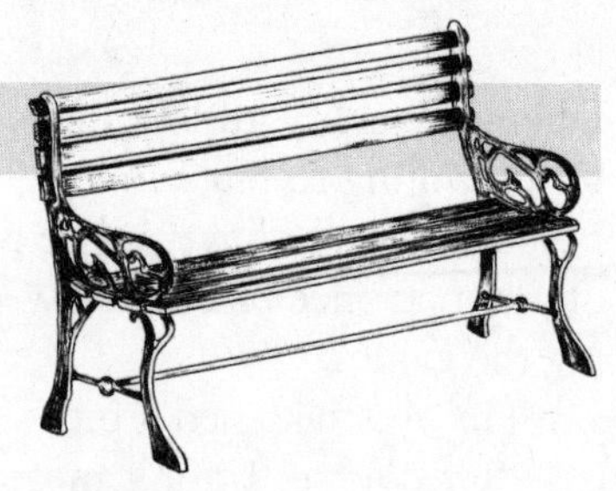

Monuments

Friday couldn't come soon enough. After the Monday football practice, the week slowed to a snail's crawl. I felt like a kid during the week before Christmas. Game day couldn't come soon enough.

I returned to the practice field every day after work. It quickly became my habit to be as close to the team as possible. Most days the team didn't practice in the stadium. It was reserved for the games. The practice field was across town—on School House Hill. I had stopped by the practice field the night of the murder. It was located right next to the Bryson City cemetery.

During the practice I'd quietly walk around, observing and learning. Watching how the coaches and kids interacted. Looking for limps that might disclose an old injury—or maybe one that was being covered up. It was the closest I could come to being part of the team. It felt good. Real good.

I also began to get to know Boyce Dietz. My experience as a team physician while at Duke had taught me that head coaches are in an unusual position. Often they don't have anyone to share with, to be vulnerable with. To share with assistant coaches or with players risks appearing weak or indecisive. Most have wives who tolerate their profession and its sacrifice of family time—at least during the season. Nevertheless, most of these women don't want to hear anything about football in the brief amount of time they have with their husbands. That leaves the team doctor—who often becomes the coach's sounding board, confidant, adviser, physician, and friend. It was a relationship I enjoyed at Duke and hoped to enjoy with Coach Dietz.

During those first days I could sense him testing me. He'd come to the sideline after going on the field to fix a problem he'd seen, and he'd ask me a question or two. Partially probing my knowledge of football, football players, and sports medicine, partially probing my ability to communicate. Would I be an uppity know-it-all doctor? He'd seen far too many of those. Would I be a coach wanna-be—deluded into thinking I knew more football than he did? He heard from far too many of them every week, especially at practices.

"Doc," he said, "Tony Plemmons, my quarterback, likes to ice his ankles after practice. You think he ought to use some heat?"

Careful, I thought. Coaches without team physicians on the sideline had to learn a lot of practical day-to-day sports medicine. They had *their* ways. And they certainly didn't want some newcomer upsetting their ways or challenging their authority. I knew I'd have to tread lightly.

"Well, Coach, the college and pro trainers really debate this. Some like to use ice, some prefer heat. One of the newer approaches is called contrast therapy, where you alternate icing and heating, but you start and stop with ice. If you want, I can tell you what I think."

He looked interested—or perhaps amused—as he lobbed the ball back into my court. "Well, I think I *am* interested in what you think."

Careful, I thought again. "Well, Coach, I think you've kinda gotta go with what works best out here, not just with what worked best at Duke. What have *you* found to be the best treatment?"

He smiled. I was guessing I had gone the right direction by giving him some options and then deferring to his experience and expertise—which he was glad to share. "I've found that the ice packs work best. I think if it's OK with you, I'll stick with that."

"Sounds good, Coach."

He smiled.

A little later he came back to where I was standing and continued the test. "Thinking about adding a triple wham. Sylva's got a huge defensive end on the right side. Hard to double-team him. What do you think?"

Now he was testing my football knowledge. When you wham blocked, you used two guys, usually running backs, to block a single defensive player. A triple wham was almost never tried, because it left too many other players unblocked. "What's their tackle and linebacker on that side like?" I asked.

He nodded his head. "They're big, but slow. And the cornerback can be taken away pretty easily."

"Can your tight end set it up OK?"

"Think so."

"Coach, I haven't seen a triple wham since my sophomore year in high school."

"I don't think Babe Howell [the Sylva coach] has ever seen one either. Might like to have it ready."

Having passed question two, I watched him run out on the field and teach his team a new trick. Boyce loved new tricks and always had a few in every game plan. He was an intensely driven man, and his drive resulted in both significant football success and consequential acid reflux. I noticed him almost constantly chewing on Tums tablets, and over time I learned to read his pained facial expressions. I could sense when he was angry, disappointed, or simply experiencing heartburn.

During Wednesday's practice I was standing on the sideline watching the scrimmage. Coach Dietz had become livid about a poorly run play and had gone into the offensive huddle to fix the problem himself. After things were running smoothly again, he came back to the sideline and walked over to me. But instead of turning toward the field, he kept his back to the action. After a moment I turned to see what he was looking at. He was staring up the hill at the cemetery.

"Doc, you ever think about death?"

I nodded. "Coach, in my profession we think about it more than we want."

His next question took me by surprise. "Doc, you ready?" He paused. Then he looked me straight in the eye. "I mean, if you knew you were going to die today, would you be ready?"

Now it was my turn to pause. I looked down at my feet for a moment and then up at the hill of headstones. I thought about having just started my new profession and about my young family. I thought of Kate—a whole life in front of her as a disabled adult. I thought about Barb, now pregnant with Erin Elizabeth—and we didn't even have life insurance. I thought about my personal relationship with God, a relationship that had begun in my college days. I enjoyed my times of Bible reading and my quiet times, and our worship at church too. I felt *spiritually* ready for death but not financially or psychologically ready. It was my turn to choose. Would I be vulnerable? Would I be transparent?

"Coach, I don't think so. I feel like the Lord's got a lot of things for me to do just yet. So . . . I don't think I'm ready. At least not today."

He took a deep breath and let it out slowly. "Me neither, Doc. Me neither. But one day I'm gonna take some time and go walking up on that thar hill. Suspect them stones got some stories to tell." He turned back to the field. "Speaking of dead, Doc, this team's a lookin' a bit dead to me. They're lookin' a bit beat. Whatcha think?"

I paused for a moment. For a coach to ask a question like this was not surprising. But to ask so early in our relationship *was* surprising. *Was it a test? Or did he really want my opinion?* I wondered. Yet, if he could discuss eternity with me, why not the physical and psychological condition of his kids? But they were *his* kids, not mine—at least not yet.

"Coach," I replied, carefully, "I don't know your players very well yet. I don't know their spirits or their limits. But they do look a bit whipped. They've got a big game Friday night. Might be encouraging to them to hear a good word from you, get a little reward. And a rest might not hurt them. Tomorrow you can polish up the game plan with them. But I'm just guessing. It's your call."

The diplomatic dilemma of a confidant: How do you offer advice without being pushy or bossy? How do you inform or correct without hurting or offending? How do you support and befriend without intruding or repelling? When do you draw close, and when do you stay away? I knew all of this had to be learned over time and with experience.

"Doc, I think you're probably right. Let's shut things down a bit early today."

He blew his whistle and called the surprised kids and coaches around him. When they were quiet, he explained, "Men, you're tired and you're trying too hard. I appreciate your effort. You know how bad I want to beat Sylva. I know how bad *you* want to beat Sylva. But right now you're beating yourselves. We're gonna call it off early. Captains, after showers I want you to have a team meeting. Seniors, this is your last chance at those Sylva boys. The rest of your life you're gonna have to live with the results of this game. You're probably gonna be working with these boys the rest of your lives. I want you all to talk about it a bit. Then I want you to spend some time tonight thinking. Really thinking. What can *you* do—what *must* you do to do *your* part to beat those Sylva boys this week? Friday's game will be the most important game of your life."

He was quiet. You could hear the crickets in the grass and the deep breathing of the exhausted players. Then I saw the first of a hundred examples of great coaching.

"Men, whether we win or lose, I want you to know something." He paused to look at each one of them, eye to eye. "I want you to know just how much I admire you as a team and as individuals. I'd be proud to have any one of you as my own son. I want you to wake up Saturday morning knowing that, no matter the final score, you gave your all, you done your very best. You do that, you'll have kept my admiration and you'll have earned my respect." He nodded his head, and they silently turned and began to walk toward the locker room.

As the stands and the fence line emptied of spectators, Coach Dietz and I were alone on the field.

"Doc, mind taking a walk?" He turned toward the cemetery and I followed. We walked up the stadium steps, through a gate in the chain-link fence, and into the field of headstones. He would stop, only briefly, to look at the larger stones and monuments.

As we came up to the peak of the cemetery, the view of the town and the Smokies was both impressive and magnificent—lit up in the setting sun, ablaze with fall colors. I paused to gaze, amazed again at the beauty of the hills. He continued on as though on a mission. He paused at a huge granite rock, and I walked up beside him. Embedded in the stone was a bronze plaque:

HORACE KEPHART
1862–1931
SCHOLAR, AUTHOR, OUTDOORSMAN
HE LOVED HIS NEIGHBORS
AND PICTURED THEM IN
"OUR SOUTHERN HIGHLANDERS."
HIS VISION HELPED CREATE
THE GREAT SMOKY MOUNTAINS NATIONAL PARK.

"You know who this is?" he asked, his eyes glued to the tombstone.

"Can't say that I do."

"Maybe the most famous fella that ever lived in these parts. Educated fella. They say he studied at five universities before battling alcoholism and a mental breakdown. They say he looked at maps and books to discover what he called 'His Back Beyond.'

He wanted to find the remotest part of the country. He considered the Rockies and the rain forests of the Northwest. He thought about the deep swamps of Georgia or Florida. He finally come out here at the turn of the century—1904 if memory serves me right—and settled on Sugar Fork. That was a branch off Hazel Creek, deep in the woods west of here."

My admiration for this man was growing. I knew he knew football; I didn't know he knew the local history, especially having been born and bred in Sylva. He went on. "He recovered from his demons in these woods. And he wrote and wrote—lots of books and outdoors articles. I've read his *Camping and Woodcraft, Sporting Firearms,* and *Camp Cooking*. But the one I like the best, and the one that brought him so much fame, was *Our Southern Highlanders.*

"He'd often leave the woods and come up here to Bryson. In fact, he kept a room at what was called the Cooper House, a long-gone boardinghouse. Locals came to call it Kephart Tavern. They say that it was from this place that he took up the battle to create the Great Smoky Mountains National Park."

The coach looked up and gazed across ridge after ridge of mountains—all the way to the horizon. "Kephart hated the huge timber companies he saw as destroying the land around him. 'Why must the virgin forests be doomed for their profit?' he wrote." The coach's voice picked up in tone and intensity. "'Stop the carnage,' he'd preach to any politician who'd listen. 'I want to preserve this pristine and shrinking wilderness,' he said, 'so that others can come here and recover, as I have.'

"Let me show you another," the coach said. He took off walking and I followed. Just a bit over the ridge and to the west of the Kephart grave site, he stopped at another tombstone:

Kelly E. Bennett

1890–1974

The Apostle of the Smokies

This stone from deep within the Smokies

along with Mt. Bennett in the distance

Monuments

ARE LASTING TRIBUTES TO A MAN
WHOSE EFFORTS AND LOVE FOR THESE MOUNTAINS HELPED
IN THE CREATION OF THE GREAT SMOKY MTNS. NATIONAL PARK

He pointed to another small tombstone that just read,

DR. AURELIUS BENNETT
1861–1941

"A. M. Bennett. He was a country doctor—just like you, Doc. His son, Kelly, became the town's pharmacist and unofficial photographer—for decades. Kelly even served as a state legislator. Even though he was almost thirty years younger than Kephart, they became best friends. Together they led the efforts to form the national park."

Coach Dietz smiled, almost to himself, then continued, "Doc, these men had a passion and a mission. It gave them meaning. It gave them life. It gave us this beautiful place." He paused to look out over the town toward the national park. "Kephart became the first living American to have a mountain named in his honor while he was still alive. Can't see Mount Kephart from here. It's deep in the park out thar. A monument to his passion—to his life's work. Bennett also had one named after him—after he died."

The coach paused. "Doc, *my* monument's them kids." He turned to look at me. "For most of them, this team's the highlight of their lives. This here's their glory days. These become the lifelong memories they'll relive the rest of their lives. When they're working in one of the mills around here, or lumbering, or working in the furniture factory, they'll look back on these days and they'll talk about 'em. Their memories are my legacy. I just don't want to let them down. I love what I do, and I love the kids I do it for."

He took in a deep breath and then let it out slowly as his eyes turned from mine to gaze down at the gravestone. "Kephart died in an automobile accident. April 2, 1931. Died not too far from here. He was 69. Bennett lived into his 80s. Their work didn't go unnoticed or unrewarded. In 1940 ol' President Roosevelt came out here to dedicate the park. Bennett was there in the flesh, Kephart in the spirit.

"So Mr. Kephart and Mr. Bennett are both buried here, looking out over the park they helped create. But their monuments aren't really here—they're out thar." The coach swept his arm over the expanse in front of us.

"I hope that a hundred years from now, there'll be folks who'll see in my kids' kids' kids, some of me. That'll be my monument, Doc. That's what gets me up in the morning. That's what stirs my cocoa. That's my legacy." He smiled and said in a near-whisper, "My legacy's not property, it's people. When I'm gone, I'm gonna leave behind relationships. I'm gonna leave behind kids that's better than they would have been. That sound crazy to you, Doc?"

"No, sir," I responded. "Not crazy at all."

"Better be going. Don't want to keep you from your family."

We turned to leave. We walked quietly down the hillside, through the monuments to people now departed from this earth—perhaps with their legacy buried here with them. The idea of investing in others and not in oneself was amazingly appealing to me. I thought there'd be no better place to start than with my family. *After all,* I thought, *what if I get to the end of my career with a great practice and a big estate but with a marriage in ruins and kids with no integrity or character? What will I have gained? What use were all the riches I could earn if I ended my life with regret about what I gave—to my family and to others around me?*

I wasn't sure whether Coach Dietz was a religious man, but his sermon that day resulted in my praying a simple prayer of commitment as I sat on my bench that night, looking out over Kephart's and Bennett's monuments. *Lord, help me know you better. Help me make you known, first to my family and then to my patients. Lord, help me be the best husband, the best daddy, and the best doctor possible. I want my legacy to be my family.*

To this day the Lord is at work answering that prayer.

chapter nineteen

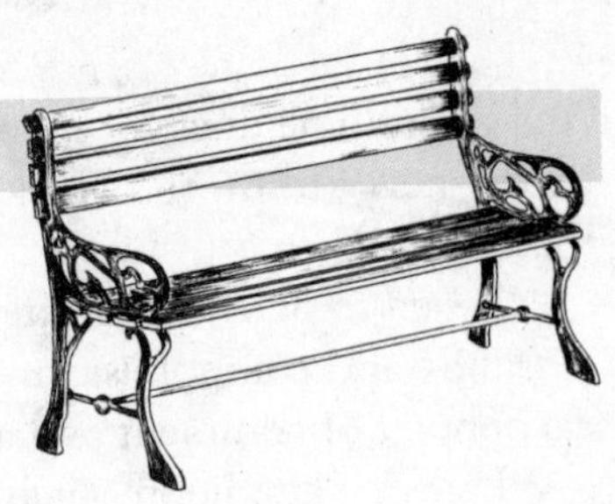

My First Home Victory

Friday finally arrived. Tonight would be my first football game as a team physician in private practice. Gary Ayers's morning news was basically all about the rivalry—past and present. He was predicting a record turnout and advising fans to arrive early for the best seats.

When I got to the office, Helen gave me a funny smile. "We've got something for you, Dr. Larimore."

I followed her to the staff lounge. There was a gift-wrapped package, with maroon paper and white ribbon—the Swain County colors. I unwrapped it under the curious eyes of the staff. Inside was a white golf shirt with maroon-tipped sleeves. Over the left chest was embroidered "Dr. Larimore" and, just below that, "Team Physician."

Leave it to Helen to burst my bubble. "Better not let Mitch see that," she warned. "They've never given *him* one like that.

And after all he does for them! I guess to get a shirt you need to be the new kid on the block, or from Duke or something like that."

I tried to defend the difference between being a sideline and a grandstand team physician, but the explanation was lost in a cacophony of comment and argument.

Late that afternoon Mitch caught me in the hall. "Heard about your shirt, Walt." He paused. I braced for the coming onslaught. I was certain his next comment would be, *You stupid?* It wasn't. "Walt," he sighed, "I think that's great. Folks normally don't take a shine to a newcomer so quickly. That's a good sign, son."

After finishing up the afternoon's paperwork and stopping by home for a quick dinner, I was off to the stadium. I arrived an hour before kickoff and was waved into the reserved parking area. Joe Benny was the attendant. "Been expecting you, Doc. We done put up a special sign for you right over by the gate."

I thanked him and drove on. Another attendant waved me into a parking spot next to the fence. "Dr. Larrimore, Team Physician" were the words on the freshly painted sign wired to the fence. I don't mind telling you that, despite the misspelling, I was feeling pretty special indeed. At least "Larimore" was spelled correctly on my coaching shirt. But I was secretly hoping that my senior colleagues didn't see this sign. I could only begin to imagine the professional jealousies. Perhaps petty jealousies, but nevertheless very real.

It was already getting dark, but the stadium lights lit up the field like day. The lighting system was as good as any college field I'd seen. Fantastic.

For a die-hard football fan, there's nothing quite like the feeling of walking out on the cool turf on a crisp autumn evening. The crowd gathering in the stands, the smoke from the hamburger-stand grills, the band warming up. I drank in the sights with childhood memories surging through my mind. From my earliest memories I have deep-seated impressions of *Death Valley.* That was the name opponents gave to the football stadium in Baton

Rouge. Games at LSU are almost always played at night, and the turf is and always has been genuine—thick and luscious. My dad and I would go to the games together, and not only can I still name my childhood and adolescent heroes, I can also remember some of their most spectacular plays.

As I walked onto the field, a thousand memories flooded my soul and my arms looked like gooseflesh. I felt at home. The kids from both teams were already on the field warming up, and to my surprise the visitor *and* the home stands were nearly full—one whole hour before the game! Fans were beginning to claim spots on the grassy mountainside. And all along the chain-link fence around the field, the men were a dozen deep.

I dropped off my medical kit in the locker room. It was a fabulous locker room—as large as some college locker rooms. On my way back down to the field, I passed Preston guarding his and Joe Benny's spots on the fence at about the 40-yard line on the home side. This was just far enough down to avoid having their view blocked by the players on the sidelines, yet close enough to yell any needed encouragement to coaches or kids.

Once on the field I checked in with Coach Dietz. He had no medical concerns to report regarding the kids, but asked, "You got some Tums in your medical kit?"

"I do."

"Can you keep some handy for me?"

"Will do, Coach."

I stood by him to watch the warm-ups.

"Doc."

"Yep."

"Doc, I'm glad you're here."

I nodded. I didn't say anything. May have been the lump in my throat. But I remember thinking, *Me too, Coach. Me too.*

As I looked across the field, I was astonished at how small our boys were compared to the Sylva kids. Our largest player, tackle Mac Gossett, was probably six-foot two, 210 pounds. He was by far our largest kid. And *most* of Sylva's kids looked bigger than him. *We're gonna get creamed,* I thought.

After warm-ups were completed, the teams retreated to the locker rooms. Each coach had his kids in a small group, reviewing last-minute details. Asking and answering questions. The kids had each been taught how to "scout" their opposing players during warm-ups and had observations on any apparent injuries. Several of the junior varsity coaches who had scouted Sylva in previous games and during the warm-ups would go from group to group to share their observations.

A referee entered the room. "Coach, I'll need your captains in two minutes." Finally Coach Dietz, who had been watching the preparations, clapped his hands. The room instantly became silent. All eyes were on the coach.

"Men, you've prepared well for tonight. There're probably four or five thousand folks who've come to see you. They've spent their hard-earned money to root for you—to see you do your best. I know that's what you're planning to do."

He paused to spit out some dip into a cup he was carrying.

"Seniors, you've never lost to these boys. And their seniors have never beaten you. That's what they're here to do. Tonight is their entire season. They've come to our house, to our backyard, to beat us up and to beat us bad. They're planning to use tonight in their bedtime stories they'll tell their kids and their grandkids until the day they die.

"Men, tonight's your legacy. This is *your* house. Don't let these folks down. Don't let your parents down. Don't let the men along the fence down. But most of all, don't let yourselves down! This is *your* house. Get out there and let's defend it!"

In a rush of adrenaline and pent-up energy, the team erupted to its feet and moved toward the door, a surging, chanting masculine mass.

What a coach! I thought.

The players tore through the paper tunnel, fire extinguishers went off, the band played the fight song, and the stands erupted in noise. I thought for sure I could feel the ground trembling. The sound was deafening. *Welcome to Swain County Football.*

At the kickoff, at each home team score, and at the times the team left and then reentered the field at halftime, the stadium thundered. But the most notable and fascinating part of the evening for me was watching and listening to the men along the fence. Their intensity was well-nigh unto fanatical—both their approval and disapproval of every play and every decision. I had been on the sidelines at every SEC (Southeastern Conference) and ACC (Atlantic Coast Conference) stadium and many others around the country during my college and residency days, but never had I seen this level of intensity, passion, and zeal.

At halftime the score was tied. The halftime sermon was intense and motivational. The third quarter was scoreless. The team and the crowd seemed to be waning in strength and energy. Sylva's size and strength seemed to be wearing down our smaller guys. Tony Plemmons, our quarterback, was a small fellow but as tough as a bobcat. Unlike many quarterbacks, he liked to run, to hit, and to be hit.

As the fourth quarter began, we had the ball. Tony took off on a run and got hit hard on the play. After the Sylva players got up, Tony didn't. He was writhing in pain. We had no experienced backup quarterback. After a collective groan, the stadium went deathly quiet.

By instinct I found myself sprinting toward him, followed closely by Coach Dietz. By the time we got to his side, Tony was sitting up and leaning forward. He was holding his right hand across his left shoulder—his left arm lying limply in his lap. He was moaning in pain.

As I knelt at his side I said, "Tony, it's Dr. Larimore. What are you feeling?"

"Doc, I think my shoulder's broken. I can't move it."

With one hand I was instinctively feeling for his pulse—which was normal—while running my other hand up his jersey to the shoulder. The clavicle was intact. But the ball of the shoulder was prominent, and he yelped when I palpated the rotator cuff. I knew what it was and I knew what I had to do, but I'd have to act quickly before the shoulder muscles began to spasm—which would only make the pain greater and the treatment more difficult.

"What is it, Doc?" asked Coach Dietz, now at Tony's other side.

"Think we're fine, Coach." I was trying to reassure him—and me too.

"Tony, I need you to lie back." He slowly lay back, moaning from the pain of the sudden motion. I could hear a hushed groan from the crowd as they saw him slump to his back.

"*What is it, Doc?*" asked the coach emphatically. "We need to call the paramedics? You need Doc Mitchell?"

I didn't have time to explain. My mind was racing. I could hear Gary Ayers the next morning. "Swain County had a chance to win the game until the newest doctor in town broke the quarterback's shoulder trying to treat a simple dislocation." Pete Lawson's headlines in the *Smoky Mountain Times* would read, "Perfect record given to Sylva by an inexperienced team physician. After the game Coach Dietz commented, 'We'd have won the game if only I had called Dr. Mitchell out of the stands to care for our quarterback. Now we've lost him for the season.'" I could feel the cold sweat dripping down my forehead and was hoping no one would notice my trembling hands.

"Tony, let your arm go real loose. Don't fight me. I need you to trust me, OK?"

"OK, Doc. Just make me better, will ya?"

"I will, Tony. I will," I said, trying to reassure us both. "Hold on now."

If my diagnosis was correct, what I was about to do would cure him. If I was wrong, if his shoulder *was* broken, what I was about to do would not only make things worse, it would put Tony in even more excruciating pain. With him now relaxing, I moved quickly. In less than one or two seconds, I was able to abruptly perform a simple manipulation of his shoulder and arm. Both Tony and I instantly experienced relief as his dislocated shoulder moved back in place.

Tony's eyes widened, and he beamed. "Pain's gone, Doc. It's gone!"

I breathed a huge sigh of relief. "Sit up, Tony. Let's get you to your feet."

As he rose, so did a crescendo of applause from the crowd as they saw him swing his recently crippled arm. The stadium erupted. The ground shook.

The referee stepped in. "Coach, you're gonna have to sit him out a down."

"No problem. No problem."

As Tony ran off the field, the stands erupted again. Their hero appeared healthy. Coach and I walked off behind him.

"Good job, Doc."

I handed him two Tums. He smiled and trotted ahead of me. I felt like I needed at least two myself!

After a quick check on the sideline indicated that Tony had suffered no nerve or blood vessel damage—and after a single play by a scared-to-death sophomore quarterback, executing his first play before his entire hometown—Tony hurried back onto the field.

His dislocated shoulder was just what he, the team, and the crowd needed. Sylva didn't stand a chance. The junkyard dog was out of the pen. We scored three times in the last quarter. The opposition never even got close to the goal line.

It was one of the most joyous nights of my life. I had made a difference. I had become, in one glorious instant, part of the team and part of the community. From that moment on, for the rest of the game, I wasn't watching *their* game, I was watching *our* game.

After the win the locker room was the scene of an ongoing celebration. Coaches, players, and parents were all slapping me on the back. There were enough cheers going around for everyone. Coach asked me to check on Tony. I did. His shoulder was in good shape. The rotator cuff seemed tight. It was his first and, hopefully, last shoulder dislocation. Fortunately it wasn't his throwing arm.

"Should I ice or heat my shoulder, Doc?"

I looked at the coach. He smiled. "I'd like you to ice it tonight and several times again tomorrow," I said. "That OK, Coach?"

Boyce grinned from ear to ear. "Doc, you say it, that's the way we'll do it." He slapped Tony on the back. "Great game, son. Tonight's part of your legacy."

"Thanks, Coach. And, Doc, thanks to you, too!"

Outside the locker room there were only a few folks left. The lights had been turned off and a sprinkler was already on—preparing the field for next week's battle with Robbinsville.

A couple came up to me. The woman spoke first. "I'm Tony's momma. He gonna be OK?"

I explained the injury and what I had done. I recommended that they bring him to the office on Monday for an X ray—just to make sure everything was OK. I told them how to care for him over the weekend and suggested that they pick up an arm sling for the next day. It would make the shoulder more comfortable and guarantee plenty of sympathy at church. They smiled and thanked me.

Preston and Joe Benny strode up. They provided a running commentary on the game, praised me for my first game's performance, and were effusive in their congratulations. It was all a bit embarrassing. When they went off, arguing about this or that play or call, I headed toward my car. There weren't many left in the lot.

I suddenly stopped. At the gate stood Mitch and Gay. I felt a chill go down my spine. *Was he angry? Should I have called him to the field?* In my haste to care for the quarterback, had I dishonored his position and experience? The questions were rushing through my brain when he stepped toward me, extending his hand. As he shook it, he asked, "Anterior dislocation?"

"Yes, sir."

"Neurovascular bundle OK?"

"Yes, sir."

"Any pain over the proximal humerus after relocation?"

"No, sir."

"Sending him for X rays?"

"To the office Monday."

"Sling?"

"Yep. Mom's gonna pick one up in the morning."

He was quiet a moment.

"Good job, son. Good job. Don't know if I've ever enjoyed watching a game this much."

He slapped me on the back as we headed out the gate.

"Should I have called you to the field, Mitch?"

"You stupid?" he asked, smiling. He paused for a moment and then laughed. "No, no. Absolutely not. Figured if you were in trouble, you'd call. Folks around me in the stands were yelling for me to go down, but I told them to just hush up. I told them there was a mighty fine physician down there. Glad you didn't let me down."

"Thanks, Mitch."

"Thank you, Walt. I'm glad you're here. Good night." They turned to leave.

"Night, Mitch. Night, Gay."

As they walked away I headed toward the car. Then something caught my eye. The scoreboard was still lit up: SWAIN COUNTY 35 VISITORS 14. And in the lights below the scoreboard, in the message section, it said, "Thanks, Doc Lattimore." My first home victory. Although my name was misspelled yet again, it was sweet indeed.

chapter twenty

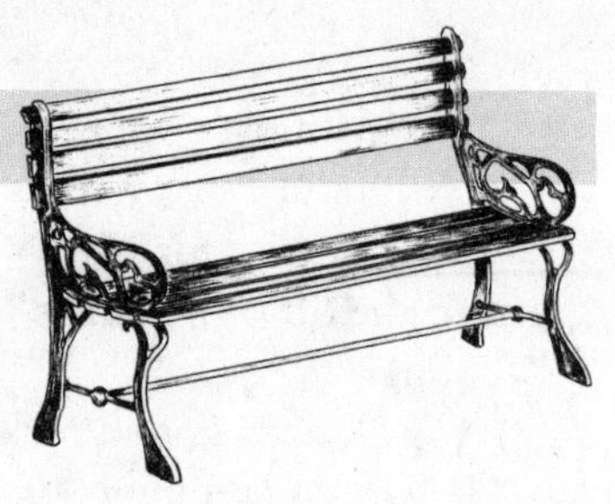

Fisher of Men

Louise and I were completing our paperwork on a minor emergency we'd just handled in the ER when we heard someone moving quickly up the hallway toward the nurses' station. Carroll Stevenson, the head technician of our radiology department, came into view and announced urgently, "Louise, the rescue squad's bringing in a full code from Fontana Village."

Don and Billy soon appeared, with a heart attack patient in tow. As the gurney came through the door, I saw a stocky man alongside the rolling stretcher, performing chest compressions on the patient.

"Louie," Don shouted, "John had this controlled with nitroglycerin and morphine before we arrived, but now the patient's not responding."

John Carswell was the head of security at the Fontana Village resort and a trained paramedic. He handled most of the resort's medical emergencies until the county rescue squad got there—nearly a forty-five-minute drive down the winding road on the south shore of Lake Fontana, a deep lake that began at Fontana Dam and ended where the Tuckaseigee River flowed into it at the western outskirts of Bryson City.

Don continued the patient's history as he and Billy guided the gurney into an ER bay. "His name is James. He's sixty-four years old. According to the wife, he has a known history of coronary artery disease, is status post two MI's, and has mild congestive heart failure and stable angina. No hypertension or diabetes. He's never smoked. Strong family history of heart disease. His last MI was one year ago. Takes Lanoxin 0.25 milligrams a day, Inderal 40 milligrams every eight hours, Isordil 10 milligrams every eight hours, and sublingual nitroglycerin PRN. He's had no cardiorespiratory symptoms in months, was at Fontana for a family reunion. After supper he had a sudden bout of severe chest pain, broke out in a sweat, vomited, and then fainted. Carswell was first on the scene."

John Carswell and I quickly greeted each other as he continued the chest compressions and elaborated on the history.

"Doc, when me and my boys got there, the family had started CPR and had put a nitroglycerin tablet under his tongue. I called for backup and for the rescue squad. Normally we'd have called for a chopper out of Knoxville, but the fog was just too bad tonight. Had to transport by road."

John paused, almost as though he knew that a long transport dramatically reduced the patient's chance of survival. "Doc, when I got to him he had no pulse or respirations, but his pupils were reactive. I started an IV and some oxygen and took over CPR. After about ten minutes we got a pulse, and then a few minutes later he began to cough and to breathe on his own. His BP was 60 systolic, and then he woke up. He was complaining of a lot of chest pain. We gave him another nitro under the tongue and a small dose of IV morphine."

Don took over the story. "Then we arrived, Doc." He gave me a brief summary as the team continued its work in ER. "We titrated morphine for the pain, which helped at first. We loaded him into the unit and took off for here. His family should be here soon. His systolic actually climbed to 80, but we could never get a diastolic. Then, about fifteen minutes out, he began having severe pain and became diaphoretic and nauseated. His BP and pulse got really low. I gave him another nitro and some more morphine, but he went into V fib and then he coded on us. Billy was driving and John and I worked on him. We've shocked him twice with the defibrillator, but he never responded. We've been doing CPR for ten minutes."

During the history, Louise and Carroll were helping to transfer the patient to the ER bed and hook him up to the monitors. Louise flew through a quick and cursory exam. I was surprised to see her doing this—in my training, it was the role of the physician. Was this local custom, or was it insubordination? I didn't know, but almost in amazement I watched her perform the exam with not a single second or motion wasted.

"Pupils eight millimeters dilated and fixed," she shouted, to no one in particular. "Extremities cool to cold." She took a reflex hammer and quickly assessed his reflexes and pain response. "No response to deep pain," she continued. Everyone on the team knew she was describing a dead man.

As Louise did the exam, the other nurses and the respiratory therapist arrived. In only seconds the patient was hooked up to the ventilator. The EKG monitor began to blink to life. It was just a flat line.

Despite television shows to the contrary, rare was the patient, at least in those days, who came into the ER in full code and who later walked out of the hospital. This one didn't either. After working feverishly for forty more minutes, I called the code and pronounced the man dead.

Louise said, "I'll call the funeral home. We'll need an autopsy. The family is in the waiting room."

"Thanks, Louise. Thanks, all. You all did a great job. I'll go talk to the family."

As I left the ER cubicle, Louise followed me out. She looked as though she had something to say.

"Louise?"

She dropped her head a bit. "Dr. Larimore, I'd be glad to go with you to talk to the family—that is, if you need me."

I thought this was an unusually sweet and thoughtful gesture. Yet, just for a moment I became suspicious. *Doesn't she trust me? Doesn't she think I'm capable—that I may not do it like an experienced doctor?* Then I thought, *Has she been asked by the older docs to spy on me? Is she looking for evidence of my ineptitude?* I quickly abandoned those thoughts. No, I concluded, she just was a good nurse who cared and wanted to help. At that moment my appreciation for her grew enormously.

We walked from the ER to the hospital lobby. We had no ER waiting room per se. Although the lobby is normally full during the day, at this hour it was empty.

I walked slowly, trying to gather my thoughts, rehearsing my lines—lines given so many times during residency, lines so very difficult to render with care and compassion, lines always rehearsed, at least by me, at the same time as prayers for wisdom and strength were silently whispered. These moments are never easy for the doctor—or for the family.

I introduced myself to the family. "I'm afraid I've got some bad news for you."

Then I paused. This was what the family had been dreading. Now their worst fears had been confirmed. Some cried. Others just looked numb. All were quiet—overcome by shock. I waited for any questions. None came—which isn't unusual at such a dramatic moment.

"I want you to know that he did not suffer. He didn't have any pain when he went to sleep. We did everything we could have done."

James's wife, Grace, smiled. Softly she said, "Doctor, thank you. Thank you for trying."

I briefly explained what had happened and how hard we had tried to save his life. I suspect that this part of the conversation was almost always one-sided—more for the doctor's benefit than for the family's. It was the doctor's way of confessing, of emoting, of rationalizing to himself and to the deceased's loved ones that the doctor had done all he could do, all he knew to do—that the passing was not *at* his hands, but *out of* his hands. It also gave the family some time to get ready for what would come next.

I then explained the legal and practical details. Under North Carolina law an autopsy would have to be performed, but it could be done, most of the time, without removing the brain. Grace seemed to accept this. Louise and I answered her and the family's questions.

Then Grace asked, "Can I see him? Be with him a moment?"

"Of course," I said. "Of course. If you would allow us a few moments, Louise will come back and get you. Is that OK?"

She nodded.

Louise and I walked back to the ER. James was covered with a blanket to his neck. He looked peaceful. The nursing staff had cleaned him up and replaced his cover sheet with a fresh, clean one. Don and Billy were doing paperwork. John was sitting by the outside door. After checking to see that all was in order, Louise announced that it was OK for the family to see James.

"Louise, if it's OK, I'll go escort them."

"Of course," she said.

I went back to the lobby to escort them in. Like most families, they wept. They gently stroked James's cheeks and touched his head. His boys—he had two of them—bent over to kiss him good-bye. It was my custom to stay with the family during these private moments. To be still and respectful and available. Often families will use this time to share a story or two. Sometimes they'll ask more questions. Sometimes they'll be very quiet. I would be there with them and, if possible, try to bring some solace into a dreadful situation.

The last thing I was expecting was for James's wife to comfort me.

After she kissed his cheek and held his hand, Grace looked at me. Her eyes were puffy, but she seemed unusually calm and peaceful.

"Doctor," she explained softly, "my James has had several heart attacks. His father died at the age of forty-five of a massive MI. His dad's dad and granddad both died before the age of fifty from heart attacks. He's sixty-four and has lived longer than any other man in his family. He was a great dad to our five kids and a wonderful husband to me—my best friend."

She stopped to wipe away the tears. Then she went on. "I am so grateful to have known and loved and lived with this beautiful man. And the Lord has given us so many more years than I ever expected. But, Doctor, best of all, because of his faith in the Lord, I know for sure that he's in heaven. I know for sure that he'll never feel pain again. And I know for sure that I and the kids will see him again."

She paused. I was overwhelmed by her faith, her peace, and her gentleness. Even in my short career, I had seen many grieving families. Yet, in my experience, it only seemed to be those with a deep and unshakable faith in God who were able to face death with such grace and assurance.

"Doctor," she continued, "although professionally he was an attorney, he really called himself a 'fisher of men.' He didn't really lead people to God, like so many clergy or missionaries try to do. James just loved people wherever they were at—warts and all. He didn't try to force them to God; he just gently and lovingly introduced people to his Lord. And more often than not, they would see his life and his example and his character and his giving spirit, and they would want a relationship like he had. He saw so many begin a personal relationship with God because of what God did through him. Now it's time for him to go home to the Lord he loved and served. I'll miss him so much, but he loved me so much. He loved others so much."

She bowed her head and gently wept. I found myself having some very selfish thoughts. Instead of thinking about James or about Grace, I found myself thinking about me. I wondered what others would say about me when I would walk the same path that James walked. I felt that I knew God. I'd had a personal relationship with him for nearly ten years. But did I know God the way James knew God? And could others see God's love at work in my life? I didn't know.

I walked over to Grace's side and reached down to take her and James's hand in mine. My tears were now as obvious as hers were. I wanted in some way to return to this kind woman the same kind of gift I sensed she had just given me. I thought back to my prayer with Harold and Doreen, and how they had appreciated a doctor praying with them. I felt compelled to offer the same to this precious woman.

"May I pray with you?" I asked, with slightly trembling lips.

She gently, almost imperceptibly, nodded her affirmation.

I said a prayer of thanks for James and for his rich life. I prayed for his wife and his children. I prayed for myself—that my love for God and for others might someday look a bit like James's.

After the prayer, Grace gave me a hug and looked into my eyes. "James would tell you to be strong in the Lord. He would have encouraged you to come to know the Lord more deeply, to spend time with him every day, and to make him known to others. He would have been thankful for all you did. I know I am. Thank you, Doctor." Then she and the family turned to go. Their last family outing with James was over. But his impact on me would be eternal.

I whispered, "No, thank *you*."

After the family left, I walked over to the nurses' station and started to do my paperwork, but I paused and put my head in my hands—my tears and silent sobs obvious. I had witnessed death before—many times—but had never been touched by a death like I had been by this one. I cried for my own inability to save James—and for my own lack of faith, compared to this man's. I knew I wanted to make a difference with the patients I saw and cared for. I was learning that this would be possible only if I could be competent both clinically *and* spiritually. I wanted to be able to care for the body, mind, *and* spirit—to care for the whole person as part of a family and as part of a community.

I felt a hand rest softly on my shoulder. Louise whispered, "What you just did, Dr. Larimore, it was . . . beautiful." I felt her lean over to kiss the back of my head.

"Thanks, Louie," was all I could say. But no words could reflect the depth of my appreciation for her at that moment. From that moment on, to me she wasn't "Louise," she was "Louie." But *never* in public.

I finished dictating my notes on James. The report contained all the necessary clinical details. It began, "This sixty-four-year-old married white male . . ." This was the usual and customary dictation technique, yet this was *not* the usual and customary case. I had been deeply and indelibly marked by this man whom I had never really met, had never known. Yet, to this day I carry his imprint on my soul.

My involvement in the ministry of medicine—incorporating faith into medical practice—in many ways began with this man, a loving man I never knew.

chapter twenty-one

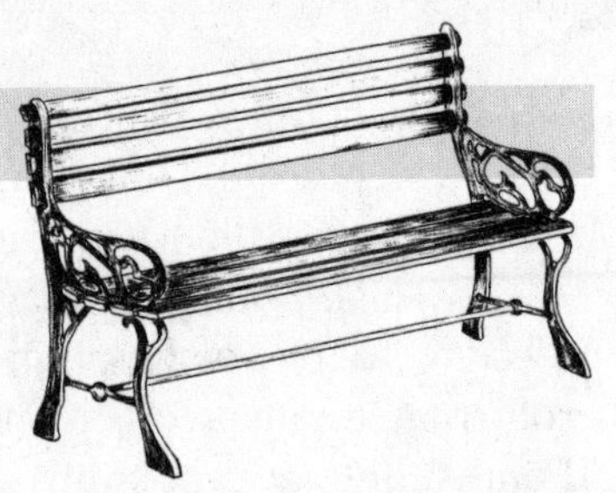

Fly-Fishing

After completing the dictation about James's case, I stepped back into the ER. Don, Billy, and John were waiting. I again thanked them for their hard and competent work.

"Doc," commented Don, "me and John and Billy seen a lot of docs come and go around here. We've worked a long time with them that's stayed. But you're about as good as any of them. And that's sure enough the truth."

I didn't know what to say. Obviously they hadn't yet heard of the "skintight cast" fiasco. I had no doubt that they would. Equally certainly it would bring their opinions back to earth. All I could mutter was, "Well, thanks, guys, but you really did all the work. I'm just sorry we couldn't save him."

"Doc," said Billy, "I don't think Saint Peter hisself could have saved that man. He was gone when we got there. I knew it. Sometimes you just know these things."

We all nodded in agreement. Then John turned to me. "Doc, if you're ever interested, I'd like to invite you to come out to

Fontana Village. I'd love to show you around a bit. Maybe we could take some time to go fishing out by the dam. It's mighty fine fishing down thar."

Don, not to be outdone, said, "Doc, Carswell here don't know how to *really* fish. I mean, he can lake-fish, but if you really want to learn how to fish, I need to take you fly-fishing."

Carswell broke in, "Doc, you go with him, all you're gonna catch is some little skinny trout. I want to teach you how to catch some real fish. In *my* lake we have monsters compared to the babies in the streams. We got bass, walleye, pike, muskie, perch, sunfish, and crappie. Fontana's a fisherman's heaven. You come on the lake with me, and you'll do some *real* fishing. And the lake fish are about as good a eatin' as you can find!" He rubbed his protuberant belly as he smiled and licked his lips. Obviously this man liked to fish as much as he liked to eat.

Billy and I sat back to watch this escalating battle of opinions, which went on for several minutes. Finally, however, Don settled matters with what seemed to my nontheologically trained ears to be a fairly ludicrous theological argument.

"Carswell, it's obvious you don't know the Bible. Why, Jesus picked the very most unlikely men to be his very first disciples, and they were lake fishermen. Jesus took them away from the lake 'cause he was a fly fisherman."

Not being a churchgoing man, John was obviously taken aback by Don's comments, as well as uncertain of the biblical prowess—or lack thereof—of his antagonist. But before he could speak or even sort out his thoughts, Don launched another salvo.

"Although the Bible doesn't say so for sure, I believe that Jesus was a dry fly fisherman—'cause wet fly-fishing is only second best for a real fly fisherman. Boys, Jesus was a fisher of men, and he made his disciples fishermen—and the best fishermen are fly fishermen—so obviously, Jesus was a fly fisher of men." He crossed his arms in front of his chest, took a deep breath, and looked very proud of himself.

"Don," ventured Billy, haltingly, "I'm not sure that's all in the Bible, but anyway, after his resurrection, didn't Jesus help the disciples catch fish in the lake?"

John chimed in, "That's shore 'nuff right. So, Don, how do you explain that? Sounds to me like Jesus was blessing lake fishing. I knew it. I knew Jesus was a lake fisherman." He smiled broadly and crossed his own arms over his chest.

Don smiled. "Boys, you all haven't been a readin' your Bibles closely enough. 'Cause it says that the disciples hauled in 153 of them lake fish. But you know what? They didn't eat a one. When they got to the shore, Jesus hisself was already cooking up some of them tasty fly-fishin'-caught fish. He just wanted them to see that all those lake fish wouldn't hold a candle to his stream trout."

If three men could look any more astonished than we looked, I can't imagine it. Don puffed out his chest, smiling like a Cheshire cat. "Boys, it's crystal clear. Jesus was telling the boys not to be fishers of men like lake fishermen, but to be fishers of men like fly fishermen. And that takes skill. It's God's work at its best."

He paused only long enough for his sermon to sink in.

"Doc, tell you what. Tomorrow's Saturday. I'll pick you up at 8:00 A.M. and take you fishing. You'll have a ball."

He turned to his fellow paramedic. "Come on, Billy. Let's get back to the shop." Then he was gone, whistling the old tune "Onward Christian Soldiers"—Billy trailing behind, pushing the ambulance gurney, piled high with their equipment.

John looked at me and smiled. "Son, after you tire of that sissy fishing up a creek or two, come on down to the dam and we'll do some real fishing. It will be my treat."

He held out his large hand and I shook it. He looked straight into my eyes. "Doc, pleased to meet you. I'd be right honored to send folks from Fontana to see you up here, if you'll have 'em."

"I'd be pleased to see anyone you refer."

He nodded and turned to leave. I reckoned he'd just given me about as big a compliment as I would get from anyone in the area.

At 8:00 A.M. sharp the next morning, Don Grissom pulled up in his pickup truck and honked. I grabbed my sweater and overcoat and ran out to meet him. We drove down Hospital Hill toward the river and then made a quick stop at the new Hardee's in town. We picked up some sausage biscuits and coffee to enjoy on the drive toward Cherokee. During the entire drive Don sustained a nonstop lecture on fly-fishing. He gave me a crash course in its history. He addressed the different types of fly-fishing poles and reels, and he waxed eloquent about dry flies—those designed to float on top of the water—and wet flies—those designed to sink below the surface. He explained the difference between hand-tied and machine-tied flies and why the former is significantly superior to the latter. He was so confident about our impending success that we even discussed his favorite recipes for mountain trout. Then he explained the three species of trout in the national park (rainbow, brown, and brook). Only the brook trout is native, and Don elucidated how the others were imported to western North Carolina. I was duly impressed by his extensive knowledge but was hoping he knew more about trout than he did about the Bible!

We drove into the park for a mile or two and then pulled over just off the road. Don had an extra pair of chest-high waders and enough fishing equipment for us both. "Doc, we're going to be way back in the rhododendron. The streams up there are small and the bush thick. Instead of using a classic fly-fishing technique, we'll use a 'flipping' technique. You'll just let out about five to eight feet of the tippet and flip the fly upstream, letting it float down toward you. Since the fish face upstream, you have to flip the fly ahead of them and then let it float down naturally. Just let the stream deliver their dinner to them. Then look out, 'cause they'll attack like tigers."

"Hey, Don, I forgot to ask. Do we need fishing licenses?"

"Nope, not if you're local, like us," he assured me.

It sounded good: *local, like us*. So, feeling dutifully assured, I followed him across the road and across the narrow Oconaluftee

River. Soon we were in fairly deep rhododendron. Don led the way to a clearing where two tributaries fed a small creek.

"Doc, since it's so cloudy and cool today, there won't be any hatches of larvae. So dry flies probably won't be so good today."

Hmm, I thought to myself. *Was this the same man who preached only last night about the theological merits and technical purity of dry fly-fishing?*

As though reading my mind, Don justified his apparent turnabout. "Doc, the Lord used different approaches as he fished for men. Sometimes he just asked questions, like he did with the woman at the well. Other times he asked and answered questions, just like he did with Nicodemus. Other times he preached to crowds, other times he taught a single person. A fisher of men, just like a trout fisherman, matches the message to the hearer. That's just the way it is. So, no use preaching to these trout with a bait they can't see. Instead we're going to be using a wet fly that looks like a yellow jacket. It's black with a yellow stripe on its tail."

He had now bent over and pulled a small can out of his pocket. He was using his pocketknife to open the can. Before taking the lid off, he drained out some liquid and then opened the top to reveal kernel corn. "Doc, to help weigh down the fly and to add a bit of color and smell, I've brought some corn. It's an old Indian trick. The trout around here are addicted to corn. We'll be having a mighty fine dinner tonight. Mighty fine!"

Don pulled two sandwich bags out of his fishing vest and divided the corn into the two plastic bags. After handing me one, he gave me a small container of wet flies and showed me how to tie them on to the end of the tippet. Then he spent some time demonstrating his unique style of fly-fishing and giving me several pointers, which rapidly increased my skill and comfort level. With my first cast, I flipped the corn kernel-weighted wet fly upstream and then let the line out to allow the fly to bump along the bottom—from rock to rock. All of a sudden, a silver streak flashed from the edge of the stream, and before I could react, the little trout had taken the bait and taken off upstream—at least until he hooked himself and the line tightened.

I couldn't believe it! The excitement and exhilaration of my first trout! I gently lifted up the end of the rod to guide it into my net. He wasn't more than six inches long, and the beautiful silver bottom, speckled and glistening with a rainbow's worth of colors, allowed even me, the novice, to recognize this for the rainbow trout that it was.

"Way to go, Doc!" shouted Don, slapping me on the back and dancing with glee. "Way to go!" I was just hoping it wasn't beginner's luck.

"Don, he seems so small. Should I let 'im go?"

"No way, Doc, no way! The smaller ones are the best eating. That's just the way it is. And we can keep all we catch, as long as we eat 'em and don't waste 'em. I'd recommend you try to catch fifteen or so. That will make a real nice supper for you and Mrs. Larimore."

We agreed to meet each other two hours later at the clearing. Don took off up the left fork, and I began my trip up the right.

With the exception of the gurgle of the water, the silence was deafening. The rocks were slippery and the bushes closed in on each side of the stream. The land was steep and the flow of water quick. I often had to detour around small canyons, making a trail where none existed. Between the bubbling runs through the small canyons stood silent pools. They could be six feet or thirty feet across. Some were only one to two feet deep. In others, I couldn't see the bottom.

I would slowly sneak up to the downstream end of the pool, sometimes working my way around the side of the pool if it was a larger one. Then I'd bait the wet fly with the corn—sometimes trying two kernels instead of one—and flip it into the stream above the hole and let it float into the upstream end of the pool. The trout would gather at this end of the pool, facing into the water flow, awaiting the dinner that would invariably float their way. It almost seemed too easy. Within an hour I had caught fifteen—none longer than seven inches. Eight were rainbow trout, two were brown trout, and five were brook trout. I was elated.

By now the stream was noticeably smaller and the terrain flatter. As the bush thinned, I could see that I was in a small valley. The trees were tall and large. I imagined that this was a more difficult area to log, thus explaining the more virgin appearance of the forest. I sat down on a fairly large boulder in the middle of a clearing.

Then a loud thumping broke the soft symphony of water and birdsong. The sound repeated slowly and steadily. It was almost like someone was banging a hammer against a tree limb high in the trees. Then a raucous call, *Kik-kik-kikkik*. The sound repeated. Then it appeared. Flying from one tree across the clearing, over my head, was the largest bird I'd seen since arriving in the Smokies. Bigger than a crow, with slow sweeping wing beats, the large black bird had a flaming red crest with bright white underwing feathers. It landed far up a tree and began pecking again. This was the largest woodpecker I'd ever seen—a pileated woodpecker—and nothing looks quite like it, at least in the Smoky Mountains.

Then I had an unusual feeling—as though I were being watched by someone. I slowly turned my head and saw the intruder. Less than fifteen yards from me was a large white-tailed deer—his rack full, his nostrils flaring as he stared at me, and I at him. He was stunningly majestic. When the woodpecker began to peck again, the deer and I both glanced up at him and then back at each other. Then the deer turned, and although walking on a carpet of leaves, his steps were almost imperceptibly quiet. Reaching the edge of the clearing, he bounded soundlessly into the bush. I was breathless.

This forest cathedral was overwhelmingly peaceful. A Bible verse I had long ago memorized at a childhood Vacation Bible School—Romans 1:20 in the Living Bible—suddenly popped into my mind: "Since earliest times men have seen the earth and sky and all God made, and have known of his existence and great eternal power." It never seemed truer to me than at that moment—a moment of profound grace.

I glanced at my watch. The time had gone far too quickly. I left the clearing, scurrying back to meet Don, who was patiently waiting at the appointed spot.

"Doc, how'd ya do?" he shouted as he stood to greet me. "I've filled my creel. We're gonna be eating well at my house tonight. How 'bout you?"

I showed him my creel. "Can't believe you caught so many brookies. My man, brookies—they're the sweetest-eating trout ever created. All I got was rainbow. You done well, Doc, you done well!"

He slapped me on the back, and off we went to return to the car. Back through the woods and across the Oconaluftee. But as we looked both ways before crossing the road, I saw something that made my blood chill. Coming down the road and slowing to a stop was a patrol car driven by a local law enforcement officer. *Come on,* I said to myself, *you've done nothing wrong.* Nevertheless, perhaps based on some reckless times when I was a young man, I still harbored a primal fear of the uniformed authorities.

"Don Grissom, how in the dickens are you?!" shouted the officer.

"Jim, you old coon dog, what are you up to?!" replied my friend.

"Just keeping our envir'ment clear of the criminal elements and our roads safe for the law-abiding citizen, my friend. 'Justice for all' is my cry for the day."

Both laughed deeply and long as they shook hands—clearly good friends.

"Hey, Jim, have you met the new doc in Bryson City? This here's Doc Larimore—one of the best I've ever seen. You shoulda seen him last night—nearly pulled someone right out of the grave, I'd say! Jim, if you're ever planning to have a heart attack, then I'd recommend you get under his care, lickety-split!"

The officer, now freed from Don's massive paws, extended his hand to me. "Mighty glad to meet ya, Doc. My pleasure."

He turned back to Don. "Hey, son, what you all doing in this neck of the woods? You're not taking all the fish from our streams, are ya?" He winked. "How'd you all do today?"

For some reason I felt sick. Somehow I just knew I needed a license, and there must be a limit on either the size or the number of fish or the type of fish I was lawfully allowed to catch.

"Aw, Jim, we did just as bad as we usually do. And worse yet, the streams were murky, the sky gray, and there was no hatch. Not hardly worth going out today, if I do say so myself."

"Well, you let me know if you ever want to learn how to *really* fish, and I'll be glad to give you some lessons."

"Jim," chortled Don, "you'd have trouble catching a cold!" They both laughed again.

"Tell you what, Doc," Jim said to me. "My wife's been looking for a good doc. I'll bring her over your way next time we need to see someone. In the meantime, watch the company you keep!" He pointed a thumb toward Don and erupted in a belly laugh. "You all take care. I'm off to catch criminals."

He revved up the patrol car and took off down the road. As he drove off I breathed a deep sigh of relief. For some reason I felt I had just been the recipient of the gift of mercy.

"Doc, that's one nice guy and one good officer. They don't make many like him."

We climbed into Don's truck, and on the way home he once again explained his favorite way to prepare the trout. "Doc, these guys are too small to fillet—and you don't need to anyway. Their bones are too small and too soft to matter. So here's what you do. Just rinse them off real good with clean water. Don't even have to scale them or take off the head. Then slit open the stomach and remove the guts. Clean 'em out well and then wash out the cavity. Should be no problem for you, Doc. After all, that's what you do every day!" He laughed at his picturesque characterization of my profession.

"Then you take some lemon pepper and sprinkle it over the entire fish, inside and out. Then take a pat of butter—don't use that margarine stuff—just a pat of butter, and place it in the cavity. Then wrap each fish in aluminum foil. Get your grill going at about medium heat and grill the fish for about ten minutes on each side. Boy, oh boy, you are going to eat like a king."

I thanked him for his kindness and for a wonderful day. While waiting for Barb and Kate to return home from their Saturday errands in town, I began to clean and prepare the fish. That night we had our first meal of genuine Smoky Mountain trout. Barb cooked green beans and corn, along with yeast rolls. The wonderful aroma in the house matched the sweet evening we spent as a family—an evening of storytelling and laughter, an evening that defined what family was all about. The warmth of that evening wafted through all of Sunday and on into the evening.

First thing Monday morning, however, the feeling completely morphed into horror. The radio clicked on at the prescribed 6:00 A.M., and then I heard it—from the mouth of Gary Ayers himself.

"Good morning, folks. Boy, law enforcement over in Cherokee was busy, busy, busy yesterday. Seems a bunch of tourists were caught coming out of the woods with creels of illegal trout. Yep, folks. These guys had caught a bunch of brook trout. Not only did they catch an endangered species, but all of the fish were under the eight-inch minimum, and they went over the six-fish limit. Worse yet, these guys didn't even have licenses. And if that's not enough, they were found to have used kernel corn—and you all know that the park only allows fishing with artificial bait. Well, folks, law enforcement will be buying some new patrol cars this week. They arrested these guys, and they're in jail, without bail, over in Sylva. Looks like they'll get a $1,000 fine per rainbow trout, $2,500 for each brook trout, $2,500 for fishing with bait, plus $1,500 for trout fishing without a license. Folks, we'll need an adding machine to figure out the damage.

Not only that, officers have confiscated the criminals' cars. Now for this morning's weather report . . ."

I was mortified. I felt a cold sweat break out on my brow.

"Honey," murmured Barb softly, as she lay curled up beside me in bed, "didn't Don tell you that you didn't need a license?"

"That's right. But he also told me there was no limit on the number of fish or the size of the fish or the type of fish. He also told me that we could use bait."

I paused to consider the implications—and then the headline in the *Smoky Mountain Times*: "Local physician buried under the Sylva jail after murdering ten endangered brook trout caught without a license and with illegal bait."

I barely made it through morning rounds at the hospital. The first thing I did after arriving at the office was to give my fishing mentor a call.

"Don, did ya hear 'bout those boys being arrested over in Cherokee?"

"Yep, sure did. Mighty unfortunate for them. Mighty unfortunate."

"For them? *For them?!* How about for *us*? Grissom, that could have been *us!* Are you nuts? Why didn't you tell me about the license? Why didn't you tell me about the size limit? Why didn't you tell me about the maximum number of fish we could take? Why didn't you tell me that only artificial lures are allowed? Grissom, we could be in jail!"

"Now, Doc. Just calm down a bit and let me explain."

I'm sure he could hear my angry breathing. *This had better be good,* I thought. *It had better be good!*

"Doc, those guys are foreigners. They were catching fish that weren't theirs. Those of us who grew up here—we know what's ours and what's not. Doc, those fish belonged to us before they belonged to the park. The park knows that, and so do we. We don't take what we don't need, and we eat all we take."

"But, Don, if Jim had looked in our creels, we'd be in jail."

"Doc, you don't think he saw our creels? You don't think he knew? It's just the way things is around here. Jim knows it. I know it. Now you know it. But if it will make you feel any better, I'll come up there at lunchtime and help you apply for your license. And, in the future, we'll catch us some bigger trout, OK?"

After I hung up I didn't feel any better at first. But as I thought about it a bit, I began to understand the feelings of the locals a little better—especially those whose parents and whose parents' parents had grown up in Swain County, especially those who had lost their property to the government when the national park was formed. Many still considered it, in a way, their land—and land that still provided them food.

After that day I didn't ask where the turkey or deer or hog or bear meat I received in payment for medical services came from. I just accepted it with a grateful heart. And I was thankful for an afternoon in the woods, seeing and hearing some things that refreshed and invigorated my spirit and soul. I wouldn't have been there except for Don. I was thankful for one of the best meals of my life. I wouldn't have enjoyed that except for Don. I was thankful that at least this one local fellow was starting to consider me one of the "locals." I was also thankful for the mercy shown to me by a law enforcement officer who understood the *spirit* of the law as well as the letter of the law.

Louise and Mitch had begun to teach me the ways of mountain medicine. Don began to teach me the way of the land. Jim showed mercy. I thought of the words of wise King Solomon in the Old Testament:

> There is a time for everything,
> and a season for every activity under heaven:
> a time to be born and a time to die,
> a time to plant and a time to uproot,
> a time to kill and a time to heal,
> a time to tear down and a time to build,
> a time to weep and a time to laugh,
> a time to mourn and a time to dance,
> a time to scatter stones and a time to gather them,

a time to embrace and a time to refrain,
a time to search and a time to give up,
a time to keep and a time to throw away,
a time to tear and a time to mend,
a time to be silent and a time to speak,
a time to love and a time to hate,
a time for war and a time for peace.

A time to die, a time to live. A time to learn, a time to be thankful. And, I thought to myself, *That's just the way it is!*

chapter twenty-two

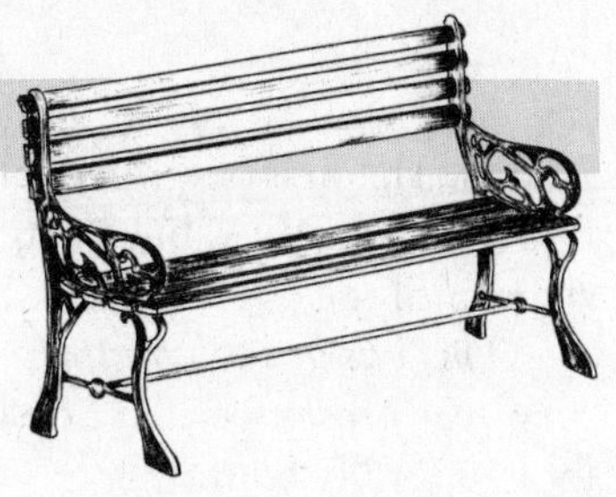

Something Fishy

I was on my way out of the operating room, having assisted Ray with an emergency appendectomy on a young newlywed. She and her husband had been honeymooning at one of the local inns. Suddenly Louise burst through the OR doors.

Ray and I looked at each other. *Who was she after this time?*

"Dr. Larimore," she squawked, "I need you in the ER. You won't believe what I've got. I've been here in this hospital for *a lot* of years, and *I* don't even believe what's in there!"

She turned and tried to escape through the rapidly closing doors, which caught her squarely on the shoulders. She gave the doors a shove and shouted back over her shoulder, "Now!"

Ray and I looked at each other again. "Mind if I join you after I get the patient settled in the recovery room?" he asked.

"Sounds like it might be interesting. Come on down," I chuckled as I sped through the OR doors.

When I got to the ER, things seemed calm. Louise was writing a note at the nurses' station, and two of the three patient bays had drapes pulled around them. There were no paramedics to be seen.

As I walked in, Louise stood up. "There's two patients, Doctor. The first one will live but needs a lot of suturing. The second one was DOA, but the first patient will not let her out of his sight until the game warden arrives."

This has got to win the prize as the most unusual patient history ever presented to a doctor, I thought to myself. I must have looked totally confused.

She continued. "Before your jaw completely dislocates, come look."

The smile on her face was devilish. She pulled the curtain of bay 2 open, and my eyes beheld something they had never seen before nor ever seen since in an emergency room. It was a fish. Now, not just any fish but a *gigantic* fish! The ER gurney is about seven feet long, and this fish occupied at least two-thirds of its length. It was massive. My jaw dropped. The jaws of the fish were also open, with horrific-looking teeth and some blood on the sheet by the mouth—I presumed from being hooked. Louise was snickering.

A voice from bay 1 spoke, "That's one monster of a fish, ain't it, Doc? I've ne'er seen a muskie so big. Think she's shore 'nuff a record. Maybe even a worlt record."

"What's this *fish* doing in our ER?" I asked.

"Well, Doctor," Louise piped up, "Mr. Crisp here would not be evaluated unless I agreed to let his fish accompany him."

"Doc, that thar is a record fish. Can't let her outta my sight till she's properly measured and weighed. I caught her fair and square. I'd rather bleed to death than let her outta my sight."

"Bleed to death?" I inquired.

"Oh, yes, sir," exclaimed Louise. "Come looky at this." She pulled the curtain back to reveal a white-as-a-sheet Mr. Crisp, who otherwise looked just fine—aside from his right arm, which was covered with a bloodstained hospital drape. Louise went to the patient's right side and slowly peeled back the sheet that was clotted to his arm. He winced.

"What happened?" I cried—trying not to sound as shocked as I really was. The arm looked as though it had been through a meat grinder. No bones were showing, but there was clotted blood from just above the elbow to the wrist.

"Well, Doc, I was down near the Almond boat dock, jigging for crappie. The lake's down a good forty feet, so to get to the shore you've got to walk down the edge. Thar ain't no trees or stumps 'round the cove thar, just the water's edge. But I know a place where thar's a rock. When the water's that low, you can get to the rock. On the side of the rock thar's an underwater cliff, about fifteen or twenty feet straight down. Great place to fish."

His eyes bored into mine. "Doc, you ain't gonna tell no one about my spot, are you?"

"No sir, Mr. Crisp, your secret spot's safe with me."

"Well anyhow, I was just standing there at the edge of that rock, a jiggin' for crappie, like I said. Had caught a bunch of them critters. Had them on a stringer in the water. But I had the end of the stringer under my foot, since thar warn't no place to tie it to."

"Go on," I encouraged. The story was getting more curious by the minute.

"Well, I commenced to hearin' a slurpin'."

"A slurping?" I asked.

"Yep, Doc, a slurpin'." He then mimicked one deep long slurp, followed by another.

"What was it?"

"Well, I tell ya, Doc, I didn't rightly know m'sef. Ne'er heerd such a noise. Then I realized it was at my feet. I just plumb froze. Then, while that slurpin' continued, I slowly aimed my eyes down at my feets. And thar was the most unusual sight my eyes had e'er beholded."

I couldn't believe what my mind told me was coming, but he sure enough said it anyway.

"At my feets, which were thar on the edge of the rock, thar was that muskie." He pointed to the fish in the bay to his left. "Doc, that's a deepwater fish in Lake Fontana. They don't ever come up to the surface. You've gotta troll real deep for them. But thar she was, a comin' up right at the surface with her mouth wide-open, just like a big ol' shark, and then she'd just suck in one of my crappie and then she'd a close her jaws and just fillet that thang while she backed up. Just filleted 'em one at a time, and then she'd come back for the next one. Why, I've ne'er beholded such a thang."

He was quiet for a moment, almost in a trance.

"Then what happened?" I asked.

"You *won't* believe this, Doctor," Louise commented, shaking her head from side to side. "Just won't believe this a'tall."

"Well, Doc, I only had three crappie left on that stringer," Mr. Crisp continued. "So I had to commence my planning real quick-like. I slowly bent down and took my pole—and very, very slow-like passed it from my right to my left hand while I was continuin' to stoop. That muskie then slurped up my second-to-the-last crappie. But she either didn't see me or didn't care, 'cause she backed up and then came up for the last 'un. But, Doc, I was ready."

"You were ready?"

"Yes sir, I was ready."

"So what happened?" I was scared to ask. I knew the answer. Not only could I not believe it when I *thought* it, I still couldn't believe it when he said it.

"Well, Doc, when she opened them thar jaws to come up an' suck up my last crappie, well I just jammed my right hand through her jaws and up through her gills and then jumped back real fast 'afore she could pull me in and drown me."

He paused as he relived this once-in-a-lifetime event—taking in and then releasing a deep breath. "Well, Doc, she shore didn't like me a pullin' her outta that thar lake. She was a thrashin' and a floppin'. I backed up like a crab, a pullin' her along with me—when all of a sudden-like my brain yelt at me, 'She's a bitin' you, boy!' I looked down at my arm, and every time she thrashed she done gored me again. Thar was blood a flowin' out of her mouth—and I realized it were mine!"

"Then what happened?"

"Well, I kinda panicked and pulled my arm outta her mouth real fast, but I think that just caused more gashes. Anyway, I threw myself on her and we wrestled a bit. I warn't gonna let her a back in that thar lake. Finally the fight kinda left her. I got my stringer and real careful-like passed it through her gills and done drug her back up to my truck. Come straight up here. Knew Louise would know who to call."

"What in tarnation is going on?" a new voice blurted out. As the curtains separated, the exclamation continued, "What the blazes ..." and trailed off as Ray entered the room. "Well, I never ...," he muttered as he looked back and forth between the two patients.

The story was told again, with perhaps even more gusto and bravado. As Ray listened to the tale, I examined the gory mess. The patient's hand was intact, and all the arteries and nerves were uncut and fully functional. But he had row after row of fairly superficial lacerations and a few that ran deeper.

"Looks like you're going to be sewin' awhile, champ," encouraged Ray.

"Don't you want to stay and help a bit?"

"I'd love to, buddy, but I promised Nancy I'd be home for dinner." With that and one last chuckle, he was off.

I commenced to cleaning, numbing, and sewing. I don't remember just how many dozens and dozens of sutures it took to close up Mr. Crisp, but it took a couple of hours of nonstop work. I took several breaks to see other patients. It was a good thing the afternoon was light—as we only had one available patient bed in the ER.

After I had finished sewing, while Louise was cleaning and dressing the fisherman's arm, I was writing prescriptions for an antibiotic and a pain medication. Out of the corner of my eye I saw someone with a uniform on enter the room. As I turned, the officer introduced himself. "Dr. Larimore, I'm John Mattox with the Park Service. I think you know my daddy—the pharmacist down at Super Swain."

"Yes, John, I do. It's good to meet you."

"Well, I was heading home when I heard on the radio a call for the game warden to come over to the hospital to certify a world-record fish. The warden's hung up with a case down near Bird Town, so since I live near here, I told him I'd come and check things out."

I took John over to Mr. Crisp, who was now sitting up, his color almost back to normal. He gladly, and with even more vigor, retold his story. John listened without a word and then took a small tape measure from his pocket and measured the fish's length and girth. "Man," he muttered to himself, "that's a big 'un!"

He looked at me. "Do you have a scale?"

"For fish?"

He smiled. "No, for people."

"Oh," I stammered, "of course. Right over here." I pointed to the scale near the entrance to the ER.

"Can I weigh myself?"

What an odd request, I thought. But, ever the polite ER doctor, I said, "Of course."

He walked over and stepped on the scale, adjusting the weights. "One hundred seventy-three pounds," he said, almost to himself. He returned to ER bay 2 and hoisted up the fish in both of his arms. "Doc, come give me a hand, will you?"

What was he up to? He carried the muskie over to the scale. "Doc, adjust the scales to see how much I weigh now."

Now I could see what he was doing. By subtracting his weight without the fish from his weight with the fish in hand, he could come up with an approximate weight for the fish. As he saw the weight, John's eyes widened, and he whistled. "Man, oh man, this could have been a world record."

"Could have been?" I whispered. He nodded his head and carried the fish back to her bed. With my help we got her situated again.

"Is that a record, Mr. Ranger?" asked Mr. Crisp anxiously.

John walked over to the sink and washed his hands. "Excuse me for a moment, gentlemen. I need to radio this information to the game warden. I'll be back in a moment."

I also stepped out to finish my dictation on the case. Soon I heard a yelp, as Louise administered a diphtheria-tetanus booster to our fisherman.

Ranger John returned, and I joined him in the ER bay.

"Mr. Crisp, I've got some good news and some bad news. First of all, if this fish is weighed on a certified scale, it's likely a world-record weight, but . . ."

"But what?" croaked our now pallid fisherman.

"Well, that's the bad news."

"*What's* the bad news?"

"This fish won't qualify for any records."

"Just why the blazes not?" shouted Mr. Crisp.

"Since you didn't catch it with a rod and a line, it won't count. You caught it with your hands. They won't certify a fish for a record unless you catch it with a regulation rod, line, and bait. I'm awfully sorry."

Mr. Crisp's face registered the terrible shock. His lower lip began to quiver. He bit it as he fought back the tears. He looked at his arm for a moment, sniffled, and then looked over to the fish.

"Well, she's going to make one nice barbecue, I'll tell you that. Might have to find me a pig grill to cook her. I think the Rotary Club might just rent their cooker. Gonna be one nice meal."

John and I said our farewells to the patient and walked out of the ER together.

"For a minute there I thought I might have to write a prescription for an antidepressant," I chuckled.

"Well, he's not the first around here to catch some large fish with his hands."

"You're kidding."

"Nope. We've got people who go fishing with underwater electrocuting devices. Even had an occasional fellow using underwater detonation devices. Kills off or shocks a mess of fish and then he just scoops 'em off the surface of the water. Every now and then one of them will try to claim a record fish. Pretty easy to figure out."

I just shook my head in disbelief.

"Aw, Doc, that's just the beginning of the stories I could tell you." He winked, and off he went.

I headed back to the recovery room where Mary, the newly operated-on newlywed, was with her husband. She was groggy but responsive. Her vital signs were strong, her abdomen was soft, and her bowel sounds were active. These were all good signs.

As I was leaving, Mary's husband walked out with me. "Dr. Larimore, is she going to make it?"

"I think she'll do fine. Just fine."

His head dropped. He seemed embarrassed. "Doctor, will this affect our ability to have children?"

"Oh, no. Not at all. The fallopian tubes, the womb, and both ovaries looked good—good and healthy. Most patients with a ruptured appendix like this are able to conceive without a problem—at least the women, that is."

He smiled. So did I.

"I would expect her to do fine, but I'm glad you got her up here when you did. Just in time."

"That's what Dr. Cunningham told us."

Ray and I are both learning, I thought. "Let's just take it one day at a time, OK?" I turned to leave.

"OK. It's just a sad day for us. I had so many high hopes about this honeymoon. Now it's been kinda ruined."

I turned back to him. "Let me share something with you." I paused to gather my thoughts, then continued. "I'm learning that the Lord seems to have a reason for the things he allows. I'm also learning that if we'll trust him, he'll often take the things that appear bad, and make good come from them. Let me encourage you and Mary to look for the good in this. I bet you'll find it. What do you think?"

He tried to smile. “I hope you’re right, Doc.”

“I’ll drop by later this evening to see how she’s doing.”

Mary’s husband took a deep breath and suddenly furrowed his brow. “Hey, Doc. What’s that smell? Smells like something . . . fishy.”

I smiled. “Probably just a smell of sadness coming from the ER.”

He nodded in empathy.

chapter twenty-three

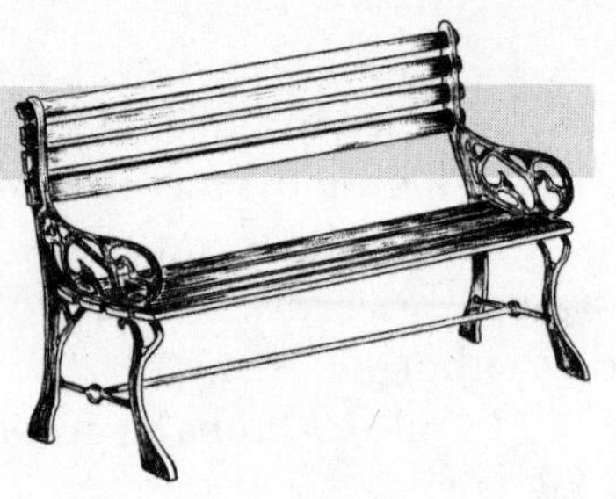

A Good Day at the Office

November 17 fell on a Tuesday that year. Barb and I had not yet had our usual weekly date night since moving to town. Today was our eighth wedding anniversary, and we were looking forward to the evening alone. Barb had tapped Dorinda Monteith to be our baby-sitter. She was young but came with very high recommendations. Besides, Kate was an easy child to care for.

Gary's voice woke us at the usual time. I listened to the day's news as Barb snuggled close. I melted into her waking embrace. There was a special way we just fit next to each other—content, warm, and relaxed. Our eight-year habit of waking up in each other's arms would, it looked like, survive into yet another year—although a growing Erin Elizabeth was making the fit a bit more challenging.

Suddenly I felt Erin give a swift kick. "Ouch!" Barb responded, as she moved back a bit to "unsquish our little girl." She giggled at her comment. I began to sing, "Happy anniversary to you, happy anniversary to you, happy anniversary, dear Barb, happy anniversary to you."

She let out a contented purr, gave me a sweet kiss on the cheek, and sighed.

"Penny for your thoughts?"

"Oh, Walt, I was just thinking, every time I hear you sing, I realize how good Billy Joel *really* is." We laughed and embraced again.

I asked Barb where she wanted to go for a romantic dinner. The culinary choices in Bryson City were a bit limited. The downtown grills and cafés, although adequate for lunch, weren't really fitting for a special evening. As much as we had enjoyed our stay and the food at the Hemlock Inn, the family-style seating didn't seem conducive to a romantic evening. We were really left with only three choices—the Frye-Randolph House and the Fryemont Inn in town, or the Holiday Inn over in Cherokee, with a reputation for fine dining. We narrowed our choices to the ones in town and decided on the Fryemont Inn, since we'd already enjoyed a five-star evening at the Frye-Randolph House with the Mitchells and the Cunninghams more than a year before. I called to make the reservations.

"Fryemont Inn, this is Katherine. How may I help you?" came the friendly greeting.

"Hi, I was wondering if you might have room for two in the dining room this evening."

"I think we might! What time would be best for you?"

"How about 7:00?"

"That will be fine. What name will you use to place the reservation?"

"Larimore."

"Is this *Dr.* Larimore?" came the reply.

I wondered why she was asking. *What had she heard?* Carefully, I answered, "Uh, yes, it is."

"Oh, you and Dr. Cunningham helped save the life of one of our guests who was in the honeymoon suite. She had a ruptured appendix. I've been wanting to meet you."

"Well, I'll look forward to meeting you also. We'll be celebrating our eighth wedding anniversary tonight."

"Oh, wonderful!" Katherine exclaimed. "Do you and your wife like prime rib?"

"We certainly do."

"If you want, I can prepare that for you. I just need to know ahead of time."

"That sounds fine to me."

"Well, Dr. Larimore, expect us to be prepared. We'll see you all at 7:00."

Expect us to be prepared. As I hung up, I wondered what those words meant.

After completing the morning's hospital rounds, I arrived at the office a bit early. Since Mitch and Ray were in surgery much of the time, most mornings I was the only doctor in the office, and my practice was getting busier and busier—for which I was grateful. Rick would be arriving in a week or two, and he'd be able to help carry the load. In addition, we'd be able to begin our maternity care practice. I was looking forward to attending births in our new birthing center.

I had just entered the office when I heard Helen's voice, "Oh goodness, glad you're here. I think we've got a fracture in here." I followed the shrill warning to the X-ray room.

There was a tremulous young mother with an even more tremulous three-year-old child in her lap. The tot was holding her right arm against her chest.

"She won't let me move it to take an X ray. I tried, because I wanted to have it ready for you. But you came here too early, and she's not cooperating very well," came Helen's sharp rebuke—directed at everyone in the room but herself.

"Let me have a look, Helen."

She backed away—I suspect quite unhappily.

I knelt down in front of the scared-to-death pair. I tried to be warm and friendly. No use in getting them any more wound up. It would only make things more difficult later. "Hi there. My name's Dr. Walt." I smiled at the mom.

She returned a small smile. "I'm Debra Fortner. This here's Julie Lou."

I looked at the little girl. Right arm pinned to her chest and abdomen. Left thumb deeply sucked into her mouth. I began to touch her shoes. "These are *beautiful* sandals, Julie Lou. Dr. Walt likes them a lot. Can I have them?"

She removed her thumb only a bit, to smile and then to remark, "No. You're too big."

I smiled back. She was warming up. "Dr. Walt thinks you're right." I sat on the floor next to her and removed my loafer. Helen was apoplectic. Her mouth hung open in mild horror. I placed my loafer next to Julie Lou's sandal. "Yep, you're sure enough right, Miss Julie Lou. My foot is way bigger than yours. I could never wear your sandals. No way."

She giggled and then looked up at her mom. The thumb was out of the mouth, but the right arm had not moved.

"He's a funny man, Mommy."

"Harrumph. I'd say so, honey," remarked a still somewhat horrified Helen.

As I put my shoe on, I asked, "Mrs. Fortner, what happened this morning?"

"Well, Doctor, I'm not rightly sure. Me and Julie Lou were walking from the barn. I was holding her hand when she slipped or tripped and nearly fell in the mud. I jerked on her arm to keep her out of the dirt, and she screamed and began to cry. She said her arm hurt and she wouldn't move it. I tried an onion poultice, but it weren't no hep. No hep a'tall."

Without even knowing it, Mrs. Fortner had given me the diagnosis and confirmed that I was about to cure her child—which I suspected would surprise everyone in the room. But I continued my chitchat. "My, oh my, I've never been taught about an onion poultice. Tell me about it."

Helen sighed audibly. She had no tolerance for this type of banter. She considered it a complete waste of time. "No way a doctor could see sixty patients a day if he just sits and jaws with every one of 'em," she would complain.

I began to softly massage Julie Lou's legs. Mrs. Fortner seemed to visibly relax. This was good. When a mother relaxed, the child on her lap or in her arms would also relax as well. By now my right hand was holding Julie's right hand. I felt her relax a bit as her mom explained, "Well, you just boil up an onion till it's real soft. Then you puts it in the foot of a ladies' stockin'. You mash it up real well. Then you press it on a sore area. The heat and the juice of the onion'll heal most anythang." She smiled confidently.

"Makes sense to me," I commented as my left hand crept ever so slowly toward Julie Lou's elbow—an elbow I was sure was not fractured. I was thinking that Debra's idea about the onions really *did* make sense. The heat would be good for increasing blood flow, which can reduce pain and inflammation—although I, like Coach Dietz, personally subscribed to the "use only ice for the first twenty-four hours" theory. Also, the softness of the onion mash and the hose would allow it to conform to the curves and crannies of the body. Several years later I would publish information about Mrs. Fortner's "smashed onion poultice" in a medical journal—*The American Family Physician*. Subsequently, I've read about it in a "medical tips" section of another respected medical journal.

With my right fingers I could feel that Julie Lou's hand was warm. Her radial pulse was strong. She gave my hand a little squeeze. These were all good signs. Julie Lou's circulation and nerve function seemed fine.

"Well, let's take a look," I commented more to myself than anyone. Before anyone could move, I gently squeezed Julie Lou's elbow with my right hand—my thumb on the front of the elbow, and my fingers on the back. I applied pressure with my thumb as my left hand grasped her hand and turned it outward, and then I quickly flexed the elbow, followed by quickly extending it. There was an audible *POP*.

I let go of Julie Lou and quickly stood and backed away. Both the mother's and daughter's eyes were as wide as saucers. So were Helen's. Julie Lou let out a shriek and then instinctively pivoted on her mother's lap and reached out with *both* arms for her mother's embrace. Mrs. Fortner hugged her as Julie Lou wailed on her shoulder.

Helen spoke first. "What did you *do?!*"

"Let's see," I said. "Mrs. Fortner, can you put Julie Lou down in front of you—see how her arm is now?" Mrs. Fortner looked at me very suspiciously but then very slowly pried Julie Lou away and placed her on the floor in front of her chair. Still crying, Julie Lou reached up to her mom with both arms, flexing and extending her fingers in that universal sign language of all kids that meant, "Come here, Mommy. I want you."

"Oh, Doctor, it looks like she's fixed," Mrs. Fortner exclaimed. She ran her fingers along her daughter's elbow, flexing and extending it. "That's amazing!" she said. She then looked up at me. "How *did* you do that?"

"It's really nothing. Quite elementary. We call it 'nursemaid's elbow.' When a small child's arm is suddenly extended, like when a nursemaid or nanny jerks on the arm of a child she's walking with—or like when Julie Lou fell and you jerked her arm—it causes one of the two bones in the forearm to come out of place just a bit at the elbow. It's fairly simple to fix. I usually do it without explanation. It's easier for me, the child, and the mom. I hope you didn't mind the surprise, Mrs. Fortner."

"Why no. No. I certainly don't. I cain't thank you enough, Doctor."

Helen had recovered from her shock and surprise. Apparently she had never seen this before.

"Well, do you need me to X-ray the elbow, Doctor?"

"Nope, Helen, no need for that."

"How about a sling for the arm?"

"Nope. Won't need that either. She's as good as new."

I turned to a beaming Mrs. Fortner. "Thank you, Doctor. Thank you," she said again.

I leaned over to a now quiet Julie Lou—whose lower lip was still quivering but who was moving her elbow without pain.

"Can I have those sandals now?"

"No!" was the emphatic answer, spoken over a poutingly protruding lower lip.

I suspected both Julie Lou and her mom would be back for future visits. I think Helen was secretly impressed—although she never let on, at least to me.

As I left the office that afternoon, I reported on my hospital patients to Mitch, who was on call for the county, and told him of our evening plans.

"You and Barb have a good time. A good evening."

As I turned to leave his office, he continued, "Oh, by the way . . ."

I turned back to face his desk.

"Helen told me about that Fortner girl. Good job, son. Good job. I think you taught the old girl something—and *that's* something in itself. She's been around a long time. I'm pleased."

Mitch rarely gave such direct praise. It was a special gift. I nearly floated out of the office.

chapter twenty-four

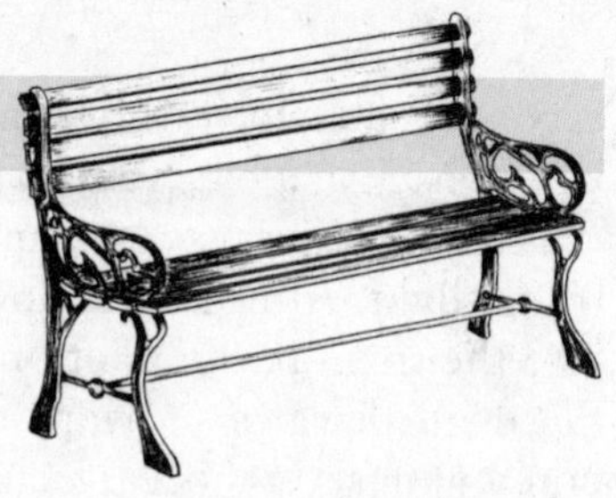

An Evening to Remember

As I walked up to the screen door at home, Kate wasn't there waiting, as she usually was, but I could hear Barb humming in the kitchen. This is always a good sign. When's she's humming, she's happy. Barb's joy always lifts my spirits. Before I got to the door, I could smell her fragrance—it was *Tatiana*, her favorite perfume. I didn't think it was too bad either!

As I opened the door, she was there to meet me. She was all ready to go. Her hair and makeup were perfect. Her simple but elegant maternity dress was stunning. Wow, she was beautiful! She gave me a hug and a long kiss. Wow, again!

"The sitter took Kate out for a walk in her stroller. It's just us."

"Want me to cancel dinner reservations?" I asked suggestively.

Barb backed up a bit and smiled, her arms still resting on my shoulders. "Take your time, big boy. Your lady and your baby are ready for a night on the town." She affectionately rubbed her expanding abdomen with both hands. "Besides, Dorinda and Kate will be back in a bit. Now go get ready and let's blow this joint."

We drove across town and up the hill just south of the main traffic light. After a little dogleg around the library, we pulled into the small parking lot of the Fryemont Inn. We strolled up the front driveway toward the main entrance—a large front porch with several occupied rocking chairs and a nearly endless view up the Deep Creek Valley. The famous Smoky Mountain haze was setting in as the sun retreated behind the distant peaks. The air was cool. We stood in each other's arms for a few minutes, slowly and deeply breathing in the crisp, clean mountain air. The view, the surroundings, and the air were all invigorating.

How welcoming to then step into the large, warm sitting room, with rocking chairs and overstuffed couches scattered comfortably about. Several were arranged in front of the large stone fireplace. We followed a long narrow hall that led to the dining room. The foyer outside the dining room displayed framed articles from scores of food critics and travel correspondents lavishing praise on the inn and its chef-owner, Katherine Collins. The pictures showed a lovely woman who possessed a beautiful smile and long sandy blond hair.

Finally we opened the old entry doors into the dining room. In the background we heard the croonings of a 1940s-sounding album. The dining room was nearly seventy feet long and about forty feet wide, with a floor of wide maple planks. Large dark timbers supported the vaulted ceiling. We were the only people there. As we moved into the room, we saw it: a massive stone fireplace with a large fire roaring inside. In front of the fireplace, perhaps ten to fifteen feet away, was a small round table set for two. It had a bouquet of freshly cut flowers and a scented candle.

After a few moments, a young woman came from the back and greeted us. "Hi, I'm Elizabeth Ellison. Are you the Larimore party?" We smiled, as the reservation book was otherwise empty. As we were escorted to our seats we felt like a king and queen.

"Katherine has asked me not to provide a menu," Elizabeth explained. "She will be cooking a special meal for you."

Elizabeth left us alone to enjoy each other, the fire, and the relaxing environment. We reminisced about our first months in Bryson City. In many ways, it wasn't what we had expected, but we weren't really sure we had known what to expect in the first place. We laughed about my first delivery and the missed world-record muskie. We contemplated my first patient who had had a miscarriage and the couple whose honeymoon had been derailed by a ruptured appendix. We reminisced about my experiences with Louise and Millie. I mused about how delightful it is to practice with Mitch and Ray—and to get to know Dr. Bacon—but also how unwelcoming and unfriendly Drs. Mathieson and Nordling had become. Barb bubbled as she discussed the imminent arrival of Dr. Rick and the not-yet-imminent arrival of Erin Elizabeth. But we spent most of our time talking about how most of the townsfolk were making us feel so welcome—especially the football community.

"You really enjoy working with that team, don't you, darling?" asked Barb, as she reached out to hold my hand.

"The coaches, the kids, and the parents have all made me feel so welcome. I *do* love working with them."

Barb smiled her beautiful and sparkling smile. I squeezed her hand.

Then, out of nowhere, someone was at our side—radiant, warm, and friendly. "You *must* be the Larimores." She offered her hand first to Barb and then to me. "I'm Katherine Collins. I'm pleased to meet you and delighted that you've chosen to come to the Fryemont Inn for your anniversary."

"Is it usually this quiet?" I asked, wondering if maybe the food might be suspect.

She threw her head back as she laughed. "No, no. In the summer, we're booked solid from Memorial Day weekend through Labor Day weekend. Then we fill up again for two or three weeks during the color season. We close the inn after Thanksgiving and don't reopen until the first of April—although this year I'm thinking about keeping the dining room open all year long. Anyway, this is our quiet time. We use it to freshen up the old place—and to welcome new friends."

She continued, "It will be my pleasure to serve you a special feast tonight. I've prepared my favorite specialty—slow-cooked prime rib. But first, Elizabeth will bring out some appetizers. How does that sound?"

We nodded eagerly.

"Fine," she said, "I'll let Elizabeth keep an eye on you, and I'll go to work on the rest of the dinner."

In just a few moments Elizabeth appeared with two small plates. "This is smoked Smoky Mountain rainbow trout. We smoke them using an old family recipe. On top is a puree of caviar and capers and on the side some homemade thin croutons. Enjoy."

We did. When Elizabeth reappeared, our plates were empty.

The next course was what Katherine called her Silver Queen corn chowder, a thick creamy chowder that was slightly sweet and a bit spicy. The soup was accompanied by freshly baked, piping-hot sourdough rolls and honey butter that melted in our mouths.

Each course left us more and more enchanted with the inn as the evening progressed. Others came into the dining room but were seated near the windows, away from us. We felt as though we had the place to ourselves.

The salad dish was fresh milk mozzarella cheese on top of thick ripe beefsteak tomatoes that Katherine grew in her vegetable garden at the inn. When topped with freshly ground pepper and dried basil, it was magic.

As the salad dishes were being cleared away, Katherine reappeared. "Are you still hungry? In a moment I'll bring the main dish. The A-1 prime rib comes from a farm near here where the grain-fed cows are raised without chemicals or hormones. The beef is lean and so tender you can cut it with a fork. I've been slow-roasting it all day, over salt, in my oven. Would medium be acceptable?"

We felt our mouths watering and nodded in eager agreement as she disappeared, soon to return with two giant plates. On each one was a huge slab of prime rib surrounded by mashed potatoes, crisp steamed garden green beans and snow peas with a small section of zucchini and squash.

"The potatoes are Yukon Gold—the best—slow-cooked and mashed with a bit of garlic, fresh sour cream, and pepper. I steam the peas and beans. They're fresh from the garden, so expect them to be a bit sweet and crisp. The zucchini and squash casserole is a recipe from my grandmother. And no, I won't share the recipe with you!" She mocked sternness, and we all laughed. This royal service was infusing our evening with an even deeper sense of celebration for a marriage and a career that were both launching into a hopefully pleasant and enjoyable future. We had no way at that point of seeing the storm clouds forming on the horizon—clouds that would threaten my very ability to practice medicine. But at this particular and special moment, we were celebrating.

We were left alone to enjoy the best prime rib we had ever tasted. Indeed, you *could* cut it with a fork—and it was over an inch thick. We simply couldn't finish it—but we savored each bite. As we ate, we laughed and conversed. Barb talked candidly about what it was like to be a doctor's wife, and I confided in her about how my initial feelings of ineptitude and stupidity were being transformed into a slowly building confidence.

When Katherine came to check on us later, she laughed. "Can I get you folks a doggie bag?" Her eyes sparkled in the light from the fire that was being stoked by Elizabeth throughout the evening. We nodded in agreement and settled back. The atmosphere was *beyond* romantic, and the service had been superb—attentive, yet giving us the privacy we needed to talk and to revel in each other's company.

Katherine appeared with a tray loaded up with ten or twelve desserts, each one looking better than the other. We finally decided to share a freshly baked peach-and-blackberry cobbler, smothered in vanilla-bean ice cream—a laudatory cap to a wonderful evening. I was apprehensive to think what the bill might be, but when the check came, we were shocked at how little this feast cost. We thanked Katherine for the lovely evening. She graciously thanked us for being her guests and invited us to return. We would—many, many times.

"If you all are interested, why don't you go out and sit on the front porch. There's a nearly full moon that will rise over the valley in a bit. There's some blankets right by the door, and I can bring you some hot chocolate, coffee, or tea."

We decided to take her up on the offer and had comfortably settled into a rocker for two when Katherine arrived with the hot chocolate. This time, instead of disappearing, she inquired, "Mind if I sit a spell with you?"

We welcomed her to pull up a rocking chair. As the moon rose and illuminated the Smokies, she told us about the history of the inn and how her family had purchased it for her and her husband, Jim. They were recently divorced, so Katherine was now the sole proprietor and chef. She described her upbringing in Sylva and went on and on about her travels, yet how she was always drawn back to these mountains. "There's just something about the Smokies. Mysterious. Romantic. Wild. Lush. Untamable, yet not too large, not too immense."

I could, even after only a short time in the Smokies, understand her sentiments. Looking out over the moonlit hills—almost silvery in radiance—the dark sky seemed glittered with countless sparkles. This masterful showpiece was ours to just sit and enjoy. Yes, these hills were definitely taking hold of me at a deep level.

Then Katherine spoke, almost in a whisper:

> The heavens declare the glory of God;
> the skies proclaim the work of his hands.
> Day after day they pour forth speech;
> night after night they display knowledge.
> There is no speech or language
> where their voice is not heard.

I looked at her. She was staring out at the hills and sky.

"A bit of ancient wisdom from the Psalms." She cocked her head toward me and smiled. I wondered if she was blushing. "Not real sure where that came from. It just seemed appropriate."

We sat for a bit longer, enjoying the sights and the silence. Barb touched my arm. It was her signal that she was ready to leave. So we stood to go. A simple thank-you seemed inadequate for a woman who had made our anniversary so memorable and us feel so welcome. As I pondered how to put our gratitude into words, she spoke.

"Dr. Larimore . . ."

"Walt," I corrected.

"Well, OK. Walt . . ." She paused to look at the valley. Her eyes were misty in the full moonlight. "A lot of us young people leave town to get our medical care in Sylva or Waynesville—or even drive to Asheville—at least those who can afford it. But since Dr. Cunningham arrived, some are starting to stay. Now that you're here, I think others are going to stay, too."

She was quiet for a moment, her hair gently moving in the evening breeze. Then she turned to face Barb and me. "I'm glad you're here."

I took in a deep breath, not really knowing what to say. In just a few words she had deeply encouraged me, almost empowered me. With the arrival of Rick and the support of our patients, maybe, just maybe, we could overcome the resistance of some of the old-timers, especially some of the doctors who were still so antagonistic about my presence.

While looking out over the seemingly endless mountains, shimmering under the full moon's silver light, I slowly exhaled. "I'm glad we're here, too, Katherine."

Barb whispered, "Me, too."

chapter twenty-five

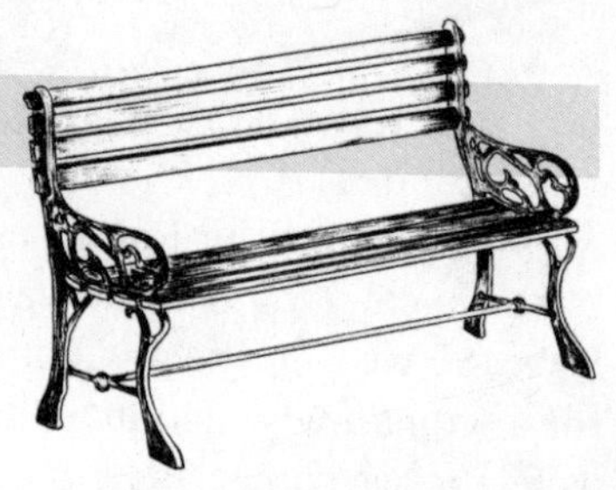

ANOTHER NEW DOC COMES TO TOWN

Today was the day. Rick Pyeritz, M.D., would be joining us in practice. I was elated, as I had been anticipating this day long before we had arrived in Bryson City.

When I entered my family medicine internship at Duke University Medical Center, I was one of only four men in my class of twelve—and the only one from the deep South. My welcome to the world of the erudite, academic, Ivy League non-South was abrupt and, to say the least, memorable. During our first day of orientation, the first-year residents walked over to the hospital for brunch. On the way back, I was walking with Lloyd Michener, M.D. Lloyd was a Harvard graduate who many years later would become the first residency-trained chair of the department of family medicine at Duke University. We were chatting about how varied our medical school experiences were. At Harvard he had *seen* a lot of medicine but hadn't had much hands-on experience.

In contrast, during my medical school days at Charity Hospital in New Orleans I did *everything*. Well, maybe not everything, but I did a lot. I had delivered over two hundred babies, participated as first assistant in dozens of operations, sewed up countless lacerations in the emergency room, set fractures, drawn blood, started intravenous lines—even in large veins in the neck and trunk—all procedures usually reserved at most medical centers for residents in training. However, at Charity Hospital there was more work than there were residents, so the students in those days were able to gain much firsthand experience.

Dr. Michener and I were engrossed in conversation as we approached the door of the Family Medicine Center. Behind us were two female residents from Ivy League medical schools—both clad in Birkenstock sandals and both obviously braless. To me and my narrow way of thinking, both of these were markers of either a hippie or liberal lifestyle—or both. Nevertheless, without even thinking, and simply doing what I had always been taught was proper to do, I opened the door to the center and stood back to allow the women to enter before me. Lloyd cruised past me without a word. However, the two women stopped and stared at me as though I were loony.

One of them stepped forward, got chest to chest with me, and glared up into my eyes. I was stupefied. *What had I done?* It became instantly apparent. She practically shouted, "Just what in the blazes do you think you're doing?" Well, actually that's not an exact quote. She added a number of rather colorful words to her query.

"Just . . . just holding the door open for you," I stammered.

"I don't need a *man* to do that for me!" she nearly shouted. Her face was as red as a beet and her fists were clenched. I was stunned.

She and her friend stomped into the building, leaving me looking, I'm sure, ashen and shaken.

Eric Pyeritz, M.D., one of my classmates, walked in next. Once I got to know him better, I just called him Rick. I was still holding the door open, jolted and frozen. "You're lucky she didn't slug you," he laughed as he walked by. That was my first memory of Rick Pyeritz.

The second memory, no more enjoyable, occurred that afternoon and forever branded me among my classmates as an incorrigible chauvinist at worst, or a dumb backwoods southerner at best. The resident psychologist for the training program was showing us three- to four-minute videotaped vignettes of patients telling a story. We were supposed to react to the stories and share how we felt about the story or the situation. Since my dressing-down earlier that day, I was being exceptionally quiet . . . at least until the video vignette of the rape victim.

This vignette was a very close-range face shot of a woman describing the experience of being raped. It was a *very* emotional and disturbing tape. The response was, to me, quite instructive. The women in the group were, to a person, *very* angry about what they had seen and heard. They emoted about how terrible this was and about what needed to be done. The men all seemed to think that the woman was fabricating the story. I noted that the contrast in these two observations was, at the very least, stark.

At that moment in my contemplation, the psychologist asked me, "Dr. Larimore, you've been quiet this afternoon. Would you like to share your thoughts?"

So I shared my perceptions with the group. As I did so, several of the women began to become distressed. But it only took one silly comment from me to cause them to erupt. After sharing my observation, namely, that the women in the group were responding to the emotion of the story and that the men were quite objectively seeing an actress at work telling a story, I asked, "Well, what do you girls think?"

I had no idea that anyone viewed the term *girls* as offensive. In the South, boys were boys and girls were girls—or sometimes guys and gals. But neither term was pejorative—merely descriptive and respectful. In the North, at least at the Northeastern medical schools and universities, this was apparently about as insulting a term as a male could ever use. The explosion was as vehement as it was immediate.

At the end of our session, everyone left the room except for Rick. His helpful observation: "Boy, that sure was a stupid thing to say!"

I laughed, and then we laughed together.

Rick and I began to build a friendship, as did he and Barb. Since Rick was single and a long way from home, Barb became Rick's surrogate sister, comforter, confidant, and friend. The three of us did many things together. Finally, during our third year of residency, we decided to go into practice together as soon as we could. So I was chomping at the bit for Rick to arrive in Bryson City. During my first few months here, I'd been learning the ropes of private practice, settling into this mountain community, gaining, ever so slowly, a sense of confidence in my own style of practice. But Rick's arrival would propel me into a higher gear. I just knew it! At last I'd have a relationship here in Bryson City with shared roots and history, shared experience, mutual respect, comparable training and medical perspective, and a similar outlook concerning the value of faith. The thought of Rick and me hanging out our shingles together seemed to me a declaration that we were ready to make a real contribution to the town.

It was a Saturday. Barb had all the windows open, and the cool autumn air was cleansing the house of some of the cooped-up odors that inhabit older homes—especially those that are heated, as ours was, with fuel oil. I was playing with Kate on the dining room floor and Barb was busy in the kitchen, humming as she worked. She was *very* pregnant and had that rosy look and disposition often seen late in the second trimester and early in the third trimester with pregnant women. The discomforts of the end stages of pregnancy—the heartburn, lower back pain, bladder pressure, small stomach, difficulty sleeping, and the like, had only just begun. But today was bright and pleasant.

I heard the truck—a rented Ryder—struggling up the hill. It was Rick and all of his belongings. The hospital owned an empty house on the opposite side of the hospital from us, and it was Rick's house-to-be. Following the Ryder truck, in two cars, were

Rick's good friends Andrea and Ben Gravatt. Both were doctors, he an anesthesiologist and she a pediatrician. We had all known each other in residency, and the Gravatts had begun their practices in Asheville earlier that summer. Andrea was driving Rick's car and Ben was driving theirs.

"Barb, Rick and the Gravatts are here!" I called out.

Her eyes brightened and she quickly took off her apron. "Let's go!" She was out the door before me. I picked up Kate and followed. The hugs and greetings were warm and intense. It was so good to see friendly and familiar faces!

"Are you glad I'm here?" Rick asked.

"You have *no* idea," I said.

The afternoon was spent helping Rick move in. During the afternoon Kim and Mike Hamrick dropped by to help, as did Ray and Nancy Cunningham. Even Louise dropped by, before her shift began, to inspect the new doctor. I suspected that her observations would be spread around the hospital fairly quickly. *Funny,* I thought. *None of the other doctors even came by. Hmm.*

By midafternoon, Rick was settled in. Barb had made up his bed, and she and Nancy had the kitchen in order in no time. The Hamricks and Gravatts left by late afternoon. We were sitting in Rick's living room when Barb brought up the topic of dinner. Nancy quickly spoke up, "Oh, Ray and I are cooking supper for us all, if that's OK. How about 6:00?"

"You bet, Nancy, that'll be great," I said.

We left to go home and clean up for supper. At about twenty minutes before six, Rick was knocking on our screen door. Barb was feeding Kate, so Rick and I stepped out back and took a seat on the bench. The views of the valley were as lovely as ever, especially now that all the leaves had fallen. The normally clothed hills now revealed their crags and scars, their waterfalls and rock faces. It was a less soft, more rustic view—one that was a good fit for the coming months of snow, cold, and gray skies. Winter in the mountains, not often experienced by the three-season visitors, can be downright dismal, discouraging, disheartening, and depressing. The gloomy season would come to be my least favorite in the Smokies.

"What do you think of the place, Walt?"

"Well, Rick. The views are stunning. The fishing is fabulous. The hiking and birding are amazing." I knew that Rick was an expert birder. During residency he had taught me to bird-watch, and I had been surprised at how much I enjoyed the hobby.

"How's the doctoring?"

I quickly recounted just a few of the stories—the murder trial, my first delivery, the miscarriage, the anal angina story. We laughed together. "I *knew* it'd be interesting," he commented, "but I had no idea your road would be that full of adventure." We talked a bit more about football, politics, the scrumptious food at the local inns, and the medical staff.

"Are they really *that* resistant?" asked Rick about the staff.

"Well, working with Ray is a dream," I said. "You'll love him. Harold Bacon has been terrific. Mitch is a tough taskmaster, but he's totally supportive of our being here. Paul Sale has been friendly, but a bit standoffish. Drs. Mathieson and Nordling have been downright ugly at times. When I'm walking down the hall toward them, they hightail it the other way. Patients and staff tell me that their comments about my living here and my practice style are less than complimentary. Hopefully you'll have better luck than I've had."

"I'm not sure. The dentist that came by this afternoon . . ."

"Mike Hamrick?"

"Yes. His wife told me that some of the doctors in town don't like you or Ray. You know, Walt, you'd think they'd be glad to have some help."

"I know. I guess they've just been at it for so long it's hard to give up what they've always had or to let in any new blood."

Rick added, "This afternoon Louise told me that none of the older doctors ever take time off."

"That's true. Paul Sale takes a week twice a year, but he tells me he forces himself to stay away so that by the time he gets back, he can't wait to get going. I'm not sure I've ever seen Mathieson or Nordling take time away. Gay forces Mitch to go with her—once in a while. I'm not sure Dr. Bacon has ever left town."

"They really are married to their medicine, aren't they?" Rick mused.

"I think that's right, Rick."

For a moment we looked out over the mountains.

Then I laughed as I remembered a story Louise had told me. "Rick, once you get to know her, I think you'll love Louise. She told me the cutest story about Dr. Bacon. She said it happened way back when he was a younger man. He had been going day and night for nearly a week. Between delivering babies and dealing with an outbreak of typhus, he had been forced to keep up his round-the-clock visits until he became nearly exhausted. He finally reeled into his house late one evening and crashed into bed next to his wife. He told her, 'Don't let anyone wake me up unless it's life and death.'"

"So," asked Rick, "what happened?"

"Well, in the middle of the night there was a knock on the door. A neighbor told Mrs. Bacon the story, who then scurried to the bedroom. It took her a bit to rouse the good doctor, but when she did, she told him that a woman who lived only a few doors down from Dr. Bacon's house was having a heart attack.

"Dr. Bacon groaned and pulled himself out of bed complaining, 'She's the most obese person in the county and she's always thinking she's having a heart attack—but she has the heart of an ox. If it *is* a heart attack, she won't survive long. If it's not, I'll commence to tell her off—like I've been meaning to do for some time. Either way, I'll be back soon!' Louise said the woman reportedly weighed over 300 pounds. She rarely got out of the house, and she was always suffering from one medical affliction after another. She seemed to take great delight in having the doctor visit her at home.

"So Dr. Bacon staggered sleepily down the street, following a frightened family member into the house and to the bedside.

He was so tired that he pulled up a chair by the bed to take a history and to perform a brief exam. The patient was a massive mound of flesh—but in no apparent distress. Dr. Bacon asked a few questions, determining from the history that her discomfort was almost certainly not from her heart. He took her pulse, examined her eyes, nose, tongue, and throat, and then placed his right ear on the left side of her chest in order to listen to her heart—having left his stethoscope at home.

"Dr. Bacon asked her to start counting. To start with one-two-three and to continue until he told her to stop. 'Madam,' he instructed her, 'count *very* slowly.' Being one to *always* follow the doctor's directions, she began her counting."

Rick began to groan and laugh as the story drew to its inevitable conclusion. "The next thing Dr. Bacon remembered was feeling the morning sun on his face and hearing a fatigued woman's faint voice saying, 'Six thousand four hundred, six thousand four hundred and one.'"

Rick began to double over in laughter. Soon we both were laughing so hard we were crying.

"Boys, it's time to go to the Cunninghams," shouted Barb from the dining room window.

"Well, Walt," Rick summed up, "should be an interesting practice."

"Indeed!"

chapter twenty-six

'Twas the Night before Christmas

Barb and I had talked a number of times about what our first Christmas in Bryson City might be like. We had wondered, *Would we would be enjoying our new home? Would we feel welcome? Would this feel like home?*

Now it was only two weeks until Christmas. The town was decorated to the nines. Lampposts were adorned with garland and festively lit Santas and reindeer. Christmas lights and stars crisscrossed up and down the streets. The store windows were decorated with window paintings, trees, and displays. Even Sneed's Café, perhaps the most tacky of the local cafés, made an attempt to be merry—though, of course, tackily so.

On Saturday Rick, Barb, Kate, and I went downtown for the annual Christmas parade. Kate loved being carried by her "Uncle Rick." As we strolled the streets I imagined we were in a Currier and Ives scene—without the snow. The streets were lined on each side with, it seemed to us, everyone in town. We were surprised to discover how many people we knew and how many knew us. To stop and chat with patients and friends, to have them welcome Rick, to have them talk to and tickle Kate, and to have them offer their best wishes and prayers for Erin's coming arrival all contributed to making us feel at home.

The parade began and included cars with public officials, the sheriff's cavalry, the high school homecoming court, and high school marching bands from Robbinsville, Cherokee, and Bryson City. We cheered and clapped as floats from a variety of community groups—each one throwing candy to the kids—passed by. I found myself hoping that Kate and Erin would be able to ride on one of these floats one day.

For most of the parade we wandered. The folks without kids wouldn't just stay in one place. They'd walk and talk and visit and laugh. We did the same. Kate was now riding in her carrier on my back, and she took it all in—squealing with joy at each passing float, holding her hands over her ears at each passing band. We met a number of new folks—including Monty and Dianna Clampitt, who owned Clampitt's Hardware Store. Monty was also the chief of the rescue squad.

"The squad's been around a long time," he said. "We're housed in the volunteer fire department, and our guys are trained in all the search-and-rescue techniques. I'm sure you've already met our ambulance crew—Don and Billy. We do everything from extractions of people from automobile accidents, to searches for lost hikers in the park, to rescues of folks that's been hurt or hobbled in the backwoods. And because of all the water, we have to know river and lake rescue techniques, too."

"Sounds pretty intense."

"Sure is. We're always in training. Guys get together every week to learn new skills and to keep the old ones up-to-date. We've also got to keep all the equipment in shape and ready to go at an instant's notice."

"Do you all get much medical training?"

"Yep, my guys are all trained in basic life support—basic cardiopulmonary resuscitation. All of the guys are trained in basic first aid—and most are certified in advanced field and wilderness first aid. We see about everything from severe trauma to hypothermia to near drownings. Like I say, it can be intense."

"Do any of the local docs work with you all?"

He cocked his head and looked at me a bit queerly. "No. Why?"

"I just thought that with all the medical stuff you have to do, you might have some of the doctors involved."

"Hmm. Well, to tell you the truth, none of them have seemed that interested in what we do. Don't get me wrong, they all support us financially, but I don't think any of them, excepting Dr. Bacon, have ever been down to the station—and Dr. Bacon hasn't been down for a few years now!"

We watched the Cherokee High School marching band go by, playing "In Excelsis Deo." Then he looked back at me. "You sound interested, Doc."

"Well, I'd like to come to a meeting or two and learn more about what you all do."

"After the holidays I'll call over to your office and have you come down for a visit."

Bringing up the end of the parade was Santa's float. Kate squealed with delight. We all felt filled to the brim with holiday cheer.

The week before Christmas I ran into Nancy while rounding at the hospital. "What are you and Barb going to do for a Christmas tree?" she inquired.

"I'm not really sure. I guess we'll just go to the Christmas tree lot down by the river and pick one up."

"Oh, I wouldn't do that."

"Why not, aren't they any good?"

Nancy laughed. "No, that's not what I meant. It's just that there are folks who sell live Christmas trees with their roots intact. That way you can plant the tree after the holiday."

"Are they expensive?"

"Not really. The Shulers sell them for less than the cost of some of the cut trees."

During lunch with Kate and Barb I mentioned Nancy's suggestion. Barb loved the idea. So after work we drove up to the Shuler place in a small valley cove. Their home place was at the top of the cove, and there was a small trailer home at the entrance to the cove. Across the hill was a well-manicured orchard of four- to five-foot-tall Norwegian spruce trees. We parked by a sign next to the trailer. A couple about our age came out to greet us.

"Howdy," the man said as he approached, offering his hand, "my name's Greg Shuler. This here's my wife, Myra."

"Hi, I'm . . ."

Before I could finish, he interrupted with, "Dr. Larimore. Yep, I know 'bout you. I done hear'd 'bout your fishin' trip with Don Grissom over thar in Cherokee." He smiled. "It's real good ta finally git ta meet ya."

I couldn't help but wonder, *What had he heard?* But rather than ask, I introduced the family. "This is my wife, Barb, and our daughter, Kate. I hear you have Christmas trees for sale."

He smiled as his hands spread toward the expanse of trees. "Just a few."

We walked among the trees, looking them over and chatting, until one caught Barb's eye. While we were looking, an elderly man walked down from the home place. He had a slight limp and seemed frail. "This here's ma pappy." Greg introduced us. His family had been in Swain County for well over a hundred years. As we talked, the senior Shuler was whittling a small stick. I found myself wondering about his life. Then, without a word, he handed the knife to me to examine.

"It's a mighty fine pocketknife," I commented. "It looks old."

"It was my pappy's. It's a Buck. 'Bout as good as you can get."

"Mighty fine gift. Your pop must have been something special," I said, looking the knife over and imagining what it must have meant for a boy to receive such a gift from his daddy. I handed it back, and it was then that I saw his eyes staring at me, filling with tears. He turned on his heels and walked away silently. With nary a word he had told me volumes—about himself and his pappy. I wanted to know more.

Greg was watching his dad limp back up toward the house. "Sometimes he gets like that. I think he knows his time is short. To him, family is everything." Greg sighed and turned to me. "You come back tomorrow, and I'll have her dug out and the root ball bound in burlap."

"Any chance I could get it delivered?"

"Yep. But I'll have to charge ya another five bucks."

"No problem. It's a deal." I shook his hand and turned to leave.

"Oh, one thing, Doc."

I turned to face him.

"Don Grissom's a real nice fella and all, but he's not much of a fisherman. My family's been in these here hills a long time. I know some of the better spots. I'd love to take you fishin' sometime—if you're interested."

"I'd love to go. Just let me know when."

"Maybe after the holidays." He paused. "One more thing, if'n it's no problem." He looked at his wife and placed an arm around her shoulder. She looked down. "Myra here. . . ," he paused again, looking for just the right words. "Myra here's thinkin' of givin' my pop some grandkids. If'n we're gonna have one, we'd be right proud if you'd be our doctor."

"I'd be delighted, Greg. Delighted."

We shook hands. They both smiled ear to ear.

"Bet she's already pregnant," observed Barb as we were driving away.

I nodded.

By Wednesday our family preparations for Christmas were complete. Greg Shuler had delivered our tree into the living room. Barb and I thoroughly enjoyed decorating it and had invited Rick over for the occasion. Although we had been married less than a decade, we already had a number of well-established holiday traditions. One was our collection of ornaments from all the places we had lived and visited. Hanging them and decorating the tree was a precious family time for us. As each ornament was hung, we would reminisce about the location from where it came and feel gratitude for the memories we had carried through the years. At one point I sat down and watched my wife and daughter and my partner, each hanging ornaments, telling stories and laughing. Rick held Kate up high as she placed an angel on top of the tree. I had a deep sense of comfort in my soul.

Barb was *very* pregnant with Erin, who was due in another month or so, and she was *so* beautiful when she was pregnant. Her laughter filled our home. And that it was—*our* home. Decorating the tree this way took so much longer than just throwing the ornaments on, but it was such a special time for us all.

Two nights before Christmas I had been on call for the county and had made several trips to the ER—which meant I had slept *very* little. Fortunately, Thursday was only going to be a half-day in the office, so I was looking forward to a "long winter's nap" on Christmas Eve. Better yet, Gary's weather report on WBHN that morning predicted that a cold front would be coming through that afternoon and that it would be snowing by evening and continue through the night.

Barb exclaimed, "We're going to have our first white Christmas!" Having grown up in Louisiana, neither of us had ever experienced one.

After hospital rounds, I arrived at the office in the costume I was to wear each Christmas for the next two decades—a Christmas tie and festive holiday socks. My staff and patients got a kick out of the doctor's unusual garb.

Midmorning I walked into an exam room to see a four-year-old girl who had a sore throat. Of all my daily visits in the office, I was discovering that I liked seeing kids best. They were so honest and disarming. I loved their candor, their lack of pretentiousness. Plus, there was a lot of kid left in me!

"How's work?" I asked my little patient that morning.

"Dr. Walt," Erica giggled, "I'm a kid, I don't work!" Mom and daughter and doctor all laughed. Then Erica saw my socks. Her eyes widened in surprise. "Dr. Walt . . ." She paused for a moment, looking from my red Christmas socks to my face. "Dr. Walt," she repeated, "I *love* your panty hose."

Now it was time for my eyes to widen as Erica's mom doubled over in laughter.

Suddenly there was a knock on the door.

"Come in," I said.

Rick stuck his head in. "Excuse me, Dr. Larimore. I need you for a moment."

"Excuse me," I said to Erica and her mom as I stepped out. Rick motioned me back toward Ray's office.

"Walt, sorry to disturb you," he said, "but Barb came in for an office visit. She was concerned that after her shower this morning, she couldn't keep dry."

"Keep dry?" I inquired. "What do you mean?"

Rick put his head down, and I felt a lump rising in my throat as my heart began to speed up.

"What is it?"

"Well, she came over to be checked, and, believe it or not, she's ruptured her membranes."

He was quiet for a moment. He suspected the sudden terror that was gripping my soul. Barb was only eight months pregnant. We had had Kate a month early—and she had cerebral palsy. Barb's membranes had suddenly ruptured over a month before Kate was due. All at once I felt almost faint.

Rick's voice softened as he placed his hand on the arms crossed across my chest. "Walt, all of Barb's tests and exams have been normal. The ultrasounds have shown us that your little girl is growing well and doing well. I don't expect *any* problems whatsoever."

"Thanks, Rick." I let out a sigh of relief. "Well, what do you think we should do? Wait and watch? Or would you prefer to go ahead and induce labor?"

I asked because these were the two options we usually considered when a woman who was beyond thirty-five weeks gestation experienced rupture of membranes when not in labor. With Kate, Barb had chosen to "wait and watch." When labor did not begin after twelve hours, Barb's physician had offered her induction with an intravenous drug called Pitocin. Most of my patients choose induction and, given the choice again, I thought Barb would, too.

"Neither," Rick answered.

"*Neither?*" I was shocked.

Rick walked over to the window. "Walt, it's starting to cloud up. We've got a cold front and a possible snowstorm coming through this afternoon." He paused for a moment. "I'm not at all worried about Barb. Actually, getting her through labor is the easy part. What I *am* concerned about is your little girl. Thirty-five- or thirty-six-weekers usually do well. I know you know that. However, we've only had our new nursery up and running for a few weeks."

I could sense my partner's concern.

"Walt, if there's a problem with Erin and we're in the middle of a blizzard, I simply won't be able to get her to the care she'd need or get any necessary care to her."

"Rick, what are you saying?"

"I think I want to refer Barb up to Asheville to deliver. Barb is not now in labor, and her cervix is only two to three centimeters dilated. If you leave now, you can be there in an hour. In case of any problems on the way, the hospital in Sylva is only twenty minutes away and the hospital in Waynesville is only forty minutes away. Also, if you leave now, you'll beat the storm. I've talked to Ray; we'll cover your patients. I've talked to the OB group in Asheville and they not only agree with this course of action, but they'd be delighted to take Barb as a patient."

My mind was racing. I had *so* wanted Erin to be one of the first babies born in our new birthing unit. I wanted our nurses and staff to see that the doctors trusted them and the hospital. That we didn't *have* to travel to Asheville to deliver a baby. I felt like a traitor for even *thinking* of leaving town for the delivery of my own child.

As though reading my mind, Rick continued, "Walt, there's not a person in town who won't understand my sending you all to Asheville. It's the right thing. If anything were to go wrong, it might hinder our chances to see our dreams come true—to have a great maternity care service right here in Bryson City. I haven't been here that long, Walt, but, like you, I'm sensing that some of the older doctors might like nothing more than for us to make one big blunder. I think they'd go after our hides in a minute."

He was making sense. I was *not* sure that a majority of the doctors would be supportive if there was a misstep of some sort.

Rick continued, smiling. "Worse yet, would you want to hear Gary Ayers airing our dirty laundry on WBHN?"

I smiled. "Guess you're right. Should we talk to Barb?"

"I already have. She's up at the house packing her things and getting Kate taken care of."

"OK. I guess this is best."

He walked over to me. "It is, Walt. It is."

"Thanks, buddy."

"Look, you drive safe, OK?"

"OK." I smiled and turned to leave.

"Walt!"

I turned back. Rick reached out and placed his hand on my shoulder. "I'll be praying for all three of you."

"Thanks, Rick. That's the most precious gift you could give us."

His gesture of faith and solidarity sunk deep into my soul. To have a compatible practice partner was a joy. To have a true friend with whom to work, one who was a fellow adventurer on the pathway of faith, was even more invaluable.

By the time I got home Barb had an overnight bag packed. She was sitting by our Christmas tree. When she heard me enter the house, she called out, "In the living room!" She stood as I entered. We hugged. "Nancy Cunningham is off today," she said. "She came to pick up Kate and will keep her as long as we need. I've packed for you and me. We can go anytime." She paused, turning her head to look at our Christmas tree. Then she began to cry.

"Aw, honey." I hugged her tight. "Everything's going to be all right. It's going to be all right."

"I know," she sobbed. "I'm just so sorry we can't deliver here. I know how important it is to you. This is our home. This is where we're putting down our roots. I'm so sorry."

I pulled back slightly, keeping my hands on her shoulders. "Honey, your and Erin's health is far more important to me than anything. I don't care if we have to drive to Emory or Duke. I just want you and Erin to get the best care—and I want her to be safe and healthy."

Barb smiled and wiped her tears away. "I know, Walt. I know. I just wish there was some way to deliver here."

"Thanks, honey. I do too."

I put the bags in the car, and we piled in. I started up the little Toyota and pulled away from our home—suddenly realizing that I was driving out of our *hometown* as well. In this hour of uncertainty and anxiety, disappointment and anticipation, I was more aware than ever that our connection with this small town was strengthening and becoming very important to us.

As we pulled onto the four-lane in the middle of the afternoon, it became darker and then began to snow. *Would we make it to Asheville? Would Erin be safe?* I didn't know what our immediate future held, but more than ever I felt certain about who held the future. I smiled. I was beginning to learn how profoundly important faith is during a medical emergency—and wondered again how people without faith made it through things like this.

chapter twenty-seven

A Surprising Gift

We arrived at Memorial Mission Hospital in Asheville in a driving snowstorm. I dropped Barb at the emergency room entrance and parked the car. By the time I arrived in the ER, Barb had been whisked up to the obstetrics unit and was already being evaluated by the admitting nurse, who had spoken by phone with the admitting physician—Sedrick Porter, M.D.

Our admitting nurse, Marie, had been a labor and delivery nurse for her entire career—all of which had been at this hospital. "I am *so* glad you're here," she said warmly. "It's been unusually quiet. We haven't had a delivery since yesterday, and you all are our only guests—at least for now."

Admission labs were drawn and a detailed history taken, and then Dr. Porter showed up. He struck us as a quiet and gentle man whom we instantly liked and trusted. What I liked the most was his simple explanation of the options *we* could consider. I was used to physicians telling us what to do, not doctors willing to empower us to make our own decisions. Whether he did this because I was a physician or whether he did this routinely with all his patients, I don't know. I do know, though, that I was forever influenced by his example. I would go on trying to emulate Dr. Porter's approach throughout my career.

"Walt and Barb, there are a couple of options open to you. One, we can wait and watch. You can walk around a bit, Barb, and if labor gets going, hey, that's great. The advantage of this choice is that we won't need to start an IV or use Pitocin. The disadvantage of waiting is that, since your membranes are ruptured, the longer we wait the greater the chance of you or Erin getting an infection—which would prolong your hospitalization and increase your costs. Fortunately, the real risk for this doesn't start increasing until the membranes have been ruptured for eighteen to twenty-four hours.

"The second option would be to begin Pitocin now. The advantage is that your baby almost certainly would be born sooner. The disadvantage is that Pitocin-induced labors are more difficult than natural labors. But it is indeed an option.

"Does this information make sense? Does it raise any questions in your minds?"

We looked at each other. I could see Barb visibly relax. This wise physician was both reassuring and empowering.

After a moment he continued. "How about this? I need to see a couple of other folks. How about I go see them? You two can discuss the options, and then I'll drop on by and we can talk some more. OK?"

We nodded in agreement. He smiled at us both, patted Barb on the leg, and then reached over to give my shoulder a squeeze. "One other thing. I'll be here as much as you need me throughout the rest of the night, and we're going to provide you the very best care we can."

He turned to leave as I continued to take mental notes on the lessons this experienced physician was teaching me by his example.

Barb spoke first. "Honey, I think I'd like to walk around a bit. If labor doesn't start in the next few hours, then let's go with the Pitocin. What do you think?"

"That sounds OK to me."

When Dr. Porter returned, he seemed pleased with our decision. "Barb, I've never been pregnant or had to face this decision myself. But if I did, I think I'd choose what you all are choosing."

Then his forehead furrowed. "There's just one thing I need to tell you. I will only be available to you until about 6:00 A.M., and then my partner, Phil Davis, will take over. Barb, I want to tell you about Dr. Davis. He's been with our group for a number of years. My wife says that if she were young enough to have more children, she'd choose Dr. Davis to be her doctor. If you haven't delivered by 6:00 in the morning, then I'll be telling him all about you guys so he'll be up to speed."

He paused for a moment. "Any questions or concerns?"

We shook our heads no. He smiled and turned to leave. "Marie," he said to our OB nurse, "I want you to take great care of our new friends." I'm sure he must have said this to her about every patient he saw, but it sure made us feel special and important.

After dinner we were up and about—talking, walking, and then sitting. Barb continued to leak amniotic fluid but felt no cramps or signs of labor. During this time Marie came to find me. "Dr. Larimore, there's a phone call for you."

I left Barb to go to the nurses' station. I thought sure it would be Rick, calling to check on us. Instead, it was Barbara Morris. Barbara had been my intern when I was a second-year resident, and we had continued to work together when I was a senior resident. She was one of the most intelligent and fun-loving physicians I knew. She, Barb, and I had become close, and "Aunt Barb," as Kate called her, had become a dear family friend. Not only that, but during our last year in Durham she had been our personal physician. She had diagnosed our pregnancy and provided Barb's prenatal care until we left for Bryson City.

Barbara greeted me warmly. "Walt, I just called your office to wish you all a Merry Christmas and talked to Rick. He told me what had happened and where you were. How are you all doing? How's Barb?"

I updated Barbara on our situation. "Walt," Barbara responded, "if you all and Dr. Porter don't mind, I'd like to drive out and be with Barb for the labor and delivery."

"Barbara, that's nuts. One, it's snowing. Two, it's a four- to five-hour drive. Three, it's Christmas Eve!"

"Walt, one, I grew up in New York and I *know* how to drive in the snow. Two, Barb was *my* patient and I want to be with her during Erin's delivery. Three, there's no way Barb is going to deliver in the next few hours. So I'm coming!"

I knew I couldn't dissuade her. "Well, Barbara, let me check with Dr. Porter to see if it's OK with him, and I'll let you know." As I suspected, the doctor, ever gracious, responded, "Walt, I'd be delighted if Dr. Morris would come and join us. It would be a treat." I called back to let Barbara know and heard the non-surprising news that she was already on her way.

Late in the evening Dr. Porter returned. Barb was still leaking amniotic fluid and had not had a single contraction. In addition, her cervical dilation had not changed. We elected to begin Pitocin.

Barbara Morris arrived about 9:00 P.M. and stayed with us through the night. Barb's labor intensified throughout the evening as a result of the Pitocin. At 11:00 P.M. Marie said good-bye, as her shift was over, and another nurse began to care for us. At midnight we all wished each other a Merry Christmas and were now convinced that little Erin's birthday would be the same as the Christ child's.

By 1:00 A.M. I had been up for nearly thirty-six hours and could barely keep my eyes open. Barb was in a strong and uncomfortable labor pattern and had dilated to about seven centimeters. Dr. Morris had already settled down to sleep in the doctors' lounge. "Barb," I pleaded hesitantly, "would you mind too terribly much if I took a little nap?"

The hospital did not have private labor rooms—all rooms were double occupancy. Since we were still the only patients in the labor unit, I laid down in the bed next to Barb. I didn't wake up until the nurse shift changed at 7:00 A.M. Shortly thereafter two doctors showed up—Barbara Morris and Phil Davis. Phil, as had been predicted by Dr. Porter, was as gentle and kind as we could have expected. His examination of Barb revealed that her cervix was now completely dilated but that Erin's head position wasn't optimal.

Instead of being what we doctors call OA (for occiput anterior—meaning that when the mom is on her back, the baby's nose is pointing down, which is the position that is easiest for the mom, the baby, and the birth attendant), Erin was OP (for occiput posterior, or "nose up," a much more difficult position for the baby, the mother, and the birth attendant). This was not only increasing Barb's discomfort but prolonging her labor as well.

"Barb," counseled Dr. Davis, "there are some studies showing that if we get you off your back, then the baby is more likely to turn on her own. The baby is doing fine and there's no sign of any sort of trouble. So I'd like to suggest that you try some different positions. You can lie on your side to push. If you want to try some knee-chest pushing, that may be helpful. Also, if you'd like to walk, I'd be OK with that. Either way, I'm not planning to go home and open Christmas presents until little Erin is in your arms."

He smiled at us. His reassuring manner filled the room and gave us comfort.

So Barb tried different positions, but nothing caused Erin to turn. Barb pushed and worked and pushed and worked. Dr. Davis checked her on a number of occasions. "Barb, I think you *are* making progress. Are you OK? Can you keep going?"

Barb, ever the trooper, decided to continue. By 9:30 A.M. she had been pushing for over three hours. She was beginning to feel exhausted (and, not that it mattered, so was I).

"Barb and Walt," confided Dr. Davis, "I think it's time to go to the delivery room. If we can push the baby out, great. If not, I can use a little vacuum cup or forceps to help her deliver. Does that sound OK?"

Indeed it did. I hated for him to have to use an operative delivery, but if it ensured our daughter's safety, we were all for it. Dr. Davis offered to Dr. Morris the opportunity to scrub in and assist with the birth, but Barbara declined. "It was just real important for me to be here with Barb and Walt. I'll just be the assistant and the photographer, if that's OK."

Once we were in the delivery room, Dr. Davis scrubbed and got into position. Then Barb began pushing. As Erin's head began to show, I would alternate moving from up next to Barb's head—as her coach and supporter—down to her perineum watching my little girl's head begin to crown. The experience was surrealistic. It was almost as though I passed through a time warp at Barb's belly button. Above the belly button I was Walt—Barb's husband and best friend, her ally and helper. But below the belly button my medical eyes and ears kicked me into my doctor mode.

Finally, at 10:35 A.M., out popped Erin's head, nose up. She was beautiful. Dr. Davis suctioned out her mouth and nose, and she grimaced. Then, with a little push from Barb and pull from Dr. Davis, with Barbara Morris poised to capture the miraculous event on film, out came our daughter, followed by a large gush of previously dammed-up amniotic fluid. Dr. Davis began to vigorously dry Erin off—and then I noticed it!

My worst fears suddenly gripped my chest. I saw the deformity. Although the rest of her body appeared beautiful, perfect, spotless, and flawless, there was a deformity in Erin's perineum. For a moment my doctor mind went through its instinctual differential diagnosis—macroclitorus, macrolabia majorum, genital tumors of various sorts, ambiguous genitalia . . .

I looked at Barb, who was sitting up on a special birth pillow, with an angelic look on her face—that postbirth look of accomplishment and satisfaction, a look that no man will ever experience, much less reflect. She showed no concern, but only contentment.

I looked back. *She must not see the deformity. What is it? What is wrong?* My mind was reeling and boggled. I gasped, almost to myself, "What's that between her legs?"

The nurse and Dr. Davis at first looked shocked. Then they giggled at each other. It took Dr. Morris to bring me into reality. "Well, Dr. Larimore, I guess you're going to have to go back and retake your anatomy course. That's a perfectly normal appearing penis and scrotum between *his* legs."

While I was feeling more boggled than ever, Dr. Davis, who had clamped and cut the cord, handed the precious newborn, our *son*, up to Barb, placing the baby on her chest. "Congratulations, Barb and Walt. You have a little boy."

The nurse covered him up with a fresh and warm baby blanket. "Merry Christmas," she said.

"Merry Christmas," crooned Barb as she pulled our newest family member to her breast. "Merry Christmas," I whispered to her, to him, and to myself. "What a gift! What a miracle!"

When we were alone, Barb asked, "Walt, would you be willing to say a little prayer—a prayer of thanks?"

For just a moment I was taken aback. *What a wonderful request!* I thought. *After all, could there be a more natural time to pray—and to express thanksgiving—than after a safe birth? Why hadn't I thought of this before? Especially with my own patients?*

"Of course, Barb. Of course." So we had a brief prayer together—my wife, our newborn son, and I. *This,* I thought, *should become a tradition at each delivery I attend.*

Later, in the recovery room, both Dr. Davis and Dr. Morris dropped by to share some special thoughts. Dr. Morris said good-bye and left to drive back to Durham. We were *so* appreciative of her being there with us.

Then Barb and I finally had some time together with our son. He had been dressed in a gown that looked like a Christmas stocking and a head cap that looked like a Santa cap. The volunteer who brought it in was so proud. This was the hospital's first Christmas baby of the year! Barb and I were both in shock. We had expected Erin Elizabeth. At least three ultrasounds had shown that he was going to be a she. Instead, she was a *he,* and for three days he went unnamed. He could easily have been—maybe should have been—Aaron. Instead, he was named Scott Bonham—the latter a family name, the former the only name that freshly boggled parents could come to consensus about.

chapter twenty-eight

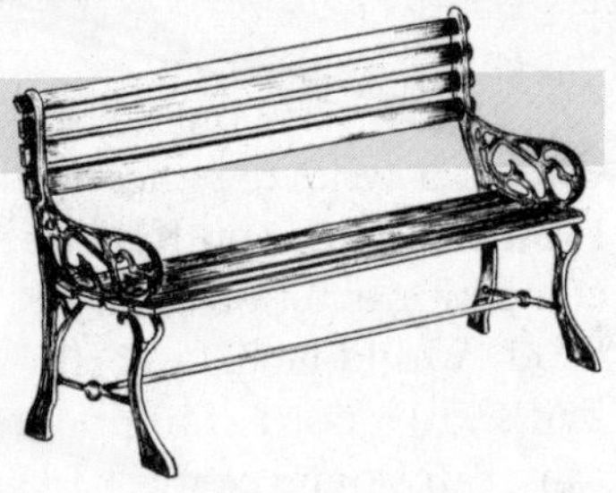

THE NEW YEAR

After driving home from Asheville through the snow-covered mountains, we went straight to Ray and Nancy's to introduce them to the newest Larimore and to pick up Kate, who was absolutely ecstatic about *her* new little brother.

As we were leaving, Ray shared some good news. "Walt, Mitch asked me to tell you to take off work until January 2. The hospital's light, we'll take your call, Rick's going to take any deliveries that come in. We feel you need some time with your new family. That sound OK?"

Surprisingly I felt a bit of guilt well up in my gut. I instantly knew that I shouldn't feel that way, but the medical profession is a selfish mistress, and she teaches you to become beholden and subservient to her—even to the point of sacrificing your own family. "You sure?" I asked, hesitating.

He smiled. "You bet. It'll be our pleasure. Enjoy your family."

"I will. Thanks, Ray."

"Don't thank me. Thank the general."

We exchanged a knowing grin.

That afternoon the three oldest Larimores opened their Christmas gifts together while the youngest slept in his crib. As I watched Barb and Kate open their gifts, I felt two distinct and competing emotions. On one hand, I was secretly worried about Scott. Would he have cerebral palsy, like Kate? The ultrasounds had shown normal brain development—but, then again, these same ultrasound exams had said he was a she. I tried not to show my concern. On the other hand, I had an overwhelming feeling of warmth in my heart. What a wonderful wife and family I had been given! What a special season this was for my family!

Before I knew it I felt tears flowing down my cheeks. I couldn't believe it. I had cried more times this fall than I had in the past decade! It had been in many ways the best few months of my life, and in other ways it had been among the worst of times. At times I felt confident and skilled as a physician, husband, and father, while at other times I felt inexperienced and inept. One group of folks loved our being in Bryson City, while others acted as though they would have been just as happy to see us leave. But as I weighed things out in my mind, I decided that, overall, I was grateful and blessed.

Barb and I had our own New Year's Eve traditions. We had never enjoyed parties on that particular evening, so we had developed the tradition of having a dinner of hot buttered corn bread and black-eyed peas. We'd spend the meal time talking about the important things we had learned that year. We'd reflect on our most special memories. We'd laugh. Then we'd go to bed early, often awaking at midnight to the sound of firecrackers.

This year we'd invited "Uncle Rick" over for the evening meal—to share in our family tradition. We expected a "plain Jane" New Year's Eve. It was not to be.

Rick called in the midafternoon. "Walt, I'd really like to take you guys out to dinner. My mom and dad have arrived in town—unannounced—to surprise me. I'd like you to meet them. Can we do dinner together?"

I paused. First of all, I was pretty sure there wasn't going to be a single restaurant in town open that evening. Our favorites were all closed for the holiday. All of the tourist joints were closed. All the local cafés had announced that they would close after lunch. *Besides,* I thought, *this is* our *family's night.*

Rick continued. "Best yet, I have a new friend who is preparing dinner for us all at her place."

Rick's been in town for only a few weeks, I thought. *Who is this new friend?*

"I know you and Barb will be turning in early, at least you always have in the past, so how 'bout I come pick you all up about six. I'll have you home in time for the kids' bedtime. Sound OK?"

"Let me check with Barb." I was hoping she wouldn't be interested, but she was. "Sounds good, Rick. We'll be waiting for you."

At the stroke of 6:00 we heard a knock on the door. Rick came in with his mom and dad—Paul and Ida. They had driven from Pittsburgh to see Rick and to get a look at his new town. His mom had a special interest in seeing that his house was in order.

"Let's go. Dinner's waiting," exclaimed Rick. As we stepped out, he whispered, "You're going to love what I've got planned." I *was* curious indeed.

"Where are we going?"

"Just for a little ride." He was smiling.

We settled the kids in their car seats, and off we went, in two cars. The destination became clear as we doglegged at the library.

"The Fryemont Inn?" said Barb, looking at me.

We followed Rick up to the parking lot and began to unload. There were no other cars in the lot. Rick smiled. "Katherine is cooking for us all."

"Katherine?"

"Indeed! While you all were in Asheville, she came into the office to see you, Walt. She had a cold or something. Since you weren't there, I saw her. We hit it off fabulously. I told her what was going on with you guys, and she said she wanted to cook you a congratulatory dinner when you were back and settled. She called a couple of days ago, and we talked for a while. One thing led to another, and she made this terrific offer. Wouldn't take no for an answer. Said she'd be alone otherwise. She loves to cook. So, that was that."

The steep driveway had been scraped clear of snow, as had two parking places next to the entrance. I carried Kate on my back in a carrier and helped Barb up the steps. She was still sore from the difficult delivery. Rick toted Scott in the car seat.

We walked into the dining room, which was cozy and warm and permeated with the smells of fir. A fire roared in the large stone fireplace. Katherine had cut and hauled into the dining room four- and five-foot-long logs and had a spectacular fire blazing. We could feel its warmth from across the room.

"Hi, everyone!" Katherine called out, sticking her head out of the kitchen door. "Have a seat. Make yourself at home! I'll be out in a jiffy."

We took off our coats. I settled Kate into a high chair. The lights were on their lowest setting, and a beautiful Advent wreath with five large candles burning adorned the middle of the dining table that stood in front of the fireplace. The gleaming hardwood floors reflected the glow of the fire. The paddle fans that hung from the raftered, vaulted ceiling were silent, allowing the snapping and popping of the wood in the fireplace to fill the dining room with its welcoming melody.

In a few moments the kitchen door swung open and Katherine appeared, carrying a tray of hot apple cider and mugs. She placed the tray and mugs on the table, threw her long blond hair back off her shoulder, and greeted Barb with a warm hug.

Then she bent over Scott, who was sound asleep. "She's so cute."

Barb, Rick, and I looked at each other and laughed.

"What are you all laughing about?"

"Long story," Rick responded, "but *she's* actually Scott."

Katherine laughed out loud. We all laughed with her. As Katherine served the cider, Rick told her the whole story.

"Well," she observed, "given your knowledge of anatomy, Dr. Larimore, maybe it's better that I saw Dr. Pyeritz in the office."

Her eyes met his, and mine met Barb's. I wondered, as did Barb, if this relationship might be—or become—*more* than professional.

After the cider had been consumed, Rick helped Katherine carry the pitcher and mugs to the kitchen, while Rick's dad and I put a couple more logs on the fire. In a moment, they returned with bowls of cheese soup. After the soup dishes were cleared, Katherine and Rick disappeared into the kitchen once again. He returned with a set of wine glasses and a bottle of wine. "From my *personal* cellar, a bottle of 1978 Sterling Reserve merlot. It's one of the best merlots made in California—and a terrific year, too!"

Barb and I smiled at each other. That was the year Kate was born. As Rick poured the wine, Katherine reset the table and then disappeared into the kitchen with Rick. Soon they came back with a massive platter of meat and potatoes.

"Ta-da," sang Rick.

"Thick center-cut pork chops, marinated, coated with a thick graham cracker crust and slowly baked," added Katherine. "Served with baked apples, candied yams, and green bean casserole."

Rick pulled Katherine's chair out to seat her and then pulled up to the table.

"Walt, if you don't mind, I think a prayer of thanksgiving is in order."

"Rick, I couldn't agree more."

He looked at his dad. Paul was a large, handsome man with beautiful silver hair. "Dad, would you say our grace?"

"Be delighted, Son."

He reached out, and we each held hands around the table and bowed our heads. "Lord, thank you for tonight. Thank you for friends. Thank you for the safe birth of baby Scott. I ask you to protect him and to grow him into someone who will make a difference—truly make a difference in this world. Thank you for

Katherine and her hospitality. Thank you that Walt and Rick can be partners. Bless their practice. Thank you not only for this last year but also for the years to come. Bless this food to us and us to your service. Amen."

Katherine took her wine glass and raised it in a toast. "To new friends—good friends—and a new year!"

"Here, here!" was heard around the table as glasses clinked.

The dinner was delicious. I reveled in the crackling logs, the flickering of the fire as it reflected off the ceiling rafters and the floorboards, the peals of laughter, and the warmth. Dessert was a warm peach cobbler with homemade vanilla-bean ice cream accompanied by mugs of strong coffee. After we had shared dessert, Rick's mom and dad set out to explore the inn. Katherine pulled her chair close to the table.

"Gentlemen," she warned, "I must tell you something." She was quiet for a moment. "You know that I'm not from around here. And until recently I've not sought medical care here." She looked at Rick and smiled. "But my business is here. I know the local people and I hear them talk." She was quiet, sipping her coffee and staring into the fire.

Rick cocked his head. "What's on your mind, Katherine?"

Her eyes suddenly glazed over. She seemed almost to shudder. She looked at me and then at Rick. "You guys are so needed in this town. You have *so* much to offer." She took another sip of coffee, then continued. "I'm not sure all the older physicians want you here. I'm not sure they're not as threatened as can be by you two. I think the only thing that's saving your hides is that you're sharing office space with Mitch and Ray for now."

Although I had suspected the same, I hadn't heard someone outside the medical community verbalize it. To me, this made the potential conflict between the younger and older physicians much more likely—maybe even more threatening. I wondered what this would mean.

"What should we do?" asked Rick.

"Your best," she responded. She looked into his eyes. "Just do your best. They'll never be able to beat that. If you are both as good of doctors as I think you are, *and* if you're as good of people as you seem to be, you'll do just fine. Just fine." She sighed. "For the town's sake—and for your sake—I hope you can ride it out."

We were quiet for a few moments. "Well," Katherine broke the silence, "let's get you all out of here." She stood and started to clear the dishes.

"Can we start the dishes?" asked Barb.

"Oh, heavens no!" pealed Katherine. "You guys get outta here!"

We gave her a hug and loaded back into the cars to travel back across town. The moon was reflecting off the snow, and it was hauntingly beautiful. At the top of Hospital Hill, Rick helped us get into our home. We said good-bye to him and his parents. By 10:00 the Larimores were all snuggled into bed.

No firecrackers awoke us at midnight, nor did we see the ominous clouds gathering on the horizon. A storm was headed straight toward us.

The first snow of the new year came on New Year's Day—about four inches of fresh powder lying on the bench just behind our house. The thermometer read twenty degrees above zero. But inside, the house was warm.

I had forgotten to turn off the clock radio, and at 6:00 A.M. sharp Gary Ayers's voice shocked us out of our slumber. As I rolled over to turn off the radio, I was surprised to hear him say, "On the home front, WBHN is proud to announce that Dr. Larimore, the team physician for the Swain County Maroon Devils, likes our little town so much that he and his wife, Barb, have decided to increase our population by one. Welcome to our newest citizen, Scott Larimore, born on Christmas Day!"

We laughed out loud. Barb confided, "Our son—almost famous!" I was just glad Gary hadn't mentioned that the birth took place in Asheville.

Now awake, I pulled on my slippers and robe and went into the children's bedroom to get Kate up.

"Katie," I whispered, "there's snow outside."

She shot straight up in bed, her eyes as wide as saucers. "Snow!" she yelped and quickly crawled from her bed to run, as best she could without her braces, to the window.

"Wow, oh wow, Daddy. Wow, oh wow! Can we go out and play?"

"After breakfast we'll go out and play, OK?" I heard a movement behind me and turned my attention to the crib. My little boy was beginning to arouse. I walked over to watch him grimace and squirm. Although he was still sleeping, he appeared to be exercising his new plumbing system.

Then I noticed it. He was the color of a carrot.

I picked him up, gave him a hug, and placed him on the bassinet to change his diaper. *He was yellow all over.* Even the whites of his eyes were yellow. *My baby was jaundiced!*

I *know* I shouldn't have panicked. After all, jaundice is common, especially in breast-fed children—particularly in premature breast-fed children. But sometimes a physician doesn't think like a physician—especially when it comes to his own children.

By 8:00 A.M. Rick was making a home visit. The lab results were in by 10:00 A.M. Scott was indeed jaundiced—not dangerously so—but his bilirubin levels indicated the need for therapy.

"I have an idea, Walt," Rick exclaimed. "Follow me."

We put on our coats and walked across the street to the hospital. Peggy Ashley was the charge nurse that day. Rick explained his plan.

"Well, we've never done *that* before," she responded. "Have you talked to Mitch or Ray about it?"

Rick's cheeks flushed a bit. "No," he retorted. "Why do I have to? I'm an attending physician here. This is standard medical practice. It's just that we're not doing it in the hospital."

Peggy thought a moment. "Well, I guess we could give it a try and see how it goes."

Before I knew it Rick and I were pushing a hospital bili light across the road and into my children's room. Years before it would become popular, we were doing home phototherapy in Bryson City.

When an newborn infant's liver isn't yet up to speed, the bile that is normally excreted by the liver can build up in the bloodstream, resulting in the carrotlike color of the whites of the eyes and the skin appearance that doctors call jaundice. If the levels of bile—called bilirubin—get too high, they may damage the brain. So while waiting for the liver to begin its life-saving work, the bilirubin levels can be reduced to safe levels by simply exposing the skin to certain frequencies of light. Back then this was accomplished with what were called bili lights—two banks of fluorescent bulbs that would be positioned over the baby. The baby's eyes would be covered to protect their eyes from any possible negative effects from the light, and the lights would be left on, day and night, until the bilirubin levels were normal and the liver was working properly.

So we set up a hospital-like nursery in our home. The nurses were kind enough to come over every four hours to check on us and on Scott. Betty and the lab techs came over twice a day to do heel sticks to check Scott's bilirubin levels. By the ninth day of Christmas the bili lights were turned off. On the tenth day of Christmas Rick and I rolled the lights back to the hospital.

On the twelfth day of Christmas we celebrated Barb's thirtieth birthday. Part of the celebration involved borrowing a large wheelbarrow and shovels from Dr. Bacon. Rick and I hauled the Larimore Christmas tree out of the house and down the road to the site of our new office building. Together we pushed the tree up to the most southwest corner of the lot—the corner that was projected to be untouched—just above what was to be the new parking lot. We dug a hole and then rolled the Norwegian spruce's ball into the hole and backfilled the tree. We stood back and admired our handiwork, a tradition we would repeat on every twelfth day of Christmas that we lived in Bryson City.

As I sat on the bench that evening, trying to keep warm in a winter coat and hat as the sun set, I reflected on the planting of the tree—and on our hopes that the tree would take root and grow.

It was beginning now to feel like our family and our medical practice was starting to take root in this small town. I was beginning to feel comfortable in my profession as a small-town generalist. We were settling into our new home and our new town—and falling in love with them both. It felt like a great start to the rest of life—a new year, and a new decade. I still did not see the bad moon rising.

chapter twenty-nine

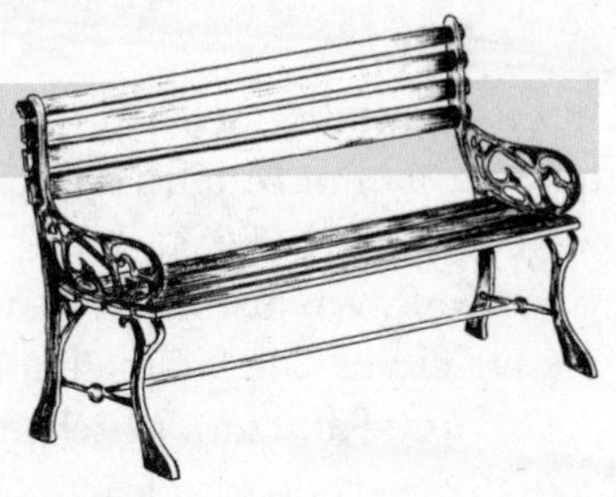

The Home Birth

Patricia Johnson, M.D., was a devoted physician in nearby Robbinsville. She had the only medical clinic in Graham County—a county that had no hospital. Patients needing hospital care either drove south to the hospitals in Andrews or Murphy, or northeast to Bryson City or Sylva. I had gone to visit her during my first weeks in town. I immediately liked her and immensely respected her. She was specially gifted to minister to her patients in this remote environment.

From time to time, maybe for a year or two at a time, a physician might join her in practice. But they always would leave. When Patricia had no physicians assisting her and when she went on vacation, the entire county was without a doctor. On these occasions, she would call one of the doctors in Andrews to cover emergencies for her practice. Occasionally she'd call over to Swain Surgical Associates.

Helen took the call from Robbinsville. "Dr. Larimore, Dr. Johnson on the phone for you."

I excused myself from the patient I was seeing and went to take the call in Mitch's office.

"Hi, Pat, how are you?"

"Walt, I'm just fine. Are you getting acclimated over there in the big city?" She laughed and I chuckled.

"I am, Pat, I am. Mitch and Ray are breaking me in, and I'm actually beginning to learn the ropes a bit. Rick's here, too, and he's been a great help."

"That's great. I've always appreciated Mitch's surgical skills, and he knows *everybody.* Ray seems to do a super job, and I'm looking forward to meeting Rick one day. You need to bring him over here to visit."

She paused for a second.

"Walt, I need a big favor. I'm taking off for a ten-day vacation. If something should come up or if my staff needs a question answered, can I have them call you?"

It seemed like a simple enough request.

"Of course, Pat, it would be a pleasure."

That night an ice storm hit and continued throughout most of the next day. The roads were a mess. Late in the afternoon the call came.

"Dr. Larimore, this is Elizabeth Stillwell. I'm a midwife in Graham County. I'm attending the home birth of a woman named Isabella Shoap, and I need some help. She's been in labor for about thirty hours, and her cervix has been completely dilated for five hours. The baby is fine, but Isabella's tiring out on me. When she pushes, the baby's head comes into view just a little bit. I've tried every position and potion I know, but I think she just needs a little help. Could you bring a forceps or a vacuum over and give me some help?"

I paused for a moment to think. I knew Dr. Johnson delivered babies at her clinic, so I presumed, wrongly I later learned, that she provided coverage for the midwives. Nevertheless, I had not been counting on something like this. Now I was facing a thirty-mile drive during an ice storm. The drive on narrow mountain roads could be tricky in good weather. In January it could be downright dangerous.

Black ice, they called it—patches of crystal-clear ice on top of the asphalt and looking as black as the asphalt. If you drove onto a large patch, you could lose control of your vehicle in seconds. If you spun off the road in a section that had no guardrails, you could end up in a deep ravine and not be found until spring—or so the rescue squad tales led me to believe. I was more than a bit uncomfortable with this whole affair.

"Mrs. Stillwell, wouldn't it be better for me to send the rescue squad over to pick you all up? We could do the delivery over here. Besides, the ambulance would be better able to handle the ice."

"Dr. Larimore, I'd love to, but there's just no way."

"No way?"

"No way. These folks have never been to any doctor but Dr. Pat. They don't like doctors, and they absolutely will *never* go to a hospital. They're staying right here."

Elizabeth lowered her voice to a whisper. "Doc, if you don't come, I think this kid could die. I'd sure appreciate your help."

I was cornered. "Mrs. Stillwell, I'll have to drive real slow. But give me the directions, and I'll get there as quick as I can."

After hanging up the phone, I walked into the minor surgery room and interrupted Mitch, who was doing an in-office procedure. I explained what was going on. He smiled.

"Walt, when I was younger, I'd make those visits over there. If I've told you once, I've told you a hundred times, delivering babies is a young man's sport."

I thought for a second. *He's never told me that!* But before I could express that thought, he continued. "Walt, don't be stupid. It's a mess out there. You try driving in this, and you're likely to hit the black ice, spin off the road, and die in some secluded ravine. And . . . ," he paused to look up from his patient, "I don't want to take your call if you die. So why don't you call the rescue squad? Their truck has snow tires and chains, and it handles ice pretty well. And then you'll have some help if you need it. You get along, and Ray and I'll finish up things here and round on your patients at the hospital."

"Thanks, Mitch."

As I turned to leave, he cracked, "Break a leg, son."

Cute, I thought. Now came the toughest call of all. I had to call Millie.

"Swain County Dispatch," she snarled.

"Millie, this is Dr. Larimore."

Pause. "Yes. I know."

"Millie, I need you to have Don Grissom call me here at the office."

"You short on appointments, son? I think it's against the law to solicit for business."

I smiled. I actually thought I might be growing to like this old curmudgeon.

"Nope. Just need him and Billy to take me to an emergency delivery up near Robbinsville."

"Your car not working?"

"Millie, it's working fine. I just may need some help up there. And to tell the truth, I'm not sure my little Toyota would do very well in the snow and ice."

Millie sighed. "Son, you thinking about investing in a new car? On a doctor's salary you might could even afford one."

Cute, I thought. "Yes, I probably do need a new one. But for now, I need to get up to this place in one piece."

Thankfully it wasn't long before I extracted a promise that she'd call Don Grissom—and in minutes he was on the phone.

"Whatcha got, Doc?" he asked.

I explained the situation.

"Doc, we do this all the time. Be glad to be your taxi out there to the mountains."

We stopped by the hospital to pick up an emergency delivery kit and then headed out of town. The mountains were covered with ice. Old-timers called it "rhine ice." It completely covered each trunk, branch, and twig. The trees looked like ice sculptures. It was hauntingly beautiful. But I was nervous about the branches overhanging the road. I knew that the heavy branches—now weighed down with ice—could break off and fall. Being struck by one can result in some pretty horrific injuries.

Fortunately the ride out wasn't as bad as I had imagined. Don explained how the older docs, especially Dr. Bacon, had done home deliveries for years. "Once Sylva brought in an obstetrician, the guys here just quit delivering the babies. So, folks wantin' a hospital delivery go over there. Those wantin' to stay home just call the granny midwives. There's only a few of 'em left, and their practices are very secretive. Tell you the truth, Doc, I think the old midwives do a better job. We almost never get called to a problem."

Billy, usually the quiet one, couldn't resist sharing some local lore. "Some folks say that if the granny midwife loses a baby, the family just buries the baby and never calls the coroner. It's never reported to the officials. The local clergy know, and they'll help with the burial and a small family service. But otherwise it's hush-hush."

"Yep," chimed in Don, "you'll see a lady, pregnant as can be, then next thing you know she's skinny as a rail and has no baby. Just says she 'took off some weight.' But everyone knows what *really* happened."

"Don't you guys have to report those sorts of things?" I asked.

Don and Billy looked incredulously at each other, then at me. In unison they chimed, "You stupid?" I laughed. Obviously they'd been around Dr. Mitchell *way* too long!

Don went on, "That'd be one sure way to get kilt. There's some things a fella's not to mess with—and this is one of them."

The ambulance became very quiet. I sensed I was treading into some fairly deep weeds.

Billy was the next to speak. "Doc, speaking of the old docs." He paused for what seemed like several minutes.

"Yes?" I prodded.

Billy looked at Don, who nodded. "Go ahead, Billy. It's OK."

Billy sighed. "Well, Doc, the way we hear things, some of the older guys really have it out for you and Dr. Pyeritz. They don't particularly like Dr. Cunningham either, but since he's hooked up with Mitch, they *have* to tolerate him. You and Dr. Pyeritz being in their building has bought you some time for now. But . . ." He paused again. "Doc, be careful. Watch your step. They've got the nurses reporting to them everything you all do. I've heard they're as mad as hornets about Dr. Pyeritz treating your son at home."

Now it was my time to sigh. "Anything we should do?" I inquired.

Don spoke next. "Well, you've got a lot of the town behind you. The athletic department and the rescue squad are in your camp. You know the park rangers like workin' with the younger doctors. But the old guys are powerful politically. I'd say you just keep practicin' good medicine and good citizenship, and you'll be all right."

"I appreciate you boys sharing this with me. I know you didn't have to."

They both nodded.

As it began to get dark we turned off the main road, up a narrow, twisting snow-covered lane. In the headlights we could still see a single set of tracks in the snow and ice from what I presumed was the midwife's car. The cabin looked decrepit from the outside, where a single car was parked near the door. There were two rusting cars on concrete blocks nearby. And there were piles of items gathered from dumpsters and other trash scattered around the front and the sides of the cabin. A small barn was off to one side.

"Doc, it's probably pretty cold and crowded in there. How 'bout we keep the unit runnin' and stay put, less'n you need us. OK?"

I nodded and grabbed my equipment bag and went to meet Elizabeth and the family. Before I could lift my hand to knock, a fifty- or sixty-year-old woman opened the door and let me in. She closed it quickly behind me.

"Glad you're here, Doc. Let me take your coat. I'm Sally Scroggins, a friend of the family. Elizabeth's in with Isabella." The cabin was small and not well insulated. But it was clean and well kept. The common room had a small kitchen on one side with a potbelly stove that had a crackling fire going. On top of it a large pot of water was steaming but not boiling. On the other side of the room several people were sitting around a small lantern. Sally quickly introduced me to the pastor and several family members—children and adults. They seemed to glare at me, and not one of them spoke a word or moved from their chairs. Clearly I wasn't very welcome here.

"Excuse us, folks," Sally declared as she took me by the arm and escorted me to a door on the back wall. "We've got some work to do." As we approached the bedroom door, the midwife stepped out and introduced herself. Elizabeth looked to be in her eighties, small, lanky, and leathery—a true granny midwife. She whispered, "Thanks for coming. You're not a minute too soon! The baby's heartbeat is starting to get slow and irregular. We don't have much time."

"Mrs. Stillwell, wouldn't it be a good idea if the paramedics came inside?"

She looked apoplectic. She still whispered, but now in a more agitated tone of voice. "No way! Absolutely not!" was her emphatic response. "It was hard enough to convince the family to let me call *you*."

"The Shoaps have a phone?" I asked, surprised.

"No, of course not. I have a radiophone that the sheriff dispatcher can patch into the phone system. Now we'd better hurry!"

We entered a small bedroom. There was barely enough room for a small bed and a chest of drawers. The woman was lying on her side, moaning. She didn't acknowledge my arrival. A man, sitting alongside and stroking her hair, stood up and faced me.

"Let me be real honest," he stated bluntly. "You're not wanted here. Not real sure we trust your type. Elizabeth here says you can save my baby's life. I'd be obliged if you did. This here is Isabella and I'm Donnie." He turned back to his wife and sat down on a small wooden chair by the bed.

"Isabella," I said, "I'm Dr. Larimore. Would it be OK if I checked your baby?" She nodded, then began to grimace as another contraction began. I reached over to palpate her abdomen. During the quick exam I had time to offer a quick prayer. *Lord, guide my hands. Give me wisdom. Protect this small baby. I know children are special to you. Great Physician, be with us.*

The baby felt headfirst and was big—my guess, somewhere in the vicinity of nine pounds, maybe more! As the contraction intensified I could see the sweat glistening on Isabella's brow, reflecting the lantern light coming from atop the chest of drawers. Her husband looked genuinely worried.

As the contraction waned I warmed the head of my stethoscope in my hands. Then I placed it on Isabella's abdomen. What I heard caused a knot in my stomach. The baby's heart rate was about one beat every one to two seconds—I guessed about forty beats per minute, the normal was more than 120 beats per minute—but was beginning to speed up.

"Mrs. Stillwell, heart rate's about forty. We've got to move fast. Let's get some oxygen started. I'm calling the paramedics to come in."

Elizabeth gave me a concerned look, but without comment she quickly set up the oxygen and placed the mask on Isabella's face.

As she was doing this I opened the door. "Pastor!"

He leaped from his seat and ran over to me.

"I need you to do two things and do them now."

He glared at me.

"Get out there and get my paramedics. Tell them I want them ready to receive this baby. Let them know the baby is in trouble."

He nodded and started to turn.

"One more thing!"

He turned back to me.

"When you get back, I need you and everyone here to pray for this baby and for Isabella."

He smiled, ever so slightly. "Be obliged."

"Pastor, one more thing."

I paused. He furrowed his brows, listening intently.

My voice softened, almost quivering, "Pastor, will you all pray for me, too?"

He reached out to place his hand on my forearm and gave it a squeeze. "Yep."

I quickly returned to the bedroom. We moved Isabella to the end of the bed and positioned her on her back. I had Mrs. Stillwell hold one leg and Sally held the other. Now sweat was beading on my forehead. I heard Don and Billy entering the cabin.

"Doc, you OK?" Don called from behind the closed door.

"Don, just set up for a resuscitation."

"You need us in there?"

"No room now. Just set up, OK?"

"OK!"

I put on sterile gloves and began to examine Isabella again. The birth canal was filled with an enormous head. Fortunately the cervix was completely dilated. Then I checked for the position of the baby's head.

"Drat," I muttered. "Elizabeth, she's OP!" This was *not* good news. The baby was in the same nose-up position my son had been in before he was born.

Elizabeth was listening to the baby's heart rate. "Doc, heart rate's in the thirties."

I felt panic starting to build. The child was in immediate danger.

"Elizabeth, can you open the forceps for me?"

"Isabella and Donnie," I continued, "I'm going to gently place some forceps around the baby's head. They will protect the head in the birth canal and will help me deliver the baby."

I was well trained in forceps deliveries, and I quickly applied the instrument. After double-checking the position of the forceps to be sure the application was correct, I waited. In just a few seconds the next contraction began. With it I began to pull and pull. The baby didn't budge. It felt stuck.

I tried gently pushing the baby back up the birth canal. Doing so would sometimes allow the head to flex and present a smaller diameter to the birth outlet or perhaps allow me to rotate the head to the normal OA position, which would then make birth easier and faster. In this case, once again the head didn't budge.

Then I quickly tried to rotate the head. I knew the odds of this being successful were nearly zero, but it was worth a try. But to no avail.

"Doctor, the heart rate's in the twenties!" exclaimed Elizabeth.

I suddenly felt nauseated. "Let's roll her back on her side."

Within seconds of getting Isabella off her back, the baby's heart rate soared into the fifties and then to one hundred beats per minute. "Much better!" I said, almost to myself. Still, the normal baby's heart rate at this stage of labor should be 120 to 160 beats per minute. We were in big, big trouble. I was thinking as fast as I could—and praying even faster.

Then a thought occurred to me. When I trained in England, where most of the maternity care and deliveries are done by midwives, we did deliveries in the side-lying position—but not forceps deliveries. I remembered one of the British midwives teaching me how to deliver OP women in the knee-chest position. She said that this position allowed gravity to pull the baby down, against the abdominal wall, which would allow the head to flex and either allow the baby to rotate or to be delivered more easily.

"Elizabeth," I queried, "did you try the knee-chest position?"

"Yes, Doctor, but it didn't seem to help."

"Well, maybe it will if I also use the forceps."

"Good idea," she confirmed.

I quickly explained to Isabella and Donnie what we were going to try, while Elizabeth and Sally arranged the pillows in the middle of the bed. We then helped Isabella roll over into a knee-chest position, with her chest resting on the pillows.

Now *I* was the one who was completely befuddled. I had used forceps many, many times—but always with the woman being on her back. This position was 180 degrees different. Now I had to think and act in the exact opposite way from how I usually did. I quickly lubricated and applied the forceps. I could see Donnie's shocked look. I was hoping his shock was over seeing the stainless steel hardware protruding from his wife's birth canal and not over my profusely sweating forehead, the look of terror in my eyes, and my lips mouthing a silent prayer, *Lord, guide my hands. Guide the head. Protect this baby!*

Isabella began to moan as the contraction intensified. I double-checked the position of the forceps.

Elizabeth reported, "Heart rate's in the twenties and falling."

It was now or never. I began to pull, but for some reason—maybe instinct, maybe intuition, but most likely God's leading—thought better of it. Instead I gently pushed the head and it moved, ever so imperceptibly, *up* the birth canal. This was a good sign, for it meant that the head might be flexing and turning to a better position.

Then I tried gently rotating the forceps, and, to my amazement, the baby's head quickly and easily turned. Then in an instant the head began to progress down the birth canal.

I quickly removed the forceps. Isabella was straining with all of her might. Elizabeth was massaging her back and shoulders and coaching Isabella's pushing. Donnie just stared at us all.

Sweat was dripping off my forehead and the tip of my nose, but I couldn't stop to wipe it off. I was using my hands to maintain the baby's head in flexion. As I pushed to do this and as Isabella pushed, the head began to show and then in an instant the baby was out of the birth canal.

"A little boy!" I shouted. I could hear, in unison, in the common room, "A little boy!" followed by shouts of "Hallelujah!" and "Praise Jesus!"

I was quickly clamping and cutting the umbilical cord.

"Elizabeth, can you take over?" I asked as I bolted from the bedroom to the paramedics with a floppy, blue, unresponsive baby. I didn't wait for the answer.

Don and Billy had set up a baby warmer on the kitchen table. They had brought in a couple of battery-powered lanterns and had the resuscitation equipment ready to go. They had also instructed the family that they must stay away from the table as we worked.

"Heart rate's less than thirty, Doc. No spontaneous respirations!" shouted Don as I vigorously dried and stimulated the baby.

I suctioned out the mouth and pharynx. Still no response.

"Start CPR?" exclaimed Don.

"Wait a second," I burst out, as I grabbed the baby's legs around the ankles and then with my other hand slapped the blue bottoms of the feet. The baby instinctively pulled up his legs and let loose with the sweetest shriek I had ever heard.

"Pulse is 120," cried Billy, whose fingers were feeling the pulse at the base of the umbilical cord.

I quickly examined the baby. He was now beautiful and pinking up just fine. He was perfect!

Elizabeth appeared at my side. "Isabella's OK, Doc. Placenta delivered without a problem. I've given her an injection of Pitocin, and there is no bleeding. How are you?"

"We're OK, we're OK!" I exclaimed as my eyes filled with tears. "Isn't he beautiful, Mrs. Stillwell?"

"He is, he is!"

Elizabeth took over, doing what she did naturally, what she had done hundreds of times before. She swaddled the baby and held him to her chest, singing a lullaby. We all simply watched. It was all I could do to choke back sobs of relief. As I watched and dabbed the tears from my eyes, I prayed, *Lord, thank you for your grace and for your guidance. Thank you for this beautiful baby. Thank you for protecting me and him!*

"I think Isabella and Donnie would like to see their baby. OK?" Elizabeth looked at me.

"You bet," I nodded.

She turned to the bedroom and then stopped. She slowly turned back to me.

"Doc. Why don't you?" She held out the baby to me.

Her thoughtfulness and graciousness overwhelmed me.

"May I?" I asked with tearful eyes.

"Yes, of course." Elizabeth smiled. So did I. As she handed the baby to me, she softly said, "Feels to me like about a nine and a half pounder, Doc."

Isabella was sitting up in bed, looking no worse for the wear. Donnie was sitting on the bed beside her, stroking her hair. When the midwife and I entered, they both turned toward the door. Isabella held her hands out. I placed the baby in her arms and then stepped back to watch this new family bond. After a few moments Donnie stood up and walked around the bed toward us.

"Mrs. Stillwell, thanks for everything."

"Donnie, I'm so glad everything came out OK."

He then turned to me and dropped his head. "Doc, I want to apologize for my words when you came here. May have been a bit harsh. But the family hasn't had very good dealings with doctors—'cept for Dr. Pat. She's about as good as they come." He paused, seemingly struggling for words. "But I appreciate you helping Mrs. Stillwell out here."

He paused for a second. Then he raised his head to look into my eyes. "Thanks for saving my baby's life."

My eyes filled with tears that tumbled down my cheeks. He stepped toward me and gave me a big bear hug. I hugged him back. When he stepped away, I was speechless. We both smiled.

I left Donnie and Isabella to enjoy their new baby. The common room was abuzz with conversation and somehow seemed brighter. Maybe another lantern or two was lit. Maybe it was the new life that had just entered the world.

The pastor approached. “I’ve never had a doc ask for prayer. Appreciate it. Appreciate being a part of your work. Mind if we say a prayer now?”

“Nope,” I replied, “that would be mighty fine.”

We all held hands in a big circle. Don on my left, Billy on my right. We were all joined in a circle—the paramedics, a mountain family and pastor, a wise old granny midwife, and a young physician—growing in experience and in spirit. The pastor thanked the Lord for the new life, for the safe delivery. Silently I was thanking the Lord for this unexpected privilege of standing in this circle of life, the stinging words of “you’re not wanted here” melting into a chorus of praise.

chapter thirty

The Showdown

Rick and I were just finishing up our last patients on a beautiful spring morning. Mitch had come in from the hospital and was in his office with the door closed. The voices behind the door were uncomfortably loud. Rick and I looked at each other. He shrugged and turned his attention to his paperwork. I tried to ignore the voices and finish my chart work.

Suddenly the door to the office flew open and out bounded a red-faced Ken Mathieson. As he saw us sitting there, he screeched to a halt and drew up to his full five-foot eight-inch frame. His eyes narrowed, and he pointed a finger at us, as if aiming down the barrel of a rifle. "You boys are trouble. Trouble, I say!"

He stormed past us. Mitch came to the door. "Boys, you better come in here."

I looked at Rick and he stared back. "Do you know what this is about?" I asked.

"Nope," Rick said.

We skulked into Mitch's office, and he closed the door behind us. I hadn't felt this way since being called to the principal's office during the second grade. That visit resulted in a paddling of my hind end—an act then considered both legally and morally appropriate.

Mitch went around us and sat at his desk. He sighed. "Boys, he wants your hides."

"Our hides!" exclaimed Rick. "For what?"

Mitch looked at me. "Walt, did you slap a young man in the emergency room?"

I was befuddled. "What are you talking about, Mitch?"

"Mathieson says he has a family he's taken care of for years. Their little boy cut his tongue. They brought him to the office because Mathieson was off. They say you saw him, Rick, and sent him home with no treatment."

"That's right, Mitch. I remember the kid. White's the name—from up Alarka Creek. He had fallen and bitten his tongue. Bled all over. They rushed him to the ER. By the time they got there, the bleeding had all but stopped. So Louise sent him over to the office. Took a look at him and saw that all the bleeding had stopped. In fact, the edges of the cut were sealed back together. We were trained to not put sutures in the tongue unless the bleeding couldn't be stopped."

"Sounds reasonable to me. So what's this slapping thing?"

Rick continued, "Well, they got home and the tongue began to bleed again. They called the office. Since we were closing, I directed them to go to the ER. That's where Walt saw them."

Mitch looked at me. "Yep, Mathieson says the parents brought him to the ER and you sewed him up. Mathieson says that before you sewed him up, you attacked him and slapped him across the face. He says the parents were so worried you broke his jaw that they had to take him to Sylva to get Dr. Dill to X-ray the kid's head."

Now I remembered the case—clearly. But it didn't happen *exactly* that way. "I think I can explain."

"I'm listening."

"I was on call for the ER, and Louise called me over to see this young boy who had fallen on his chin and cut his tongue. Louise warned me that the family had a particular aversion to doctors and to hospitals. The only reason they even saw Mathieson was because he went to their church, and the only reason they even came to the hospital that night was because they couldn't get the bleeding to stop."

"What did you do?" asked Mitch.

"Well, I went in to see the kid. He went berserk. His mom and dad looked scared to death. I suspect I should have asked them to leave, but I didn't. We had to papoose the child in sheets to restrain his flailing arms and legs, but it only made his hysteria worse. Louise had to secure his head while I dabbed the briskly bleeding tongue with a cotton swab soaked in lidocaine and epinephrine. The kid went crazy, screaming and yelling. His mom started screaming. While his daddy was holding her back, he started yelling at me to do something."

"What did you do?"

"Louise lost control of the boy's head, and he began to thrash it back and forth. I grabbed his forehead with my left hand, securing his head, and I got my face right in his. Then I just firmly slapped his left cheek with my right hand—just once and not hard at all. 'Charlie,' I said to him sternly, 'You calm down *now.* Your tongue is numb now. You won't feel any pain. I need to fix it.' Then, Dr. Mitchell, in an instant he calmed down. So did his mom and dad. I was able to sew up the tongue without the boy even whimpering. His parents seemed distant but grateful."

Mitch sighed. "I know that family. Probably not wise to have slapped that kid. I understand why you did it though."

"Well, Mitch, after they left the ER, Louise told me the same thing."

"Rick, Mathieson's after you, too."

"What did *I* do?" asked Rick.

"Did you steal some hospital equipment to treat one of the Larimore kids at their house—and then *make* the hospital nurses go to the house to do treatments?"

"You've got to be kidding me! Is *that* what he's accusing me of?" Rick was red-faced.

"Yep, that's what he said."

Rick explained the home bilirubin therapy. "But," he concluded, "I didn't *make* anybody do anything. In fact, the nurses seemed to enjoy doing the home therapy. I felt it was best for the patient, and the nurses seemed agreeable."

"Well," explained Mitch, "Dr. Mathieson wants you both brought up on charges. And that's not all. He's angry because you don't use enough penicillin."

We looked at each other. In unison we exclaimed, "What?!"

For the first time Mitch smiled. "Yep, you don't use enough penicillin."

"I don't get it," I exclaimed.

"Well, Mathieson says that when my and Ray's patients—and your patients—come into this office for a cold or a sore throat, they expect to get a shot of penicillin. When you boys think it's a virus, you refuse them the therapy they want and expect. So they just leave my office and drive up Hospital Hill to one of their offices and crowd their waiting room to get the treatment Mathieson feels they should have gotten down here in the first place."

"Mitch," complained Rick, "you *know* that most of these people don't need an antibiotic."

"Rick, I know that and you know that. But *they* don't know that! Them and their parents believe that penicillin is a lifesaver. And sure enough, sometimes it is. They still remember when half the folks who got the pneumonia would die. So they believe it works, and when they're sick, that's what they want. It may be a placebo for them, but they'll demand it till they get it."

"But," Rick insisted, "what if they don't need it? Shouldn't we educate them that they just need symptomatic care—along with a bit of time?"

"Probably should. Probably should," he sighed. "But we don't have the luxury of an audience that wants to learn that. My suggestion is that you boys just dispense a few more shots. You don't have to put much penicillin in the syringe. The needle's the same whether it's 150,000 units or a million units." He smiled.

I felt myself getting angry and defensive. I wanted to fight this suggestion but knew it wouldn't be wise to do so. I was feeling frustrated and threatened. I took a deep breath to calm myself down. "Rick," I thought out loud, "looks like we'll need to begin using that 'placebicillin.'" This was an attempt at humor—and it did seem to break the ice. Both Rick and Mitch smiled. Rick nodded his head slowly.

"Mitch," I asked, "what now?"

"Well, Mathieson says that he's going to file a complaint with Mr. Douthit. He wants the medical staff to hear the charges, and he wants your hospital privileges revoked. If he can get that, then he's planning to file an action with the state. He's going for license revocation."

We sat in stunned silence. "What can we do?" asked Rick.

"Well, we'll fight. I think that, now that I know the facts, Sale and Cunningham will be on your side. I guess it'll all depend on Bacon and Nordling. If they vote with Mathieson, there's going to be trouble."

"Why?" asked Rick. "It would be a tie."

"No, not really. Since Ray is the chief of staff this year, he can only vote at the meeting in the event of a tie. If Bacon and Nordling vote with Ken, it'll be three against you and two for you. You lose."

My mind was racing, searching for options. I thought to myself, *We can't let these guys get away with this. This is not malpractice. There were no laws or statutes broken. Oh, maybe we could have approached these situations differently—but to be brought up for sanctions! That was crazy. We'd fight, that's for sure!*

"Should we get an attorney?" I asked.

"No, no, no. That would only make things worse. Besides, all the medical staff can do is make a recommendation to the board of trustees—and they all really seem to like you boys. After all, they're building you a new office. So I think we'll win there. But it only takes two of the physicians to file a complaint with the state. Let me work on this for you all. But in the meantime, lay low. Treat the other doctors real civil-like. Be nice to them, even if you don't feel like it."

He paused for a moment, then continued, "And say your prayers."

I already was.

We received a registered letter at the office only a week later. It was from Mr. Douthit, and it recorded the formal complaint from Dr. Mathieson. The hearing in front of the medical staff was scheduled, and we were expected to be there at the appointed date and time. Our day-to-day lives were on pins and needles. Neither of us was sleeping very well. Then came an amazing day on call.

I was making my evening rounds. The days were getting longer and the trees were beginning to bud. The gray days were a little brighter and the spring flowers were starting to poke up through the dirt. Nevertheless, my and Rick's mood was still as somber as the winter skies had been that year.

The nursery had three newborns who were doing well—as were our other patients in the hospital. I was sitting at the nurses' station when Maxine Wilson, the evening charge nurse, came over and sat by me.

"Hi, Max."

"Dr. Larimore, we've got a problem."

"What's that?"

"There's a three-year-old in the ICU I think is dying."

She had my attention. "What's going on?"

"Dr. Mathieson admitted the little one, Amber, last night. She's had terrible diarrhea and was real dehydrated. He couldn't start an IV, so he started cleisis."

"*Cleisis?* What is *that?*"

"Basically it's an old, old technique. He just places a butterfly needle under the skin of the thigh and runs IV fluids into the subcutaneous tissues."

"Why would anyone want to do that?"

"The older doctors only use the technique if they can't get an IV started. This child's veins are so collapsed from the dehydration that we can't get an IV going."

I knew that Mathieson would be livid if he knew Maxine was telling me all this. She was putting her job at risk.

"What can we do?" I asked.

"Can you do a cutdown?" She was referring to the technique where a doctor will numb the skin over a large vein and then carefully cut through the skin, dissect the vein, and insert a small plastic tube for an IV access—which could save the life of the patient.

"I can, but won't Dr. Mathieson go nuts?"

"Normally he would. But he's out of town. He and Mrs. Mathieson have gone over to Asheville and left instructions that if there's any trouble with his patients, Dr. Bacon is to be called—*not* you. But we can't get Dr. Bacon to answer. So, according to policy, I've got to come to you."

"Let's look at the kid."

We walked into the ward. The young couple sitting alongside the child was obviously anxious and pensive. Maxine introduced me to them. I found out that they owned a small business downtown.

I turned my attention to the child, whose breathing was labored and whose pulse was weak and thready. My own pulse quickened. This child was sick—*real* sick. Her eyes were sunken, her mucous membranes dry and parched. Lungs clear, abdomen soft and concave. Then I saw the thigh—it was bloated and edematous, with a butterfly needle taped to the inside of the upper thigh and connected to IV fluids. Fortunately the pulse in the foot was normal.

"Max, get me a cutdown tray, stat. Also, have the lab prepare for some stat lab work."

I turned to the parents. "Mom and Dad, I'm Dr. Larimore. Your child is, as you well know, very ill. I suspect that she's septic—there's a germ growing in her system that is making her very sick. With your permission, I'd like to numb the skin over her ankle and make a small incision. Through that incision I'll try to place a small plastic tube into a vein that will then allow us to give her antibiotics and fluids. Is that OK?"

They nodded.

"I'll also need to do a spinal tap to be sure that she doesn't have meningitis—an infection around the brain and spinal cord. I'll need to take just a teaspoon of fluid that I'll draw from her back. I'll numb the skin so she'll feel no pain, and I'll draw it from the lower back so the needle can't damage any of her nerves. Is that OK?"

They nodded again.

"I'll have Mrs. Wilson get you to sign the permission forms, and then if you'll wait in the waiting room, I'll come get you as soon as we're done."

With tears streaking down their cheeks, they turned to leave. Immediately I empathized with them. I remembered Barb and I shedding tears when we handed six-month-old Kate over to the neurologist for her CT scan—the scan that would confirm a diagnosis of cerebral palsy. I remember how alone and frightened we felt as we waited in the waiting room. If we had only known then what we know now about the power and peace that prayer can bring!

"Folks," I called after them, "before you leave, would you mind if I prayed for your daughter?" I had no idea how they'd respond. I didn't even know if they believed in prayer, but I knew *I* did—and I knew that their child needed it, as did I. They looked at each other with wonder. Then the dad spoke. "We'd appreciate that, Doctor."

I walked to the girl's bedside, and her parents stood across the bed from me. I bowed my head. "Dear Lord. Little Amber is so sick. I pray that you might guide my hands as I work. Grant me wisdom as I choose her therapy. Cause her to respond well. I pray that you'd give her mom and dad peace and that you'd bring their daughter home safely to them. Amen."

I looked up. The mother was softly crying, the dad looked devastated. Maxine was standing by the door, and, to my shock, Dr. Bacon was standing next to her. As the parents turned to leave, the mother began to sob. Her husband gently placed his arm around her shoulders and walked her down the hall.

Harold Bacon, looking rather stern, stepped into the room. He took one look at the child, and his face visibly changed. "Walt, what's going on?" he asked.

"Dr. Bacon, Max called me to see this young lady when she couldn't reach you. I think she's septic, and she's obviously severely dehydrated. The cleisis that Dr. Mathieson began isn't working and she needs IV antibiotics. I had the parents sign for a cutdown and a spinal tap. I'd be glad to have you take over if you'd prefer. I know you're covering for Dr. Mathieson."

"Son, this girl looks bad sick. Bad. I think we'll be losing her if'n we don't act mighty fast. I've told Mathieson to stop doing that blasted cleisis."

I stood there, not sure what he was telling me to do. A moment later, he did.

"Go ahead, son. If you don't mind, I'll assist you."

I nodded gratefully. "Max, let's get her bladder catheterized, and get me an ABG kit, stat—with extra syringes. I'll need blood culture vials also." I pulled up Amber's gown and located the very weak pulse of her left femoral artery. Maxine returned with the kit. I unsheathed the needle and plunged it into the girl's groin. She didn't move. When the needle pierced the femoral artery, the blood began to fill the syringe—but much slower than normal. "Her blood pressure must be low," I commented more to myself than anyone else.

"Not very red, is it?" observed Dr. Bacon. "Max, let's get O_2 started. Forty percent, humidified, via ventimask."

"Yes, sir. I'll call the RT."

I withdrew the syringe. I had drawn extra blood that I now inserted into the lab tubes and blood culture broth. The rest would be for the arterial blood gases that would measure her blood oxygen, CO_2, and acidity. I handed the tubes to the lab tech who had joined us in the room. "Austin, I need the ABG, CBC, and SMA-7 results stat. OK?"

"Yes, sir," he responded, scurrying off to the lab as Maxine placed the oxygen mask on the child's face and started the O_2. Almost immediately Amber's color improved. "Her respirations are better," commented Dr. Bacon. "That's good."

Amen! I thought. I pulled her legs apart and inserted a catheter into her bladder. Only a small amount of dark, concentrated urine appeared. "Max, blow up the catheter balloon and then let's roll her over for the spinal."

Maxine expertly secured the urinary catheter and then rolled the child on her side, folding her into a fetal position. Dr. Bacon was opening the spinal kit atop a bedside tray. I found the anatomic marks that guided me to the L4-L5 interspace and marked it with my fingernail—making a small indention in the skin. Once again, Amber offered no resistance. I gloved and then prepped and draped her lower back. I raised a bleb of lidocaine just under the skin where I had made the indentation. The spinal needle passed easily into the spinal canal and the clear fluid began to drip out of the end.

"Harold, I'm not going to take the time to measure opening and closing pressure. The way this is dripping so slowly, I don't suspect high pressure and I don't think we have the time to wait."

"I agree, son," he nodded. "It does look pretty clear."

"Yeah," I agreed. "I'm sure glad it's not milky or cloudy"—either of which could have indicated a severe case of meningitis. I let about a teaspoon of the fluid drip into each of three sterile plastic collection tubes, then removed the needle and placed a Band-Aid over the puncture wound.

Dr. Bacon actually smiled at me. "You're doing good, son. Two down and one to go." I appreciated his encouragement and affirmation, but the fact was that we were still in pretty deep weeds, and the hardest procedure was yet to come.

I turned my attention to the little girl's ankle. I was thankful for my training at Duke, which gave me the education and experience I needed for these critical cases. I palpated her ankle's anatomic landmarks and made a mark on the skin above the vein I prayed would be underneath. I prepped and draped the ankle—and then regloved with a new pair of sterile gloves. I anesthetized the skin with lidocaine and then quickly made a two- to three-centimeter incision through the skin. A curved, blunt mosquito clamp allowed me to dissect the subcutaneous tissue. Then, right where it should be, appeared the large vein I was looking for.

"Hallelujah!" exclaimed Dr. Bacon, obviously as relieved as I was.

I exhaled a sigh of relief and felt a tremendous pressure ease off my shoulders. *Thank you, Lord!* The vein was flat, indicating not much blood flow, but was large enough to receive a catheter that would begin the flow of lifesaving medicine and fluids into Amber's body. I tied the catheter in place and started to close the wound. By now, Dr. Bacon had gloved and assisted me by snipping the sutures as I tied them off.

"I really should be assisting *you,* Harold."

"Nope, Walt," he reassured me. "This is just fine. Just fine."

As Maxine dressed the wound, we looked at the lab results. They were terrible. The white count was low, indicating severe sepsis as her system was running out of infection-fighting warriors. The electrolytes were grossly abnormal. I quickly calculated her fluid needs and wrote orders for frequent vital signs, fluid and electrolyte resuscitation, and large doses of three different IV antibiotics.

As I was starting to jot a brief note in the progress notes, Austin brought us the initial spinal tap results. Dr. Bacon looked them over. "No red cells, no white cells, no bacteria, normal glucose and protein."

"Good," I sighed. "No sign of meningitis."

I turned to Dr. Bacon. "Harold, since you're covering for Dr. Mathieson and since you know these folks, how 'bout you give them the good news. OK?"

He smiled and looked down at his feet.

"I've got to finish the notes and then dictate. Don't let me keep you."

He nodded and then proceeded toward the waiting room. I was finishing my dictation when Maxine stuck her head around the corner. "Thank you," she whispered. "Good job!" She was beaming like a proud mother.

I nodded. She had been a nurse for several decades. She had seen just about everything. Her compliments were given rarely and were sweet indeed for any young physician.

One week later, little Amber skipped from the hospital lobby to her dad's waiting car. Other than a sore thigh, which was still swollen, she was fine. We never knew the source of the sepsis, but many times we don't. I was just delighted that she had done so well.

Two weeks later, Rick and I sat before the medical staff as they heard our case. After testifying, we were dismissed from the meeting. We walked back across the street to my house. Barb, Rick, and I waited. We were, of course, concerned—but at the same time we had a sense of peace. We knew that we were practicing good medicine. To us this whole mess felt like a witch-hunt instigated by men seeking to protect their practice and their ways—both of which they wrongly assumed were threatened by our being there. I wondered to myself, *Would I, in the same circumstances, respond the same way?* I hoped not!

We found out later that several others were also called into the room as witnesses. The parents of the slapped child testified for over a half hour. Several of the nurses who did the home bilirubin therapy were called in for brief questioning.

After a couple of hours, we heard a knock on the screen door. It was Ray. We stood as he entered the dining room.

"Have a seat," he gestured. We all sat down.

He sighed. "Well, good news, folks. Bacon voted with us."

There was a collective sigh of relief in the room. He continued, "Two of the doctors voted against you. But the decision of the majority of the medical staff is that you all's actions were justified. There will be no disciplinary action of any kind. Nothing to blacken your record. Furthermore, there will be no report or complaint made to the state."

He was quiet for a moment, then continued. "When Bacon voted for you guys, Nordling grew pretty quiet. You know, he's been renting office space from Bacon. Wouldn't surprise me to see him leaving that situation. Mathieson blew up and just stormed out of the meeting."

He drew in a deep breath and then slowly let it out. "Walt, let me encourage you to try to avoid slapping patients in the future. OK?"

I smiled and nodded.

"Rick, if you want to do home therapy in the future, I'll need you to coordinate that with me. OK?"

Rick nodded.

"This event has shaken up the medical community a bit. But I think the shaking was needed." He looked at us. "Are you all going to be OK?"

"I think so, Ray. Are you?" asked Rick.

Ray nodded. "Gotta tell you two, you're two of the best things that have happened here—especially for me. If you left, I wouldn't be far behind. I'm glad you're here."

The next week, Dr. Nordling's office was empty. I never saw him again and was told that he had left town. Dr. Mathieson stayed in town, but also stayed away from us. For months he wouldn't speak to me—and he'd speak to Ray only if he needed surgical backup and Mitch wasn't available. He wouldn't acknowledge Rick or me at medical staff meetings and would often turn and go the other way when he saw us in the hall.

Later that spring I was walking down the hospital corridor. Ken Mathieson was walking toward me. He smiled and kept coming toward me. I froze as he walked up. "Walt, I saw Amber today in the office. She's doing great. Her parents mentioned to me what you did for her that night. For some reason I'd always thought Dr. Bacon had saved her life. I didn't know it was actually you.

"Anyway, Mrs. Mathieson, who's my office nurse, recommended that I properly thank you. So . . . ," he paused and tried to swallow, gulping in the process as he glanced away from me, looking very uncomfortable. "So . . . thank you." Then suddenly he turned on his heels and continued to walk down the hall. In stunned disbelief I watched him go. And then, I couldn't believe what I was hearing. He was whistling!

From that day on Dr. Mathieson treated Rick and me as colleagues. I have no idea what turned him around. Was it Mrs. Mathieson? Was it the fact that we started using lots of injectable penicillin? Was it something Amber's mom and dad said about a prayer from a scared-to-death physician over a nearly dead little girl? I don't know. But it was nice to have peace—at least for the time being—among our Bryson City medical staff members.

chapter thirty-one

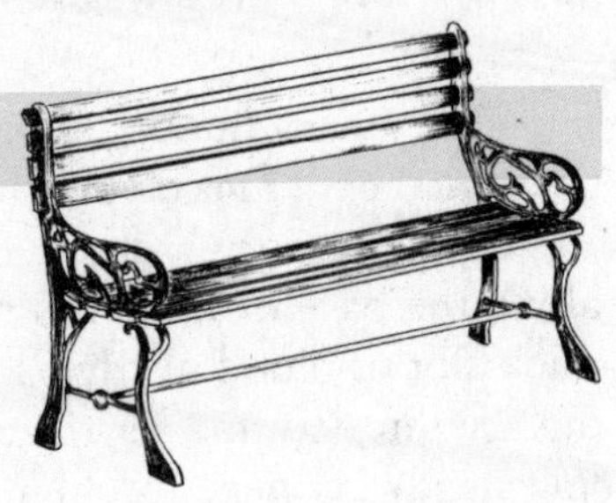

THE INITIATION

It just so happened that I was alone in the office that Thursday in July. Ray was shopping in Asheville with Nancy, Rick was on vacation, and Mitch was at his farm. I was covering a *very* busy afternoon. Helen was pulling patients back into the exam rooms as fast as she could, and I was seeing the folks as quickly as good manners and good medicine would allow.

Because of our schedule, I wasn't able to have Helen prep me for each case before I walked into each room—we were shakin' and bakin'! So, you can imagine my surprise when I walked into the procedure room to find Mitch's son-in-law, Cam, sitting alongside the exam table where a beagle was lying on a blood-soaked towel and breathing shallowly. *A dog!*

"Doc," Cam explained, "we tried to find Mitch, but we couldn't. So we did the next best thang. We brung her up here to you."

My guess is this was a compliment, but I wasn't real sure. "What happened?"

"We were a huntin' after some boar, and Queenie here got gored real bad. I need you to stitch her up if'n you would."

I stepped forward and took a look at the wound. It ran along the base of the dog's ribs for about ten inches. It had a thick clot of blood overlying the wound. Helen had already set out a suture tray and a syringe of lidocaine anesthetic. "Cam, can you steady her head for me while I work?"

"Be obliged."

I scrubbed the wound edges with Betadine and then draped the abdomen with sterile drapes. I numbed the wound edges with lidocaine. When I began to scrub the wound, Queenie stayed still. I assumed she either had a very high pain threshold or was adequately numbed. The wound penetrated the abdominal muscles but fortunately *not* the lining of the abdominal wall—the peritoneum. I'd be able to close this up.

Helen entered the room, "Sorry to keep you waiting, Dr. Larimore. What suture do you want?"

"Helen, how about a 3–0 chromic for the fascia and sub-q and a 2–0 nylon for the skin?"

"*Nylon* for the skin?" Helen asked. Oh, how I wish I had inquired as to why she was questioning my decision, but unfortunately I did not.

"Yep, nylon will do just fine."

I closed the layers quickly and then carefully closed the skin—ever aware that my boss would see my handiwork. After the wound was dressed and an antibiotic shot administered, Queenie seemed to perk up a bit.

"She should be as good as new. You can take the dressing off tomorrow and have Mitch take the stitches out in ten to twelve days. If there's any infection or swelling, please let us know."

"Thanks, Doc," replied Cam, as he picked up Queenie to leave.

Friday afternoon I was standing and writing a note when Mitch walked up to me. He stopped and looked up at me. "You stupid?" he asked.

That question *still* surprised me, even after nearly a year of practice with him. Fortunately, I was hearing it less often. Nevertheless it was still a shock to hear such an abrupt interpretation of my deficiencies. So my stunned response was the same as usual. "*What?*" I replied.

"You stupid?" he repeated.

My mouth, per usual, dropped half-open. Then I smiled to myself. "Well, given my registering Independent in *this* town, I guess you could *officially* call me stupid."

He looked astonished. "Follow me," he instructed.

He led the way to the procedure room, and I followed like a heeling puppy. Inside the room I experienced a sudden déjà vu. There on the procedure table was Queenie, her side looking like it did twenty-four hours ago—*before* I sutured the wound. It was opened up and covered with a huge clot.

Mitch lectured, "When Helen asked you if you were sure you wanted nylon suture, you shoulda thought twice. Who in the world would sew an animal with *nylon*—especially a wound within reach of her teeth? If the wound is on top of her head, then nylon's an option. But her abdomen . . ."

He paused, but the silent completion to the phrase rang across the room, *You stupid?*

"Son, you have to use steel suture in an animal like this."

"*Steel* suture?" I was incredulous. I had never heard of or seen such a thing.

"Yep, we keep it in the office for cases just like this. Well, let's get started. Before I die, I want to get you educated a bit. You may have graduated from Duke, but you've still got a lot to learn."

So I assisted my mentor—the master, the surgical sculptor, the medical maestro—as he worked. I had to admit that, even after nearly a year in his office, he was still a joy to watch. And, quite frankly, next to him I often did feel, if not stupid—well, a bit inept at least. But as I watched and then began to learn how to throw stitches with the easily bent and knotted steel suture, I smiled. I knew that once again I was learning—and learning a lot. I think I knew that I was at least somewhat less stupid than the year before, and hopefully I would be even less stupid the next year. At least that was my goal.

Delivering a calf locked in breech and sewing up a boar-gored beagle would be unusual events in the life of any first-year doctor. But for me, these events did shed light for me on the value of these animals. I was also coming to appreciate the value of hunting and fishing to the people of this area—the bond between these men and nature. Entering into this bond with new friends opened doors for meaningful connections with them that would otherwise have been impossible.

I had some of my most meaningful experiences while fishing. I was coming to especially value my fishing buddies and experiences, which took me far away from the pressures of medicine and were, in their own way, healing and refreshing. One such experience occurred on my first fishing trip with Greg Shuler, the Christmas tree farmer.

Greg came to pick me up at 5:00 A.M. in his old ramshackle truck. We were headed to Graham County to look for a very special fish—the steelhead trout. We stopped in Robbinsville at a café already packed with men—hunters and fishermen—drinking strong black coffee and smoking. Greg was not a man of many words, but I liked him. As we ate scrambled eggs with country-smoked bacon and ham surrounded by grits and biscuits smothered in butter, he shared a bit of his family's history. His great-grandfather had come into the county on a wagon and set up a farm west of the small settlement of Almond. His grandfather and father had been born on that farm. His voice slowed measurably as he told of the government coming in and taking over the farm. They clear-cut the land around the barn and home place, as the men took those buildings apart, board by board. The lumber and all of their belongings were loaded onto a flatcar and hauled over to Bryson to be reassembled on what would become the new home site—the place where we had purchased our Christmas tree. Then the valley was flooded to become Lake Fontana.

"My daddy still tells the story of'n how when he were a youngins' how he done sat on the back of that thar train when it pulled out. He war lookin' back at the valley that'd become the lake. All them trees done been cut back. The river war flowing through this terrible scar in them woods. Daddy just whittled on a stick with his pappy's Buck knife as the train pulled out. He said all his dreams war left behind in that thar valley." Greg took a sip of coffee, his eyes still looking away to another time, another place.

"He's n'er been well since then. Has to git his medicines at the VA hospital in Asheville. But he don't git no carin' thar. Just gits prescriptions." Greg emptied his mug. "He done left his dreams and his heart in that valley." We stood up to leave. There was laughter echoing off the walls of the café—but it wasn't Greg Shuler.

We drove west from the town and then up a long dirt road, finally pulling off the road as far as we could get and hopping out into the predawn silence. In the valley I could hear the hoot of a great horned owl. Day was just breaking as Greg opened the back of the truck.

"I n'er asked ya, Doc. You done got a fishin' license?"

I smiled, remembering when Don Grissom took me fishing. "Yep. Got it just after I moved here."

I could see Greg's nearly hidden smile. *He knew.* "News" like this travels fast and lingers long in Bryson City.

Later that evening, back at the Shuler home place, we cleaned our catch. Greg's pappy came down to look over our trophies. He didn't say a word. He examined our catch, and then he smiled and laughed—and continued to laugh. I wasn't really sure what he was laughing at or about, but in his laughter I heard the welcome of a neighbor. Somehow for him, I had completed a rite of passage. From that time until his death, he and his family were valued patients and friends. After his death his son brought me a small box. I opened it slowly and tenderly. Inside it was an old Buck knife, which has remained one of my most valued possessions—a sign that I had, in some small way, become part of their family.

That same summer I also experienced my most memorable social event of my first year in Bryson City. Monty Clampitt gave me a phone call—*the* phone call that was to initiate an unforgettable adventure.

"Doc, you still interested in working with us at the rescue squad?" I had taught a class one Thursday night on how to use the newly developed adrenaline syringes that could be self-administered by a person in the earliest stages of an allergic or anaphylactic reaction. I was surprised to see how many of the boys on the rescue squad I'd come to know throughout the year. I told Monty I'd be honored to work with them—as would Dr. Pyeritz.

"Well then, I'll drop by the office this afternoon with the paperwork for you boys. If you want to attend the meetings every Thursday night, we'd love to have you, but we're willing to waive the attendance requirement, knowing you all's call schedule. If you're willing to come teach an occasional class and be available to come with us on some of the calls on which we might need a doc, that'd be just fine."

"Monty, that sounds good to me."

"One other thing."

"Yes."

"There's a way that docs can be certified in advanced field first aid and in wilderness medicine. You may want to consider some of that training over the next year or two. It might come in handy if we ever need you in the field."

"Sounds good, Monty. I'd like to see the information the next time it crosses your desk."

That evening we filled out the application, not only for the local rescue squad but also for the state and national association—as well as the insurance and release forms. (Obviously the attorneys had gotten to these fellas.) As Monty gathered up the forms, he told us about a training session scheduled for that Friday evening at the station house—and that we'd be welcome to come and meet the rest of the squad.

"Well, Monty, I think I can make it."

Rick added, "I'll be on call, but I'll get down there if things are quiet at the hospital."

On Friday evening Rick was caring for a woman in labor. So I drove alone to the rescue squad building for the training session—an update on water rescue. During the session there was a sudden alarm. Monty leaped to his feet and ran over to the radio receiver to listen to the call. "Swain County Rescue, this is Swain Command Center, over." I recognized Millie's caustic voice. Now, the command center was just a little desk in the sheriff's small office—but the name sure sounded official and "big city."

"Swain County Command, this is Swain County Rescue, over." I smiled. It seemed to me that he should have said, "Millie, this is Monty. What do you need?" It would have been quicker and more natural, but admittedly and markedly less official-sounding.

"We have an overturned boat on Lake Fontana just west of the new T. A. Sandlin Bridge. One person missing. Search-and-rescue needed stat and requested by officers on the scene. Over."

"Ten-four. Swain County Rescue responding with water rescue units. Will notify you of ETA when under way. Over."

"Roger. I'll notify the officers on the scene. Over and out."

As Monty was speaking, the squad leaped into action. There was no need to sound the rescue siren, which echoed across the valley and called squad members to the station, as they were already there. The trucks, lights blazing, were pulled halfway out of the garage so that the trailers containing the inflatable rescue boats could be attached behind them. Men were grabbing their equipment bags.

"Walt, hop in the passenger side of Unit One," Monty instructed. "I'll be driving."

"You want me to go?" I shouted.

"You bet, son. You're one of us now!" He turned to run around the unit. I paused for a moment. *You're one of us now!* It sounded incredible.

"Come on!" I heard him shout. I jumped in, he turned on the siren, and we were off.

I had never ridden in the front of an emergency vehicle. In medical school, while on one of my ER rotations, I had ridden in the back of ambulances out on emergency calls—but never up front. It was exhilarating, and I could easily see how one could become addicted to the rush—seeing people pull over as you raced by them. We sped up the hill toward the four-lane and then headed west.

"Swain County Command, this is Swain County Rescue, over."

"Swain County Command here. Come on back."

This sounded to me like two truckers talking over CB units. I almost expected to hear Millie add, "Come on back, good buddy!"

"This is Unit One en route to the Sandlin Bridge. ETA 10 to 15 minutes. I do have Dr. Larimore with me. Over."

"Roger that, Unit One. Did you say you have Dr. Larimore with you?"

"Ten-four, Millie. He's on his first rescue squad call."

"Hmm!" she sighed. I had no idea what emotion she was trying to express. But she continued, "Rescue One, I've also been notified by the park service that they've launched a search boat from the Almond boat dock and will be at the search site within thirty minutes. Over."

"We'll take all the help we can get, Millie. Over."

"Roger that. By the way, Monty, there's a one-lane dirt road just before the new bridge. At the bottom of the road, around a small cove, there's a place where you can launch the boats. That's where the officers are stationed."

"Ten-four. Unit One out."

"Have a safe search. Monty, you boys be careful, OK? Command out."

I couldn't believe it. Millie's voice actually had a hint of softness in it—a touch of concern. I smiled. The old girl really did care!

As we pulled off the four-lane, the truck's emergency lights penetrated the darkness of the road leading to the lake. At the bottom, a sheriff's car, emergency lights still blazing, awaited our arrival. Deputy Rogers and the sheriff both ran up as our truck stopped.

The sheriff summarized the situation. "Monty, some fellas were drinking and fishing just below the bridge. Said their boat turned over. Two of 'em made it to shore. They say their buddy went straight to the bottom. The ambulance took 'em both to the hospital. They're near enough drowned. Don and Billy will be back here shortly."

As our other units pulled up, Monty went into action. "Joe," he called to one of his deputies, "I want you to take two smaller inflatables and place the marker lanterns. Then I want you to shore-search a half mile up-lake and two miles down-lake."

He turned to look for Ray, his other deputy. "Ray, let's launch the larger inflatable for dragging, OK?"

"Dianna!" Monty recognized his wife as she drove up. She had been monitoring the radio at home, as did most of the rescue squad wives—many of whom would be coming. "Honey, can you set up the food tent for us?" She nodded and turned to begin her work. She would erect a tent in which the spouses would prepare coffee, hot chocolate, and snacks for what I imagined could become very fatigued workers.

"Walt." Monty was walking up to me. "You ready for your initiation?"

"I guess so."

"Then I want you in the dragging boat with me. I'll show you the ropes."

I nodded, not at all sure what I was getting myself into.

First the small inflatables were launched, one to search each side of the lakeshore. The large inflatable was being launched as Don and Billy drove up in the ambulance. "Don!" shouted Monty, "you want to be in the dragging boat with me and the doc?"

"You bet," bellowed Don, as he ran over. One of the guys handed him a life vest, which he put on as he stepped into the boat. Monty started the small engine, and the three of us pushed off.

"Monty, y'all come back when the doc's tired, and we'll change off personnel, OK?" shouted Joe.

"You bet," responded Monty. "Might not be too long. Doc's fresh at all this."

"Doc'll do good, Monty," exclaimed Don. "I bet he'll set a record for a newcomer."

What were they talking about? I wondered as the little engine kicked into gear. Within moments we were in the middle of the pitch-dark lake. The only light that could be seen came from the growing encampment on the shore, the search-lights of the two small boats examining each shore, and the lanterns they had placed about fifty yards apart on each shore. Occasionally we'd see the lights from the top of an eighteen-wheeler above the guardrails of the bridge as it thundered through the night.

"Don, show Doc how to use the grappling hook, will ya?"

"You bet!" Don shouted over the sputtering of the outboard motor. "Doc, this here's a grappling hook." He pulled on what looked like an oversized treble hook, attached to about ten feet of chain and then a long rope. "Put on these gloves. Monty will move the boat back and forth across the lake. He'll be watching the shore, monitoring our progress with those lanterns on each side. He'll be using a precise pattern so we don't cover the same area twice."

"Mark," called Monty.

Don dropped the hook into the water and let the rope slide over his hands until it hit the bottom. "'Bout twenty-five feet here, Monty."

"Walt, look here. The rope is marked with tape every five feet. You'll know then how deep you are. You just jig the hook up and down. It'll slide over most of the rocks and boulders, but if it hits something soft, it'll usually stick in. You'll feel the weight, and we can pull it up. Sometimes it'll be milk cartons or a garbage bag. It's worse when we snag a log. We're done when it's the body."

I felt a shudder go down my spine.

"Doc, this is hard work. The current record for a new squad member is forty-five minutes. Want to see if you can beat that?"

"Might as well try."

So my life as part of the Swain County Rescue Squad began, dragging the bottom of Lake Fontana looking for a recently inebriated and now likely deceased angler. I didn't know how long I could make it, but I was determined to give it the old college try.

The first ten minutes weren't too difficult—except for the times when the hook would snag. Monty would have to change the boat position, and sometimes Don would have to help me unsnag the hook. Eventually I could begin to "feel" the end of the hook. I could feel the difference between a rock and a log. After about fifteen minutes my arms were beginning to burn. At the twenty-five minute mark, my neck and upper back were aching, screaming at me to stop.

"Doc, you want someone to spell ya?" Monty or Don would call from time to time.

"I'm fine," I'd reply—knowing full well that I was not.

I thought it peculiar that Don would call out the time in five-minute increments. "Thirty minutes, Doc. Want to keep going?" I noticed that the search boats were picking up the lanterns on each side of the lake. I remember wondering why. But I was seriously considering quitting, so that had become my overriding concern.

Only fifteen more minutes to the county rescue squad record. For someone who's an outsider to the county, the opportunity to set a county record was too tempting to turn down. "I'm fine," I lied once again—a white lie!

I could see another boat speeding up the river toward us, emergency lights flashing. "Looks like the National Park Service boat," shouted Monty as they passed us and headed to shore at the encampment.

"Thirty-five minutes, Doc. You OK?"

I grunted. I could barely feel my fingers they were so numb. By now the only light we could see was at the camp—which for some reason seemed very festive, especially in light of our grim task that evening. *Maybe these boys were just too used to death,* I thought.

"Forty minutes, Doc. Only five minutes till the record. You gonna make it, boy?"

Boy. In any other setting it might be a demeaning term. Not here. *Boy.* Don or Monty, I'm not sure which, called me *boy.* Not doc, but *boy.* Despite the blinding pain in my neck and back, shoulders and arms, I smiled. *I guess I was one of the boys!*

"Forty-three minutes," Don shouted. There were cheers from the shore. This *was* surreal. Here I was trying to locate a dead body, and the other boys were cheering me on to a new record. *They sure didn't teach me about this in medical school,* I thought.

"Forty-four minutes," shouted Monty. The chants on the shore began, "Go, go, go . . ."

"Thirty seconds . . . twenty-nine . . . twenty-eight," Don shouted, as the gang on the shore chimed in, " . . . ten . . . nine . . . eight . . ."

I felt a new surge of energy. Everything in me wanted to stop when he hit zero, but I didn't want to just *set* the record, I wanted to *shatter* it so that it would never be broken again. *Not likely,* I thought, *given how many records are broken and broken again, but, why not try?*

"Two . . . one . . . zero!" The crowd on the shore erupted. Sirens were turned on and truck horns pierced the dark, quiet night. Don and Monty were cheering and slapping me on the back.

"Doc, you did it!" yelled Don over the noise of the motor. "You can stop."

"Stop?" I yelled. "No way! I'm going for sixty minutes!" I screamed.

The boat was silent except for the sputtering of the small engine. Don and Monty were laughing hysterically. Finally they stopped laughing long enough for Don to bellow, "Doc, there ain't no record. You can stop."

I was stunned. "No record? What are you talking about?"

"Doc," exclaimed Monty, "this here was just an initiation, boy. There ain't no record. You just had to prove you wanted to be part of our squad."

"There ain't no record?" I asked. "Are you kidding me?"

They both rolled in laughter. From the shore I could hear a chorus of "Hip, hip, hooray! Hip, hip, hooray!"

I rolled over on my back, my arms slumped at my side. The most brilliant stars illuminated the sky. My arms were numb, but my heart was happy—perhaps as happy as it had ever been. I had been hoodwinked, but hoodwinked by friends—good friends.

Don pulled in the hook, and Monty gunned the boat back to shore. The celebration had begun. A new member of the squad had been initiated. The friendly pharmacist John Mattox had come up in the NPS boat with his son, Ranger John Mattox. Don and Billy, Deputy Rogers, the sheriff—they were all there, cheering and slapping me on the back.

An older woman approached, bringing me a mug of steaming hot chocolate. I could barely hold it in my frozen and fatigued hands. "Dr. Larimore, my name's Millie. Good to meet you—and congratulations." She actually smiled at me. She bent over and whispered, "My husband works at Cope Chevrolet. Let me know when you decide to get a new car, ya hear?" I smiled back.

As I sat down, Dianna Clampitt walked over. "Walt, from now on Barb will be invited to these initiations. Welcome to the Swain County Rescue Squad, and welcome to our community."

I remember sitting around with the men and women late into the evening. I remember the laughter. But most of all I remember the intensely satisfying feeling of belonging and of being accepted.

The next morning at 6:00 A.M. the clock radio went off and Gary Ayers's voice boomed, "The Swain County Rescue Squad was called to the site of a reported drowning last night near the new T. A. Sandlin Bridge. Turns out the call was a hoax, according to the Swain Command Center . . ."

"Walt, turn that thing off before it wakes up the kids!" exclaimed my sleepy spouse. My mind told my hand to reach over and turn off the radio, but my arms couldn't move—they were too stiff and sore. Barb had to crawl over me to turn off the radio. Before she could click it off, Gary Ayers continued, "Chief Monty Clampitt reported that Dr. Walt Larimore, officially the newest member of the rescue squad, participated in the rescue mission . . ." She clicked it off.

"Barb, don't you want to hear what happened last night?" I asked excitedly.

"Later," she whispered as she rolled back to sleep.

I couldn't move. But I smiled.

chapter thirty-two

Home at Last

Labor Day weekend was over. Kate was heading toward her fourth birthday and Scott his first. Barb and I were approaching our ninth wedding anniversary. Our marriage and our children were a joy. I was so happy to be a daddy and to be so in love with my best friend.

Our new office building was under construction. The contractor was predicting occupancy in just a few weeks. Rick and I had hired our new staff members, and they were already at work beside us at Swain Surgical Associates, learning the ropes. Dean Tuttle, wife of my football buddy Preston, was going to be our office manager. Beth, the daughter of Bryson City police chief Carl Arvey, was going to be my nurse, and Rick had hired Patty Hughes from a practice in Sylva to be his nurse. Diana Owle was also going to work in our front office. These four women knew everyone in town, and we felt *so* blessed that they wanted to work with us.

I had completed a wilderness medicine certification course and was doing more and more consulting work with the Nantahala

Outdoor Center, the National Park Service, and the Swain County Rescue Squad. I was planning to begin kayaking lessons in the fall and couldn't wait to get out on some of the county's rivers—both for boating and fishing. Rick and I had also been invited to become assistant professors and to teach the family medicine residents in Asheville, which we gladly did once or twice a month.

We were seeing increasing numbers of maternity patients and delivering more babies each month. The Shulers were pregnant with their first and had chosen us to attend the birth. Greg's dad was doing worse medically, and I would make a home visit to see him weekly. Rick was seeing Katherine fairly frequently, and her summer at the Fryemont Inn had gone very well. This budding romance in the professional community was being followed closely in the various town gossip circles. Rick was leading bird-watching hikes for both the Fryemont and Hemlock Inns.

The man charged with first-degree murder in Bryson City had been convicted and sentenced to death. However, Fred Moody appealed the case, and the verdict was overturned—to one of second-degree murder. The appropriate prison sentence—with the possibility of parole in the distant future—was not appealed by the district attorney, who decided not to run for the state senate. Barb and I remained Republicans, while Rick registered as a Democrat. We would care for members of both parties on each side of the aisle of our new building.

The Larimore's root cellar was packed with canned vegetables, fruits, honey, jams, jellies, and a variety of canned meats. We had enough food for two winters. And I had also gone ahead and purchased a lifetime North Carolina fishing license.

The spring football practices had gone very well. Tony Plemmon's shoulder was fully healed, and the two-a-day football practices of August had come and gone. The local team was predicted to be number one in the state that fall. Even Boyce Dietz had come by the office for an appointment for a "preseason evaluation" and a refill of a prescription of the oral antacid, Tagamet—

enough to last the season. Expectations for the fall were high indeed.

The tourists were gone for now—at least until the color season began in October. The air was still warm but would begin turning cool this month. I had finished my first year of practice—and what a year it had been. But the most memorable medical event of the year was yet to occur. It began, strangely enough, at the Bryson City Presbyterian Church.

Rick was in Pittsburgh visiting his brother and parents. Usually we would attend church together. Barb and I would teach the Sunday school class for sixth, seventh, and eighth graders while Rick, who was now playing the piano for the service, would rehearse.

The small church was covered with whitewashed clapboards. The steeple and steep roof, highlighted by a well-manicured lawn and overflowing flower gardens, had, to us, an almost New England look. There was an air of dignity and stability to the small building that most of the churches in the area seemed to lack.

We felt comfortable there from our very first visit, about a month after we had moved to Bryson City. We were greeted at the door by a couple and their three children. "Hi, we're the Claxtons. We're glad to meet you, welcome to our church. Is this your first visit?"

We immediately felt welcome. We sensed that we were neither an imposition nor outsiders. We conversed with the Claxtons for several minutes, liking them more and more.

"Since you all are new," said Mark, "why don't you join us in our pew? We can show you the ropes." This was indeed unique, and we accepted gladly. They escorted us to their pew, introducing us to several of their friends on the way. We had originally decided to visit the church primarily because Mitch and Ray attended there. But by the time the service began, we already felt at home. We already felt a part of the family. We continued to visit there throughout the year and eventually joined the church.

Presbyterian services had a prescribed liturgy. After the organ's call to worship, the ceremonial entry of the pastor and choir began. The members and any guests would be welcomed by Pastor Ken Hicks, who himself—as of this fall—was also completing his first year in "private practice." After a few brief announcements, he began the service with prayer, followed by the singing of a hymn. It was during the third stanza of the first hymn that it happened.

A young woman in the first row of the choir suddenly sat down. The congregation and choir dutifully kept singing, and the choir director, Peggy Ashley, one of the nurses at the hospital, kept leading. A couple of women beside the stricken woman looked down, concerned, but kept on singing.

Suddenly the woman careened off the chair and fell hard to the floor. The choir stopped, but the substitute pianist, her back to the choir, just kept playing for a few more moments. Almost instinctively and to the accompaniment of the piano, I leaped from the pew to run up front, only to find myself following Mitch.

When we arrived at the front, Mitch positioned himself at one side and Peggy at the other. I knelt down to be available for whatever might happen. They quickly evaluated her. Mitch gently slapped her cheek. "Susie, Susie, you OK?" There was no response. He pulled on her eyelids. I heard him mutter, "Oh my!" as he noticed that the inside of her lower eyelid, instead of being pink, was nearly white.

"Her pulse is over 140 and thready, Mitch. Skin is cold and clammy," Peggy calmly reported.

Mitch's hands quickly and instinctively went to the patient's abdomen. As he quickly palpated her tummy, he pushed his fingers deep into the flesh just above the pubic bone. Susie moaned.

"Heavens," he blurted out. "It's a ruptured ectopic!"

My mind was racing. How could he diagnosis a ruptured ectopic pregnancy with his hands? I would have needed a positive pregnancy test and an ultrasound showing a mass in one of the fallopian tubes. Or, I quickly thought, a culdecentesis, a procedure in which a doctor would pass a very long, thin needle through the wall of the vagina and into the abdominal cavity to see if there was blood—which can come from a ruptured tubal pregnancy. While I was considering this, Mitch went into action.

"Gay," he called to his wife and medical assistant, "get a coat or a blanket so we can keep her warm. And get her legs elevated. Let's keep what blood's left in her heart and head. Then monitor her vitals, and let me know if there's a change!"

"Yes, sir," Gay answered calmly, as she would have in the office.

He stood, like a commander in control as he continued his triage—a skill developed not only in his military service but also over years of practice. "Tina!" he bellowed at Tina Hicks, the pastor's wife and a choir member. "Call the rescue squad, stat. Tell them to get here, and now!"

He continued, "Nancy, Peg," he called out to Nancy Cunningham and Peggy Ashley, "get to the hospital, now! Nancy, get the OR ready for a laparotomy. Peggy, let the lab know I'll need six units of universal blood ready when we get there, and then you and Nancy scrub. Kim, we'll crash her as soon as she's in the OR."

Kim Hammrick shouted, "My car's out front. Let's go!" The three nurses turned to run out of the church, and members of the congregation, now crowded around the altar, separated to let them pass.

Although it seemed like only seconds since Tina had run from the sanctuary, I could begin to hear the siren of the ambulance heading toward the church—which was only about a half mile from the station. Mitch continued to look around, evaluating who was available, what skills they had, and what still needed to be done. Our eyes met.

"Walt and Ray," he continued, almost without a pause. He seemed calmer now, almost in a groove—the instincts of experience, concern, and training all flowing together before our eyes.

I hadn't even noticed Ray at my side. "Get up to the OR and get scrubbed now. Once Kim has Susie out, you guys'll have to get into the pelvis as fast as you can. Ray, clamp the bleeder, then fill her tank. I'll stay here and ride up with the ambulance." We could hear the siren outside and the squealing of wheels.

As we turned to run from the church, the crowd again separated. I could hear Mitch instructing the pastor as we left, "Ken, get the folks back in their pews, and let's begin to pray for Susie. She needs our prayers."

As we hightailed it to the car, two city policemen were running up the walk. Don and Billy were pulling their gurney out of the ambulance.

"Walt, my car's right here," Ray instructed.

We jumped into Ray's car and took off for the hospital.

"My, he's good," muttered Ray. "Gotta be a ruptured ectopic. Gotta be."

"How could he know?"

"Young woman. In great health. Married about four months ago. No birth control. They want lots of kids. Faints in a church that is cool, not overheated. Just finished Sunday school. We had refreshments. She couldn't be dehydrated or hypoglycemic. Exam shows her conjunctiva to be pale, meaning she's got a mean anemia, and pressing on her lower abdomen caused a pain response. Blood irritates the peritoneum."

We were quiet as Ray raced the car up Hospital Hill. We could hear the siren behind us.

"They probably just scooped and ran," guessed Ray—describing an emergency approach in which paramedics scoop a critically ill patient onto the stretcher and then run to put them in the ambulance. "Bet Mitch will have an angiocath in her subclavian vein by the time they get to the hospital. Wouldn't be surprised if he's got her blood drawn for the lab and a liter of fluid in her by the time we see him."

My mind was racing. The way Ray presented the case made sense, but I wasn't sure I would have reached the same conclusions had I been there alone. My thoughts frightened me. I probably would have interpreted this as a simple faint. I could hear myself trying to reassure the pastor and congregation, *Pastor Hicks, it's probably just a vasovagal episode. Very common. Not dangerous. Let's just give Susie a few minutes. I'm sure she'll be OK.*

Would I have kneeled at her side, expecting her to awaken after five or ten minutes while an unrecognized hemorrhage drained her of her life? I could hear Gary Ayers on Monday morning: "New young doctor watches patient hemorrhage to death in front of his eyes while reassuring her pastor that she was medically stable."

Ray screeched to a halt just outside the ER entrance. We ran inside, past a wide-eyed group of family members in the hospital waiting room. In the doctor's lounge we pulled our scrubs over our Sunday clothes, pulled on shoe and head covers and facial masks, and ran together to the OR. We turned on the faucets at the scrub sink, ripped open scrub sponges of Betadine antiseptic, and began our scrub. Through the window looking into the OR we could see Kim at the head of the OR bed, anesthesia machine ready, drawing up her anesthetics into several syringes. IV fluids were hanging and ready, and the monitors were turned on.

Nancy was scrubbed and preparing the OR equipment. Peggy and Louise were quickly bringing Nancy equipment and sponges. As we scrubbed, Nancy and Peggy completed the instrument count, a procedure that was carried out before any surgery. This count of each piece of equipment and sponge would also be performed after the surgery, as a way of ensuring that nothing was left inside the patient that should have been removed.

Just then there was a crash as the doors of the OR suite flew open. Don and Billy raced Susie toward the OR. Mitch was nowhere to be seen, but a nearly empty bag of IV fluid was sitting on Susie's chest. Louise and Peggy met the team at the door.

"Thanks, guys. Great job. We'll take her from here," Peggy barked as she and Louise rolled Susie into the OR and began to transfer her to the table. As Ray and I finished scrubbing, they would cut off her remaining clothes, insert a catheter into her bladder, and cover her with warming blankets. In the meantime, Kim would start additional IV lines and fluids and begin the blood transfusions. She would also begin to administer an IV agent to paralyze Susie. After Susie was immobilized, which would take only seconds, Kim would have to place a tube in her trachea to ventilate her. Kim would have only a few moments to complete the intubation. If Kim experienced delay or failure, Susie's brain cells would begin to die from loss of oxygen.

"What are her vitals, Billy?" asked Ray, finishing his scrub.

"Doc, she's afebrile. Actually a bit cool at 97 degrees axillary. We put some blankets on her. Pulse 140 when we scooped, but Mitch got the central line in, and by the time we were here, he had a liter in her and the pulse was 120. Respirations 24 and shallow. BP 60 palpable. Glad she wasn't in the national park or too far out when this happened."

"Me, too," said Ray.

"She was on her way out, huh, Doc?" Don's statement was half question and half statement.

"I suspect she'd have bled to death in just a little bit."

"She gonna make it, Doc?" asked Billy.

"I reckon she will, Billy. I reckon she will. In no small part due to you all's response time. Good thing you all were at the station and not at church."

"Yep, we're usually up at Franklin Grove Baptist Church. Would've added at least ten to fifteen minutes—and the pastor hates it when we get called out during the sermon. He always thinks we do it on purpose." Billy laughed.

"Well, that extra time was definitely not something we had. Thanks, Billy."

"You both break a leg. We're outta here. Heard on the way up there's been a little fender bender on the four-lane. May be hauling some more business for you in a bit. Keep you guys outta trouble." Billy smiled as he turned to go. I suspected we'd see him soon enough.

Ray and I finished washing off the soap and quickly backed into the OR, our hands held up and in front of us, water dripping from our hands down our arms and off our elbows. As the OR doors closed behind us, we saw Mitch, now donned in scrubs and mask, enter behind us.

"You gonna scrub, Mitch?" asked Ray as he quickly dried his hands. Nancy was already helping me gown. The answer surprised me.

"Naw. Just thought I'd watch you boys work together," he bantered. "Besides, I'm off this weekend. You're on surgical call, Walt's on ER call. I'd probably just be in you all's way."

Ray looked at me and I at him. He had been planning to be first assistant and I the second. Now we had suddenly been bumped up to first class. No words were actually spoken, but a thousand unspoken words crossed the space between us. This was a pretty high compliment in the face of a highly public and life-threatening emergency. This kind of life-saving surgery was Mitch's forte, his pièce de résistance, his reason for being and practicing. Something was up.

Mitch went on. "Once you guys clamp that bleeder, the show's really over. Besides, Gay and I have lunch reservations up at the Frye-Randolph house. The Adamses are cooking up something special for us and serving us at the private table under the gazebo. Gay will kill me if I miss that. Now you two get to it!" he barked.

While Nancy helped us with our gloves and Peggy and Louise tied our gowns from the back, Kim had started two more IV lines and was running in fluid and three units of packed red blood cells. "OK to put her to sleep?"

"You bet, let's move!" roared Ray.

We positioned ourselves across from each other. Ray quickly scrubbed the abdomen with Betadine. Normally he would take four or five minutes to do this. Today, less than ten seconds. I quickly prepared the drapes. "Boy, she's distended," he said, almost to himself.

"Lotta blood in there," Mitch commented. He was now situated next to Kim at the head of the bed, where he could see the whole operation. Front-row seat, we called it. Best seat in the house.

When Ray nodded that he was done with the prep, I threw the sterile drapes into place. Nancy expertly handed us the clasps to hold the drapes, not only onto each other, but also onto the patient.

The OR door cracked open, and Betty Carlson, the head of the hospital lab, with a mask held tentatively over her face, shouted, "Ray, her hematocrit is 16, white count 25,000 with a left shift, lytes are OK, and blood is O positive."

The hematocrit is the percent of the blood that contains red blood cells. Normally forty percent of the blood is red blood cells. Susie had lost over half of her blood into her abdomen. A normal white blood cell count is ten to twelve thousand. An elevated number like this could mean infection, but most likely not in this case. We are created so that if we have a sudden stress or accident or bleed, the bone marrow will pour hundreds of thousands of white blood cells into the bloodstream. These cells are on the lookout for foreign invaders that they can attack and kill. So, like soldiers, some are on patrol in the blood vessels, while most await action in the barracks—the bone marrow. In Susie's case, they were called into action, along with the reserve oxygen-carrying red blood cells of the bone marrow—all engaged in the effort to save a life that was quickly ebbing.

"Thanks, Betty," shouted Ray. "Kim, run in the next three units of blood as fast as you can. Walt, let's go."

For a moment the world stopped. *Walt, let's go*. Usually it was Mitch speaking. Usually, Mitch would say, "Ray, let's go!" Here was Ray in Mitch's place, and me in Ray's. *Did they trust me? They must. Wow! What a moment!* I felt fully a part of the team. No special ceremony. No certificate of advancement or completion. Just a silent confirmation that I was one of them. Goose bumps jumped up on my arms.

Nancy slapped a scalpel blade into Ray's hand, and in one clean motion he sliced from above Susie's belly button to her pubic bone, all the way to her peritoneum—the lining of the abdomen. Usually he would cut the skin first, then with a second scalpel, the fat. Then any skin or fat bleeders would be carefully and slowly coagulated. The rectus muscle, the big muscle in front of the abdominal cavity, would then be carefully separated down the middle—and then, and only then, could the glistening, nearly transparent peritoneum be seen. But in life-threatening situations when the abdominal cavity needed to be accessed suddenly, surgeons are trained to get in fast.

Instinctively, Ray and I used forceps to grab opposite sides of the peritoneum sac. Instead of being clear, it was an ugly blackish-purplish color, indicating to us a copious amount of blood beneath. In unison we lifted the sac away from the fragile bowel we knew lay below. Ray made a puncture wound in the sac. "Lots of irrigation, Nancy."

As the dark blood practically erupted through the opening, we each inserted the index fingers of each of our hands and the four fingers each instantly moved toward a different quadrant of the abdomen, ripping the tissue-thin peritoneum open. Nancy, using her right hand, began to pour in a large container of warmed saline solution that she had prepared prior to the surgery, while with her left hand she inserted a large suction tube into the abdominal cavity. Ray and I were scooping out large blood clots with our hands.

As Nancy suctioned, I grabbed an abdominal wall retainer and inserted it into the wound—both to hold the edges of the wound open and to protect the now exposed bladder. I could feel the blown-up balloon of the catheter in the bladder. Ray called out, "Louie, the catheter is in good position."

Louise called back, "We're getting clear urine, Dr. Cunningham. And don't call me Louie!"

I could hear Ray snicker as he used towels—called laps—to push the small intestines up into the upper abdomen and hold them in place. As I irrigated and suctioned, Ray quickly located the uterus. Around it was swirling a torrent of bright-red blood.

"Kim, she's well oxygenated," Ray instinctively called to his nurse anesthetist. The bright-red color meant that Kim was delivering an adequate supply of oxygen to Susie's lungs. Ray lifted the uterus out of the pool of swirling blood with his left hand, a clamp in his right hand poised above the wound. The uterus, shiny and purplish, about the size of a pear, appeared a bit larger than normal. He looked at Susie's right fallopian tube—it was completely normal.

Ray quickly turned the uterus ninety degrees so that the left fallopian tube came up out of the expanding pool of swirling bright-red blood. There it was. A mass of purplish-reddish tissue in the middle of the tube—and from that mass spouted a geyser of blood that shot out of the wound and across Susie's legs.

A new life, conceived in the middle of the tube where egg and sperm had met, for some reason did not travel into the uterus to implant. For some reason it had become stuck in the tube. Maybe there was a scar in the tube from a previous infection. Maybe Susie was born with that fallopian tube being narrower than usual. But for whatever reason, the new life, stuck in the tube, had implanted there and had begun to grow. It may have been growing for four weeks, maybe eight weeks—rarely longer. But finally the tube could no longer hold the expanding life. The tube had ripped open, and the blood-rich pregnancy began to hemorrhage. The preborn child quickly died, but the hemorrhage continued—and, in Susie's case, intensified. Before she knew what had hit her, over half of her entire blood supply had drained into her abdomen, robbing the oxygen and blood pressure that her brain needed, and she fainted—all in all an uncommon but not rare presentation for a ruptured ectopic pregnancy.

In a flash Ray passed the jaws of his clamp in front and behind the tube, right next to the uterus, and closed the jaws. Immediately the bleeding stopped. I could hear an audible sigh from behind his mask. "Thank God," he whispered. I echoed his relief. I continued to irrigate and suction, and in a moment the blood in the pelvis was gone.

"Ha, I knew it. Boys, I knew it. Couldn't be anything else," bragged our senior observer from the head of the table. "I think she'll be fine. While you boys are moppin' up, I'm gonna go join my beautiful bride for lunch."

As he turned to leave, he commented, "Kim, Peg, Nancy . . . ," he paused for effect. "Well done!"

He began to move, then stopped in his tracks and turned to Louise, who was sitting on a stool by the wall. "Oh, and *Louie* . . . ," he snorted, "good to see you." He began to laugh.

"That's *not* funny, Dr. Mitchell. You can just go ahead and leave *my* hospital right now. You go ahead and get out of here. These young boys don't need your poor example. You've been here *far* too long not to know better. You're about to get me irritated and mad. So get on out of here, you hear?"

Mitch was just laughing, his eyes sparkling behind his surgical mask as he looked back over at me and winked. "Louise, I'm leaving. But there's not a lot I have to teach these young university-trained docs anyway." Then he was gone.

We closed Susie up. By the time she was in the recovery room, her hematocrit was over thirty, and her vital signs were normal. Her left fallopian tube was resting comfortably in a small container of formaldehyde. The pathologist would in a day or two confirm the ruptured tubal pregnancy. Susie would recover—and go on to have several more children.

As I walked back to our house, I decided to take a detour to look at the new office building. It was coming along nicely. The Norwegian spruce we had planted after Christmas was doing well, with plenty of new growth. The view from the office up the Deep Creek Valley was magnificent. I couldn't wait to move in.

I made my way back to our little house by the hospital and went around back to sit on our bench. I was looking out over the Smoky Mountains. I could just begin to see the change in the colors of the leaves—or was it only my imagination? Nevertheless, before long the hills would be ablaze again, as they were one year ago, as they had been for countless falls and would be for the falls of the future. I took a deep breath. The clean, crisp air was cool in my lungs—the mountains and the seasons appearing to me as they had to my professional predecessors for over a century.

After that day I was no longer the same. My initiation into this small town was complete. I felt fully on board with the medical team and was beginning to feel a welcome part of this small, closed mountain community. I also felt an intense admiration for a group of aging but skilled physicians who had taught me so many lessons that could never be learned from a textbook.

My life now bore the thumbprint of the folks of Bryson City. Their pleasures and tragedies, their wisdom and faith, their traditions and stubbornness, their loyalties and wounds, their preferences and prejudices—all had shaped the man, the husband, the father, and the physician that I was becoming.

I now knew why they called it the *practice* of medicine. And I was coming to understand that my skills in medicine, in faith, and in life itself would never be mastered. I'd just have to keep practicing and practicing and practicing . . .

MORE TALES OF A DOCTOR'S PRACTICE IN THE SMOKY MOUNTAINS

BRYSON CITY *Seasons*

WALT LARIMORE, M.D.

Read an Excerpt from *Bryson City Seasons*

chapter one

Dead Man Standing

It was one of those swelteringly hot summer afternoons the Smoky Mountains are known for—sticky and unyielding. Not even the heavy, sultry air was moving.

"You didn't tell me about this!" my bride of nine years complained.

"About what?"

"About this heat! If I had known it was going to be this hot in the mountains, I might have just stayed in Durham and let you come up here by yourself!"

Barb turned to smile at me—one of those "you know I'm kidding" smiles I had grown to love. She turned back to face the mountains. "At least I would have asked the hospital to put an air conditioner in the house!"

We were sitting on the park bench we had placed in our backyard when we moved to Bryson City, North Carolina, over a year ago. It looked out over an exquisite view across the rolling hills of Swain County Recreational Park, then up and into Deep Creek Valley, and finally all the way to the distant mountain ridges—deep in the Great Smoky Mountains National Park—that separated North Carolina from Tennessee.

The view was mesmerizing, and we had now seen it through each of the four seasons—my first four as a family physician—since finishing my family medicine residency at Duke University Medical Center the year before.

"I didn't know it would be this hot," I commented. "But then, there were so very many things I didn't know, weren't there?"

Barb threw her head back and laughed. My, how I loved her laughter!

"True enough!"

We both silently reflected on our first year of medical practice. I had left residency so full of myself. Indeed, I had been very well trained—at least for the technical aspects of practicing medicine. But when it came to small-town politics and jealousies, the art of medicine, the heartbreak of making mistakes and misdiagnoses—all piled on top of the difficulty of raising a young daughter with cerebral palsy, dealing with one strong-willed, colicky little boy, and transitioning a big-city girl into a rural doctor's wife—well, the task was not only daunting but had been totally unexpected.

Barb turned to look at our house for a moment. She was listening for the children. Kate and Scott were both lying down for a nap. We had the windows in our air-conditioner-less house open—both to capture any passing breeze that might come our way and to hear the children if they were to awaken.

Rick Pyeritz, M.D., my medical partner for nearly a year and also a classmate in our family medicine residency at the Duke University Medical Center, was on call this day for our practice and for the emergency room. In this small hamlet, the on-call doctor was truly on call—for the hospital, the emergency room, the sheriff and police departments, the national park, the coroner's office, the local tourist resorts and attractions, and the area nursing home. But the fact that one of us would cover all the venues in which medical emergencies might occur made it very nice for the other six physicians in town who weren't on call.

"When the kids get up, how about we all take a stroll up Deep Creek?" Barb asked.

"Sounds like a great idea!"

We looked across the valley. I looked at Barb as a small breeze caught her hair and blew it across her forehead. She swung her head to flip it out of the way. "But until the kids get up," I inquired, "maybe their parents need a nap, eh?"

"Just what do you mean by *nap*?" Barb wondered out loud.

It was my turn to smile and silently look up at the ancient creek and across the ageless mountains.

Suddenly we heard a loud sound that startled us both. We turned to see a car screeching around the hospital and barreling down Hospital Hill toward town.

"Wasn't that Rick?" asked Barb.

"It was! Wonder where he was going?"

It didn't take long for me to find out.

Rick Pyeritz, M.D., even though on call that Saturday afternoon, had found some time to lie down on his couch for a nap.

He and I had been friends since our internship at Duke. Our varied backgrounds, interests, and character traits—he a New Englander and I a Southerner; he a single man and I a married one; he a backpacker, naturalist, ornithologist, and jogger, and I a sedentary family man; he an introvert and I an extrovert—almost drew us together like opposite ends of the magnet. Our bond had grown stronger through our shared love of family medicine and our desire to serve the families that had chosen us to be their physicians.

Sometime in midslumber, the shrill ring of the phone snatched him from his sleep.

"Dr. Pyeritz," barked the official-sounding voice, "this here's Deputy Rogers of the Swain County sheriff's department. We're at the site of a terrible accident and need the coroner up here. Mrs. Thomas in the emergency room has notified me that you are the coroner on call. Is that correct, sir?"

"That's right," Rick replied, in his most official, trying-not-to-sound-just-awakened, coroner-type voice.

"Then, sir, we need you at the scene as soon as possible."

"Where's that?"

"Where's what?"

"The scene—you know—where's where you're at?"

"Not sure I can tell you, sir."

Rick paused for a second—as he tried not to laugh. Smiling, he continued, "Well, Deputy, if you can't tell me, how am I supposed to get there?"

"Well, sir, that's what I'm tryin' to tell you. I mean, I'm not sure I can explain it. We're up in the national forest—up on Frye Mountain. It's not far from town, but it's not easy to get here. Well, at least it's not easy to tell someone how to get here. Especially if they're not from here—uh—sir."

Rick was beginning to get irritated. "Well, Deputy, you tell me. Just what *am* I supposed to do?"

There was silence for a moment. "I reckon I have an idea, Doctor. How 'bout you drive down to the station and catch a ride up here with the sheriff. He's a comin' up here. And he's from here. So he'll know how to get here. But you best git on down to the station purty quickly. The sheriff's gettin' ready to leave 'bout now.""

"Sounds good. Let me phone Louise, the nurse in the emergency room, and let her know, and then I'll be right there. Okay?"

There was silence on the other end for a moment. Then this warning: "Doc, it's purty gruesome up here. Best be prepared."

Rick was glad he had ridden with the sheriff.

Indeed, the site of the death was not far from town as the crow might fly. But the accident scene was far up the rugged side of Frye Mountain, and the sheriff had to navigate a number of small, winding, steep lumber roads and frighteningly tight hairpin turns.

During the trip up the mountain, the sheriff was, as usual, quiet and nontalkative. He was concentrating on driving, and Rick didn't bother him.

Finally they pulled up behind another patrol car—which was parked behind an old logging truck. Beyond the truck, Rick could see the crime scene tape, about four feet off the ground and strung from tree to tree, surrounding the logging truck and then going up a small ridge.

Rick and the sheriff got out of the car and walked past the other vehicles. The sheriff lifted up the tape to let Rick walk underneath.

The deputy was walking down the hill toward them.

"You won't believe this one, Sheriff. Never seen nothin' like this, I'll tell ya!"

"What happened?" asked the sheriff.

"You jest come look. You gotta see this." Deputy Rogers turned and began hiking up the hill. The sheriff and Rick followed.

They crossed a small ridge. When Rick saw the scene below him, it stopped him in his tracks. *What is this?* he thought. His eye squinted as he stared—almost gawking—at one of the strangest and most surreal sights he had ever seen.

His first impression was that he was seeing a scarecrow. There was what appeared to be a human body standing straight up. It had been dressed in old overalls and a denim shirt—the standard dress of the lumberman in the western North Carolina mountains. *But*, Rick wondered to himself, *where are his lower legs?* The man appeared to be standing on his knees—with both arms hanging down at his sides—his gloved hands nearly touching the ground.

"What in tarnation?" muttered the sheriff, who had stopped beside Rick.

"I told you!" the deputy exclaimed. "I done told you! I ain't never seen nothin' like this here. Never!"

Rick and the sheriff began to walk toward the body. It was standing straight up—with no support whatsoever. *This can't be a body!* Rick thought to himself. *It's got to be a fake!*

As they slowly walked up to it, Rick noticed that the man's hard hat was nearly crushed flat—almost like a beret—and was resting on his shoulders. But there was no head! Rick bent down to look more closely. He could not see a head, and the shirt was terribly bloodstained front and back.

"Who is this?" asked the sheriff.

"Clyde Frizzell. Has his home over in Graham County—not far from Robbinsville. Been lumberin' in the national forests out here his whole life."

"What happened?" asked Rick.

"His partner is Bobby Burrell. Bobby done said he was using his chain saw to cut down this big ole poplar tree." Rogers pointed to the tree that was about three or four yards in front of the body—not far from its freshly cut stump.

The deputy continued, "When the cut tree began to fall, Bobby done yelled 'Timber!' jest like he always did. Clyde was standin' right here, leanin' against this tree. He should have been safe here, but he jest couldn't see that the tree Bobby was fellin' was connected to this one jest behind him by one big ole vine."

The deputy pointed out the vine and continued, "When that vine pulled tight, it snapped off the top of the tree that Clyde were leanin' against and that trunk crashed down and fell right smack-dab down on top of Clyde's head. It jest bonked him on the head and drove him straight into the ground, jest like you see him. He done never seen it comin'!"

"Where's Bobby?" Rick asked.

"I sent him on to the hospital. He was purty tore up. Figure he needs a serious sedative. The men had been lumberin' together the best part of four decades."

Rick sat his black bag on the ground and opened it. He reached in and removed a set of latex gloves. Then he stood and began to slowly walk around the body as he pulled on the gloves. When he came back to the front of the body, he first reached for the man's arm. It was still supple and moved easily. *He hasn't been dead that long*, Rick thought. He felt for the radial pulse he didn't expect to feel. Indeed, there was none.

Then he slowly reached out toward the hard hat. It was driven into the tissues of the shoulder and took a bit of wiggling and pulling to remove it. When it slipped free, Rick gasped and fell back. He could not believe his eyes—as an overwhelming sense of nausea overcame him.

chapter two

Eyes Wide Open

The phone rang, waking me—but not Barb—from our afternoon nap. I rolled over to answer the phone.

"Hello," I muttered. Unlike Rick, I tried to sound as tired as possible. I wanted whomever this was who was disturbing my nap to know she was doing so. Admittedly, it *was* a rather selfish tactic.

"Don't you play like you're sleeping! I know you've been sitting outside on your bench with Mrs. Larimore."

It was Millie on the other end of the line. Every doctor knew Millie. She was one of the dispatch officers for the Swain County Sheriff's Department. Millie knew just about everything about every doctor in the county—all seven of us. She always seemed to know where we would be and what we would be doing at almost any time of any day. Equally important to me was that Millie knew every road and every nook and cranny of the county.

"I *was* sleeping!" I complained.

"No you ain't. Louise Thomas in ER told me she seen you and Mrs. Larimore out on your bench behind your house."

"Millie!" I tried to sound irritated. "Once again, Louise is wrong. Mrs. Larimore and I *were* on that bench, but that was over an hour ago. More recently, we were trying to lie down for a nap."

I heard her snicker.

"Millie, you've been reading too many of those romance novels." I tried to snarl at her, but not very effectively.

She replied with her typical and very condescending, "Yes, I know." She continued, "Well, anyway, the sheriff and Dr. Pyeritz just called me here. They want you to come help 'em at a crime scene."

I sat up. "I saw Dr. Pyeritz light out of here a little while ago. What happened?"

"Logging accident. One dead. No others injured."

"What does he need me for?"

"How am I supposed to know?"

"Millie, it seems to me you know most everything around here."

"Well, I ain't no smarty-pants, know-it-all doctor, I'll tell you that!"

I realized I was treading on thin ice. "Where's Dr. Pyeritz located?"

"Dr. Larimore, I'm not even sure I could get up there. It's up near the top of Frye Mountain. But if you get down to the ambulance squad, you can ride up there with them. So you stop your romancing that beautiful wife of yours and git moving, ya hear?"

I felt like I was being lectured by my mother. I hung up and got out of bed. Barb was sound asleep—as were our children. I slowly closed the kitchen screen door behind me as I left the house.

I met Don Grissom and Billy Smith, two of Swain County's finest paramedics, at the sheriff's office. They had the ambulance cooled down and ready to go. The air-conditioned unit felt wonderful. I hopped into the back and pulled down a small seat so that I could sit just behind and between them. On the way up the mountain, I told them all I knew about the case.

Billy commented, "Sheriff and Rogers both say hit's the strangest thang they done ever seen."

Dave chimed in, "That Rogers just got a soft belly. Don't take much to get him green-faced."

"Yeah," added Billy, chuckling. "Kinda like you were in your first coroner's case, Doc."

That crime scene was seared into my memory. Two men were drunk and got into a fight. One of them pulled out a loaded shotgun. The two wrestled over the gun, it went off, and one of them had his head blown off and his brains splattered all over the walls and ceiling of a small bedroom.

Chagrined, I admitted, "I did get green on that one."

"'Member when we first met you?" Don asked.

I thought for a second and then smiled. "Yep. It was my first home delivery. Millie called me out on my first night on call here in Bryson City. I asked her to call you guys to come back me up."

Billy laughed. "I'd have liked to have seen yer face when you walked in that barn with that ole farmer and saw his white-faced heifer locked in breech. I'd pay anything fer a picture of that moment."

"Yep, my first home delivery was quite an education."

"Doc, ya know if Clem still got that calf?"

"He does. In fact, I just saw her last week."

"Did you shore 'nuff?"

"Yep. I go see her from time to time—after all, Clem did name that little calf after me."

"No way."

"He did. Named her Walter."

The two paramedics broke out in laughter.

"Seems like so very long ago, doesn't it?" I commented, more to myself than to them.

"Well, time does fly when you're having fun!" commented Don, "But, Doc, I'll tell ya this—you'll be needin' to git a lot more miles on ya. One year of practice out here is jest a beginnin'—at least compared to your colleagues."

I smiled. "I know." As Don drove up a steep valley, I thought about the other physicians in town. Harold Bacon, M.D., was nearly eighty and the dean of the medical community. Bill Mitchell, M.D., was in his seventies and a general surgeon who had served as a captain in the Army in World War II. We all called him Mitch. Along with Ray Cunningham, M.D., who was a Bryson City native, they formed Swain Surgical Associates.

Ray was a much younger surgeon than Mitch and was the only residency-trained and board-certified physician in town besides Rick and me. Mitch and Ray had helped recruit Rick and me to the area and were allowing us to practice medicine with them until our new office was completed.

The ambulance bumped as it left the paved road and began climbing up a narrow, graveled mountain road. I thought about the other local doctors. Paul Sale, M.D., was just about fifty years old and a general practitioner. Like Harold and Mitch, he had practiced in Bryson City his entire career. However, Ken Mathieson, D.O., had retired from practice someplace else and settled in our hamlet to set up what would be his last practice. Like Rick and me, he was still considered an outsider.

The ambulance strained as it climbed the steep lumber roads.

"Good thang this here has four-wheel drive," Billy commented—to no one in particular.

Finally we arrived at the scene.

Rick had heard the ambulance struggling up the mountain road and met us at the tape.

"What's up, partner?" I asked him, as I hopped out of the unit.

"I've never seen anything like it, Walt! Just wanted you to see. You know, create a memory together." He tried to smile—but couldn't. He turned, and we followed.

The four of us walked over the ridge where the deputy met us—the sheriff having left to return to town. There was no banter, as we all turned to fix our eyes on the body and the shocking scene in front of us. As we walked around it, Rick explained what he had learned. "Obviously, the cause of death is blunt trauma to the head."

"How's he still standing?" asked Don.

"I wondered the same thing," Rick answered. "The blow clearly drove his lower legs deep into the mud. And it must have crushed his spine in such a way that he's stuck upright. Of course, having the tree right behind him helps."

Don commented, almost to himself, "Seems like he'd bend over frontward at the hips, don't it?"

"I agree," I said. We three continued to walk around the body—not believing what we were seeing.

Then I noticed the crushed hard hat sitting on the shoulders. I looked at Rick. "Have you taken the hat off?"

"I did. But you may not want to, Walt. It's pretty ugly."

The deputy chuckled. "I thought Dr. Pyeritz here was gonna toss his lunch. He got even greener than you did at the Crisp shooting, Dr. Larimore."

"Well, Rick," I muttered, "at least our reputations are established among the law enforcement community, eh?"

"I'm just kiddin' you boys," the deputy said. "Don't take no offense. Happens to every new doctor comes out this way. You jest don't see these types of things in the city, do ya?"

"True enough!" I responded. "Well, let's take a look."

I took a deep breath and then lifted the flattened hard hat off the shoulders of the dead man. I'm sure my instant shock was apparent to anyone not transfixed on what I was seeing. It wasn't the skull, squished like an eggshell, that stunned me. It wasn't the brain, open and exposed, that surprised me. It wasn't even the dead man's face, crushed but facing up, that dazed me. It was the dead man's eyes—wide open, protruding, and staring straight up toward heaven. I slowly replaced the hard hat back on the dead man's shoulders, feeling nauseous.

"Reckon he never knew what hit him," Don whispered.

Then there was a moment of quiet. No one spoke until the deputy broke the uncomfortable silence. "Dr. Pyeritz, anything else you need?"

"I don't think so, sir."

"Well, let's see if we can get him out of the mud and over to Sylva for the autopsy. Then I'll go over and talk to his wife. It's not the best part of my job."

"It's not the best part of ours, either," Rick whispered to me.

We turned to head back to our cars. On the drive back into town I thought back on the start of my professional life in Bryson City, the sudden turns and unexpected tragedies like the one I had just witnessed, the fragility of life, and the part I played in that drama. I looked out the window and turned my eyes toward the heavens. Would I be ready for whatever was coming next? I thought, and I wondered what this new year would bring.

10 Essentials of Highly Healthy People

Walt Larimore, M.D.

A must-have resource for pursuing wellness, coping with illness, and developing a plan to care for the health needs of life!

10 Essentials of Highly Healthy People is like having your very own health mentor to guide you in your total health picture, from treating illness and navagating the health care system to developing a proactive approach to vibrant health.

You'll see how to balance the physical, emotional, relational, and spiritual parts of your life to help you achieve maximum health. Whether you're eighteen or eighty, you can become healthy—*highly* healthy.

- Master ten powerful principles for improving your well-being.
- Discover the secret to becoming your own health care quarterback.
- Chart your plan to improved health using the numerous self-assessments provided.
- Learn the right questions to ask your docotrs.
- Gain the confidence to hire and fire your health care providers
- Explore the most reliable Internet resources available.

The ten principles in this book have made a life-changing—and in many cases a life-saving—difference for countless people. They can for you too.

Hardcover: 0310-24027-1

Learn How to Take Evangelism out of the Religious Box and Weave It into Your Life at Work.

Going Public with Your Faith

Becoming a Spiritual Influence at Work

William Carr Peel, Th.M., and Walt Larimore, M.D.

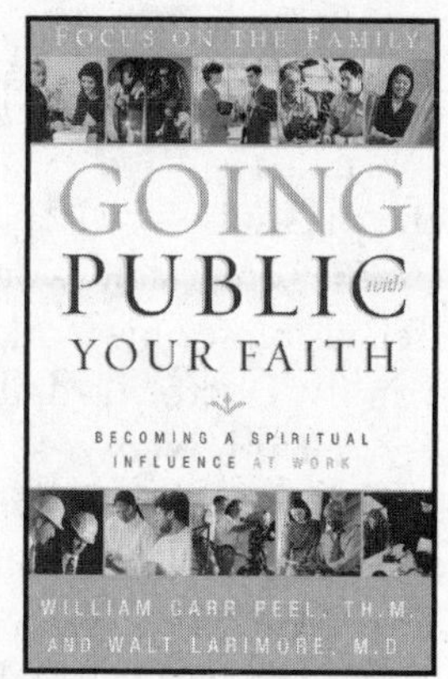

Going Public with Your Faith: Becoming a Spiritual Influence at Work flies in the face of almost everything you've ever read or heard about evangelism. Forget mechanical, aggressive styles of witnessing that treat evangelism as a one-time event. Real evangelism is a process. It's organic—a lot more like farming than selling.

Going Public with Your Faith offers a proven model for evangelism that respects the unique relationships you have with your coworkers, clients, or customers. It shows how you can be authentic instead of artificial when sharing what you believe, build trust with even the most skeptical person, and cultivate caring connections with those who have not yet come to a saving faith in Christ.

If you've ever wanted your life to count for the kingdom, *Going Public with Your Faith* will show you how your God-given gifts and talents can easily and naturally draw customers, clients, and coworkers to a personal relationship with Jesus Christ.

Softcover: 0-310-24609-1

Abridged Audio Pages® Cassette: 0-310-24618-0

Abridged Audio Pages® CD: 0-310-24618-0

Pick up a copy today at your favorite bookstore!

About Dr. Walt Larimore

Dr. Walt Larimore has been a medical journalist since 1995. He was awarded the prestigious "Gracie" Award in 2000 by the American Women in Radio and Television for his work as host of Ask the Family Doctor, a daily program of the Fox Health Network. Since 2002 he has hosted a nationally syndicated radio and television health news feature. Dr. Larimore has appeared in interviews on NBC's *Today* show, CBS's *This Morning*, *CNN Headline News*, CNBC's *The Abrams Report*, PBS's *Family Works*, and several Fox News shows.

Dr. Larimore practiced family medicine for over twenty years and served for over a decade as a volunteer physician for the U.S. Olympic Committee. Dr. Larimore—who has been honored as "America's Outstanding Family Practice Educator" by the American Academy of Family Physicians and "Educator of the Year" by the Christian Medical Association—has been listed in

- Distinguished Physicians of America
- Best Doctors in America
- Who's Who in Medicine and Healthcare
- International Health Professionals and Scientists of the Year

As an author, Dr. Larimore has written, cowritten, or edited a dozen books, including: *10 Essentials of Highly Healthy People*, *The Highly Healthy Child*, *Bryson City Tales*, *Bryson City Seasons*, *Going Public with Your Faith: Becoming a Spiritual Influence at Work*, *Why ADHD Doesn't Mean Disaster*, and *Alternative Medicine: The Christian Handbook*.

He and his wife, Barb, have been married for over thirty years, have two grown children, and live in Colorado Springs, Colorado.